CONTENDING WITH WORDS

Composition and Rhetoric in a Postmodern Age

Edited by
Patricia Harkin
and
John Schilb

The Modern Language Association of America
New York   1991

© 1991 by The Modern Language Association of America

Library of Congress Cataloging-in-Publication Data

Contending with words : composition and rhetoric in a postmodern age /
 edited by Patricia Harkin and John Schilb.
        p.   cm.
     Includes bibliographical references and index.
     ISBN 0-87352-387-3 (cloth) ISBN 0-87352-388-1 (paper)
     1. English language—Rhetoric—Study and teaching.
  2. Postmodernism. I. Harkin, Patricia, 1944–   . II. Schilb,
  John, 1952–   .
  PE1404.C6338   1991
  808'.042'07—dc20   91-13016

Published by The Modern Language Association of America
10 Astor Place, New York, New York 10003-6981

❖ *Contents* ❖

Introduction

❖

*C*ontending with Words: Composition and Rhetoric in a Postmodern Age is a
collection of essays for college and university teachers of English who
believe that the study of composition and rhetoric is not merely the
service component of the English department but also an inquiry into
cultural values. We address that audience knowing that we are formed by
what we study. Our contributors, too, have been shaped by various forces in
the American academy, and at the outset we want to describe at least a part
of that shaping. In an effort to understand the present and imagine a future,
we offer a brief genealogy that isolates a constellation of institutional preconditions for composition and rhetoric in a postmodern age.

We begin with the "literacy crisis" of the mid-seventies, because the
increased institutional attention to composition and rhetoric that makes this
book possible is connected to a particular account of a crisis in literacy during
that decade. It is useful to consider not simply the conditions that obtained
but also the name, *crisis*, by which our culture linked those conditions and
made them into a problem. In *Legitimation Crisis*, Jürgen Habermas, attempting to delineate a "social scientific concept of the term," writes that
"crises arise when the structure of the social system allows fewer possibilities
for problem solving than are necessary to the continued existence of the
system" (2). We might describe the freshman composition "system" in most

American universities of the seventies as one in which professors of literature (and graduate students) offered instruction in correctness and appreciation of the informal essay. Not surprisingly, that system could not cope with millions of Americans who could not read or write any language at all, with increasing numbers of students whose native language was not English, with declining scores on standardized measures of verbal aptitude, with open-admissions policies, with changing demographies, and with technological orality. Certainly, traditional humanism offered "fewer possibilities for problem solving" than people needed.

Paul Noack helps us understand how and why institutions responded as they did. In "Crisis instead of Revolution: On the Instrumental Change of Social Innovation," he points out that the term *crisis* is a powerful political instrument, perhaps because it often occurs in connection with the term *revolution*. Indeed, the terms evoke each other. Or at least they used to. Until recently, Noack notes, "it was said that the interrelationship [between the two terms] was that of cause and effect: because one type of society had reached a 'crisis,' it therefore was in 'revolution' " (68). Noack further states that although the terms *crisis* and *revolution* seem indispensable, they nonetheless lack "analytical precision" (65). His definition supplies a certain kind of precision by confronting the ambiguity: he suggests using the term *crisis* for situations wherein agencies charged with "mediating" the "postulated" values of a society are perceived as having failed (68–69).

Applied to the literacy crisis, Noack's analysis shows that the university system was perceived as having failed to teach students how to read and write according to conventional (postulated) values. But calling the situation a crisis tended to obscure both the variety of explanations for students' writing and reading behavior and the multiple reasons for the culture's perceptions. The term *literacy crisis* isolated the human beings it designated by assigning one name, one diagnosis, to their disparate situations and conditions. It is interesting to draw analogies between the literacy crisis of the seventies and the conditions Michel Foucault describes in his analyses of institutions such as prisons, mental hospitals, and the military. Foucault points out that these institutions often invidiously collected and designated people as other than normal and in need of remediation. His discussion of the Hôpital Général in *Madness and Civilization* provides an example. The persons confined to the Hôpital Général in 1656 were afflicted by a variety of conditions—contemporary science might, in its own institutional language, name these problems poverty, homelessness, and disease. Nevertheless, according to Foucault, the institutionalized thought of the Parisian administrators permitted no such distinctions. In effect, Foucault concludes, the Hôpital Général isolated the unproductive poor because they fell outside the institutionalized notion of "normal." Analogously, the term *literacy crisis* in the seventies named students who used minority dialects, nonnative speakers of English, white middle-class college students whose SAT scores were lower than those of their parents, people who lacked experience with the conventions of academic discourse, unemployed adults who could not read the instructions for filling out their welfare applications, and soldiers who failed to comprehend the instructions for making and deploying nuclear weapons. The term functioned as an umbrella to cover and isolate those persons who, for whatever reason, did not have "normal" standards for discourse. It is hardly surprising that academic institutions were unable (or even disinclined) to "mediate" the culture's postulated values to such a disparate audience.

More pressing today, however, is an analysis of the ways in which the academic systems constituted these separate circumstances a crisis and endeavored to contend with it. In this context, Noack makes another helpful observation about crisis: when people now use the term, he thinks, they envision not resolving a situation but managing it. "Crisis," he writes, "is no longer that point between peace and war, or between health and death, which will decide everything; rather, social crises today are defined by a long persistent tension" (68). In other words, to the extent that an institution succeeds in maintaining a state of crisis, it will succeed in maintaining itself: "If we define crisis as a permanent status, . . . then crisis management itself becomes permanent" (72). Crisis management as a political strategy, according to Noack, denies "the causes of the crisis by breaking it up into less threatening subcrises and thus making it more acceptable" (72).

If we apply Noack's analysis to the literacy crisis, we see how the university system in the United States "managed" the crisis—by creating new institutions, books, journals, PhD programs, and conferences to deal with smaller and narrower aspects of "literacy." Composition studies has now become a fully authorized academic field and a site of inquiry in its own right. Still, however, millions of Americans cannot read or write any language at all, college-board scores continue to fall, and discursive behavior remains a way to isolate certain members of our culture, in spite of the things they have learned how to do with words. The institution has managed to sustain itself; the problems are still there.

This book, which strives to theorize composition studies, may, of course, be seen as an attempt at crisis management. But the contributors try to interrogate, rather than merely to sustain, the processes of which they form a part. Specifically, they question the relations between composition studies and culture. They investigate the ways in which the crisis management of the previous decade has not taught students to cope with their culture. One of this book's aims, then, is to engage values critically instead of mediating them uncritically. Doing so means reexamining the conventional wisdom about composition studies.

As Richard Ohmann, Robert Scholes, and others point out (see Ohmann, *Politics* 26–41; Scholes 1–17), leisure and cultural prestige have historically been associated with literary research, whereas work and service are configured with writing instruction. Even into the mid-seventies, academic ideology deemed the labor of consuming literature innately more valuable than that of producing what Scholes calls the "pseudo-nonliterature" of freshman themes (6). For many academicians, that value differential was perceptible in part as the presence or absence of "theory." In the seventies, the prestige associated with literary studies depended on a leisure to theorize, to speculate about one's assumptions, perhaps even to change them. By contrast, the work of teaching writing usually left little time for such distanced reflection and struck many literature specialists as not even justifying it.

For many teachers trained in literature, what did change things was the condition of the job market. More precisely, they had to teach a significant amount of composition to secure any position at all. Fluctuations in the market for English teachers occasioned a situation that left many highly trained literary theorists with teaching loads largely made up of composition. Unable to teach what they had been trained to study, they experienced this contradiction, in part, as a problem of theoretical value for themselves as teachers, for the students they taught, and for the inquiries they pursued. At the same time, the founding assumptions of English departments (often, but not always, the institutional home of composition and rhetoric courses) were receiving unprecedented attention. Feminists, minorities, and other groups formerly marginalized by the traditional English department launched a critique of the literary canon and formalist criticism. Indeed, the postmodern turn of many English departments is signified partly by their new regard for the social effects of literature and the wider range of discourse in which it is embedded. Composition's concern with rhetoric has thus been extended to serve as a framework for literary study as well. This aspect of the postmodern age, however, has left writing specialists with the need to refine their understanding of the social construction of knowledge.

The job crunch faced by literary scholars also coincided with the general critique of disciplinarity most fully explored in Pierre Bourdieu and Jean-Claude Passeron's *Reproduction: In Education, Society, and Culture* (1977), Michel Foucault's *Discipline and Punish* (1979), and Jean-François Lyotard's *Postmodern Condition* (1984). After the English translations of these books had made their ways into academic inquiry, it was no longer easy to give uncritical acceptance to what Stephen Toulmin had described as "the communal tradition of procedures and techniques for dealing with theoretical or practical problems" (142). This development, too, gave new legitimacy to writing specialists' interest in rhetoric since it underscored how particular discourses seek to constrain definitions of "truth." At the same time, it suggested that both composition and literary study threaten to oversimplify writing whenever they approach it as a single phenomenon that can be authoritatively analyzed through a particular procedure. When the contributors to this volume look at writing in a postmodern context, they do not assume that composition studies as it is now practiced and professionalized is an autonomous "discipline." On the contrary, research and scholarship about the processes of writing entail borrowing procedures from several disparate inquiries, including behavioral psychology, phenomenology, psychoanalysis, linguistics, sociology and anthropology, rhetoric, history, and even biology. They see writing as overdetermined —economically important, gendered, a "basic" in certain political discourses, a "humanity" in others—but also, and perhaps most importantly, as the shifting focus of several interesting (and interested) inquiries. Taken together, the essays in this volume theorize the entire scope of composition studies, articulating alternatives to the shape a crisis mentality has given them. Instead of the phrase *literacy-crisis management*, these authors suggest *contending with words* as an appropriate description of what goes on in composition studies.

More than any other part of the academy, compositionists study the processes through which knowledge becomes communicable. More than any other part of the academy, we realize that our answers to the questions that face us can only be partial and situated. We debate alternative accounts of our situations; we do battle with language against the language(s) of oppression; we struggle to get along; we contend with words. Perhaps, then, the most useful way of introducing the contents of this volume is to explain our title, borrowed from Hackforth's translation of Plato's *Phaedrus*:

> SOCRATES: So contending with words is a practice found not only in lawsuits and public harangues but, it seems, wherever men speak we find this single art, if indeed it is an art, which enables people to make out everything to be like everything else, within the limits of possible comparison, and to expose the corresponding attempts of others who disguise what they are doing.
>
> (261–62b)

To contend is to argue. The essayists in this volume recognize that argument produces subjectivities, knowledge, and value. They realize that rhetors and audiences are not found in nature but rather made by the material circumstances in which they live and work. These authors refuse to act as the "window washers of the academy," those functionaries who teach their students to use language as a pellucid medium for referring to real things in the world. They question the notion that coexisting accounts all describe "the same thing." Rather, it is necessary to describe the ways in which differing accounts of knowledge production arise from differing accounts of how, why, and in what context we teach and write.

But to contend is also to manage, to cope, to deal with a situation, to endure, to get along. To read these essays is to find a sense of hope, not cynicism. Even as the authors refuse the complacency of traditional humanistic beliefs, they wrestle with the problems of affirmation in cultural theory. In *Language, Counter-Memory, Practice*, Foucault writes that

> humanism is based on the desire to change the ideological system without altering institutions; and reformers wish to change the institution without touching the institutional system. Revolutionary action, on the contrary, is defined as the simultaneous agitation of consciousness and institutions; this implies that we attack the relationships of power through the notions and institutions that function as their instruments, armature, and armor.
>
> (228)

The essayists in this collection "agitate" such institutions of composition studies as *The St. Martin's Guide to Writing* (Axelrod and Cooper) and the small-group workshop; they look critically at the notions that students' authentic voices can be liberated by teaching methods or that the new French feminism can be grafted onto traditional curricula, but they do not fall into despair. The sense of resistance that characterizes this volume comes from the realization that although language can be the weaponry of battles to make knowledge in a world where truth is absent, language is also the only tool we have for dealing with that situation. Language is a way of contending, in all the senses of that word, with the processes through which discourse shapes human thought and social relations in a context of change and struggle.

As a consequence, these essays do not fall easily into categories of postmodern thought. Nor can they easily be understood in terms of a theory-practice opposition. None is "theory-pure." Each addresses pedagogical questions. The map of these contents that follows, then, is necessarily schematic.

Each of the first four essays describes a kind of status quo in writing instruction and its authorizing theories. Each author then draws on various neo-Marxist authorities to describe how these itineraries might serve hegemonic ends and to suggest ways the itineraries might be changed to foster cultural criticism. Noting how Bakhtin's theory of dialogics has gripped the field, Don H. Bialostosky cautions against reducing that theory to an emphasis on disciplinary conventions, recommending instead that teachers use it to help students become conscious of differing voices in differing discursive situations. Using an account of the contexts for his professional writing as a representative anecdote, he shows that there can be no such thing as an essential self, always and everywhere the same, who writes well merely by letting individualism emerge in language that points to a stable reality. Voice is a construction that emerges from and changes with audience and situation:

"Voice is never something speakers have before they speak but something they create by defining a relation to the other voices that have already opened the discussion and to those that wait to enter into it." But Bialostosky is also wary of the other extreme, the reductive notion that we can fulfill our responsibilities merely by teaching our students a number of disciplinary languages, for such a commitment "risks teaching no more than formal compliance with those norms." He suggests "objectifying students' words and having them retell others' words in their own" as ways of cultivating "authentically" situated voice.

William A. Covino applies the term *magic* to the coincidence between power and the incantatory use of special languages, whether they reflect academic disciplines, cultural literacy, or astrology. He invokes the work of Paulo Freire and Ira Shor to examine some ways in which our students are addressed by the "coercive rhetorics" of mass culture. Asserting that working-class periodicals like the *National Enquirer* describe a tyranny of facts in a world without causality, Covino demonstrates how incantatory language and patterned behavior like "miracle" diets, self-help pop psychology, and lists of ten ways to save thousands of dollars offer a deceptive hope of some control to those whom Paul Fussell calls the "people things are done to" (44). Prevailing definitions and measurements of writing competency, Covino believes, function like the discursive strategies of the *National Enquirer*, leading students to read and write unreflectively in obeisance to "facts" and according to methods approved by superiors. Covino then suggests teaching strategies to help students discriminate the false magic of enforced doctrine from the true magic of critical thought that leads to action.

John Clifford borrows Louis Althusser's conception of ideology to describe the ways through which the writer has been conceived—unproblematically —by existing composition theory. According to Althusser, individuals are "interpellated" or "hailed" by disparate voices belonging to "ideological state apparatuses" to accept and act on certain belief systems. The academy, for example, interpellates students through institutions such as textbooks and curricula that assert the value of reason in democratic societies. Especially in the context of teaching persuasion, Clifford thinks, contemporary textbooks such as *The St. Martin's Guide to Writing* interpellate the author of arguments as a rhetor who "can somehow change the minds of others in a rhetorical vacuum freed from the pollutants of prior social alignments. This thinking is more than naive; it denies identity, represses class conflict, negates the way ideas originate in specific social configurations." By way of remedy, Clifford recommends teaching oriented toward helping our students "perceive how hegemonic rituals construct us in ways we would like to oppose," an "undertaking [that] seems . . . trivial," that calls on us to recognize Antonio Gramsci's perception that only through a " 'minute molecular process' can a transformational collective will be born." In another Marxist application, Patricia Bizzell applies Fredric Jameson's version of dialectic to problematize composition's use of the term *discourse communities*, pointing out how it disguises the role of class struggle in the university. She invokes Henry Giroux's analysis of constructive resistance to hegemony, ultimately calling for integration of this perspective into composition teaching.

Marx and Marxists, however, are not the only thinkers who help us perceive and describe our political and cultural situations. Bruce Herzberg suggests what writing teachers can learn from Foucault's emphasis on discourse as an instrument of power. Discursive practices, Herzberg believes, are the object of our teaching as well as the context of education itself. That belief leads him to observe that, although "Foucault sides with those who insist on the social production of discourse . . . this position does not automatically endorse socially oriented pedagogies" because these pedagogies may ultimately lead students to collaborate "not with one another so much as with the educational system, the disciplines, and the social forces they reproduce." Indeed, Herzberg notes, the social-constructionist approach might "amount to an attempt . . . to capture in the collaborative technique . . . the will to truth." He concludes with a warning against assuming that pedagogical techniques themselves will "guarantee critical action."

Lynn Worsham and Susan C. Jarratt examine relations of discourse and power with specific reference to the insights of postmodern feminisms. Worsham addresses recent work of Hélène Cixous, Luce Irigaray, and Julia Kristeva to describe how the epistemological attitude of phallocentric logic is historically contingent. But, she reminds us, teaching this "knowledge" to our students merely familiarizes the very situation the French feminists have sought to make strange. Instead, Worsham recommends that we understand *écriture féminine* as a strategy whose progress yields "unlearning." Jarratt examines some implications of "expressionist" pedagogies for women as students and teachers. The goal of displacing teachers' authority by evoking and rewarding authentic voice, she points out, may have the effect of enforcing subservient roles for women, as, for example, when female teachers feel called on to "nurture" a sexist voice. Our efforts to liberate students' voices, Jarratt believes, must be supplemented by a carefully theorized understanding of the ways in which power is reproduced in the classroom as a function of class, race, and gender. She uses the recent work of Joyce Trebilcot, Peter Elbow, Kathleen Weiler, and Bell Hooks to describe a pedagogy in which "feminism and rhetoric become allies in contention with the forces of oppression troubling us all."

Next, Patricia Harkin and Victor J. Vitanza turn their attention to relations of theory and praxis as they apply specifically to the scene of teaching. Harkin considers the political and conceptual question of how composition teachers produce knowledge. She invokes Stephen North's term *lore* to describe the knowledge produced by "practitioners" of composition studies. Invoking Mina Shaughnessy's work with open-admissions students as a paradigmatic instance, she argues for the postdisciplinary potential of lore as an alternative to the logical error that Stanley Fish calls "theory hope." Finally, she suggests ways we might change institutional structures to help us see and value teaching that produces, rather than merely disseminates, knowledge. Vitanza argues that composition scholars must prevent both theory and practice from becoming rigid. Invoking Lyotard's debate with Habermas, as well as the recent thought of Gilles Deleuze and Félix Guattari, he urges three theses for a "perverse comedy" or "neoanarchism." The first "(de)centers" on the issue of legitimating knowledge, either in "some universal, ontogenetic theory" (some transhistorical or metadisciplinary truth to resolve all our questions and disagreements) or "rhetorically on consensus theory" (the belief that truth can be produced by democratic consensus). Instead, Vitanza offers Deleuze's notion of "rhizome" as an antidote to belief in epistemological absolutes. The second thesis addresses the "question of author(ship)" to explain how language constitutes both addressors and addressees. The third states—equivocally— that "theory as the game of knowledge cannot help as a resource, because theory of this sort resists finally being . . . totalized." A postpedagogy, for Vitanza, is ultimately a perverse comedy that calls totalizing narratives into question.

John Schilb addresses issues that arise when composition scholars try to link the terms *postmodernism* and *cultural studies* to their work. He emphasizes that they must take into account how *postmodernism* can designate "a critique of traditional epistemology, a set of artistic practices, and an ensemble of larger social conditions" and then ponders some reasons many compositionists are threatened by the emphasis on rhetorical construction that characterizes postmodern theory. He reviews the work of composition scholars who neglect his third definition (and thus slight historical complexity) and concludes with some suggestions about how students and faculty members in composition programs can explore such issues together.

Finally, Sharon Crowley and James J. Sosnoski respond to the essays. Crowley's commentary places the volume in the context of two ongoing debates in composition studies. The first concerns the question whether composition courses ought to train students to communicate a culture's messages or to value its texts. The second addresses the question "whether writing should be taught as a process or a product." Asserting that both sides of each controversy have historically advanced liberal political agendas, she calls for postmodern teachers of writing to change the ways they view themselves as teachers and adopt a more radical stance. They need to examine the political commitments they bring to their teaching, even to the extent of noticing that those commitments might require them to "reject much of what now passes for composition theory." Sosnoski considers each essay in a context of questions about course design. He construes postmodern teaching as an attempt to reduce "the painful situations in which inarticulate students find themselves" by "total and continuous piecemeal remodeling" of the institution. After examining the essayists' proposals for contending with the disparate voices that seek to articulate the aims of composition programs and courses, he engages their accounts of relations between teachers and students. He looks at the classroom itself, predicting that postmodern courses will occur in a variety of environments, including electronic environments in which students construct their own textbooks, an appropriate gesture in the context of critique of dominant discourse. Finally, Sosnoski discusses assignments and grading procedures that might help postmodern teachers and students reduce the "painful condition of not being able to find words for the sense persons have made of their experiences."

By ending this book with responses to it, we seek to reiterate one of its major points: theorizing composition in a postmodern age should not mean worshiping certain thinkers or stances but should involve continually evaluating those stances and envisioning ways to modify or even add to their insights. As each essay underscores, this kind of analysis must address how theory relates to practice. The everyday demands of composition teaching have traditionally pressured theorists to declare how their ideas might be immediately applied in the classroom. While these essays do in fact suggest such applications, they also recognize that the teaching of writing might justifiably lead to emendations of theory. At the same time, the authors point out the complexities involved in adapting theory for the exigencies of teaching. They remain mindful that concepts and their original contexts can get lost in translation, through a drifting that Edward Said calls "traveling theory" (*World* 226–47). This possibility does not mean that composition scholars should insist on theoretical purity or resign themselves to diluting it for the classroom. Perhaps their biggest challenge in the nineties is, instead, to see what they can learn not only from "contending with words" but also from examining the ways theory and practice often contend with each other.

Liberal Education, Writing, and the Dialogic Self

Don H. Bialostosky

IN ACADEMIC writing it is conventional to revise oral presentations for publication by suppressing those figures of thought through which speakers register the presence of their auditors and the remarks of participating colleagues. Such revision deletes the signs of what Mikhail Bakhtin calls the dialogizing background of the utterance to generalize the contexts of its reception and universalize the appearance of its claims. It is also conventional to cover up the signs of such revision, presenting the argument as unified and the self that underwrites it as of one mind about it. Such silent revision enhances the appearance of authoritativeness and hides the possibility that the author did or could think otherwise. These conventions of published authority are part of what we teach in teaching academic writing, and my failure to abide by them in this paper anticipates my questioning of that pedagogy. I foreground the occasions and the revisions of my paper, then, as part of my attempt to redialogize the practice and teaching of academic writing.

I begin accordingly by talking about how I have revised this paper and revised myself for two occasions with similar audiences but diverse coparticipants. My auditors on both occasions were interested in how to think about teaching writing in a college or university, and I, on both occasions, was bringing them word of how Bakhtin's dialogic theories might clarify their purposes and inform their practices. If, as rhetoricians say, my relation to my audience governs my discourse, it might not have been necessary to revise my talk and myself from one occasion to the next, for the genre of my presentation was the same and the speaker-audience relation that determines it was the same. If the community of discourse, its conventional genres, and its commonplaces remain constant, why should I have had to rewrite my paper for a new gathering of essentially the same community? After all, the visiting pastor does not write a new sermon for each new congregation of the same faith.

Two changes between the first and second presentations of the paper nevertheless compelled me to change it, and both, I think, raise theoretically interesting questions about the notions of discourse communities, genre conventions, and commonplaces I have invoked. First, between the 1984 special session on authentic voice of the Conference on College Composition and Communication and the 1987 Chicago Conference on Interpretive Communities and the Undergraduate Writer, many members of my audience had heard about Bakhtin's dialogics. A lot of us had been saying a lot about Bakhtin in the forums many of us attend and in the publications we read, and no one needed any longer to explain who he is and how we have come to possess his work. By 1987 his name was appearing in almost every issue of *College English*, and even undergraduates were using his dialogic terms in their senior theses. So my second audience probably knew more about Bakhtin and his work's implications for the teaching of writing than my first audience did, and even if I abided by all the appropriate conventions of our community of discourse, I would have bored them if I told them what they already knew. If, indeed, the community of discourse I was addressing and the genre conventions and commonplaces of my talk remained the same, my talk could not stay the same because the history of the discussion had changed. Academic discourse is not a ritual discourse that rehearses the same commonplaces every Sunday; academic discourse moves, and we must, as we say, keep up with it.

The second change between presentations of my paper was itself double-edged: first, the voice that provoked and shaped much of my earlier paper was scarcely in evidence among the voices that addressed the participants in the Chicago conference, and, second, many of the voices that did address that conference were much closer to Bakhtin and me than was my original friendly adversary. My former colleague Peter Elbow first invited me to participate in the CCCC session he organized, and he encouraged me to reformulate his "self"-centered idea of "authentic voice" in the social and contentious terms of dialogics. Although Elbow's work was not unknown to my Chicago audience and some of its members even declared their allegiance to his position from the floor, his psychological and individualistic stance, which dominated the first occasion of my talk, was clearly marginalized on the second one. The psychologists who spoke in Chicago were more interested in problem solving and stages of development than in authentic voice, and the social constructionists who dominated the meeting already shared Bakhtin's view that our individual voices should be defined as relations to others, not as relations to ourselves. A Bakhtinian who shares the podium with Joe Williams, Tori Haring-Smith, Elaine Maimon, Kenneth Bruffee, Gregory Colomb, Linda Peterson, Richard Lanham, and David Bartholomae, among others, does not need to argue for a social understanding of discourse as I did when I shared the stage with Elbow. My earlier provocation to speech was placed in the background by the gathering of another group of speakers, and I needed to search for new provocations from other people whose positions were closer to my own. Though again the discourse community and the generic conventions and commonplaces of my paper remained constant, a change in the field of speakers involved and in the range of positions they represented compelled me to change my talk.

In my first talk I appropriated Elbow's terms for a social notion of authentic voice that I did not need to emphasize at the Chicago conference. Here is a part of the earlier paper that reveals its dialogic ties with Elbow:

> Voice, as I am defining it, is not so much a matter of how my language relates to me as it is a matter of how my language relates to your language and to the language of others you and I have heard address our topic. Voice is never something speakers have before they speak but something they create by defining a relation to the other voices that have already opened the discussion and to those that wait to enter into it. "I" am—and "my self" is—created in the course of my assimilating, responding to, and anticipating the voices of others. Language, from the time I first begin to hear it from my parents and siblings and friends and teachers, is always somebody else's first and becomes mine without entirely losing its otherness.
>
> Does this other-directed notion of voice deprive my voice of authenticity, as Peter Elbow understands it, as a resonant and effortless expression in an utterance of the person uttering it? Does my notion of voice so alienate my own voice that nothing distinctive to me remains? I think not, but I do think I must redefine what I mean when I talk about speaking in an authentic voice.
>
> If voice as I have defined it is to be heard in the speaker's responsiveness to the voices of others who have spoken on the topic as well as to the voices of those who now listen but may yet speak, then an authentic voice in my terms would be one that vitally and productively engaged those voices. It would be authentically situated, if you will, evidently aware of its place in the ongoing

conversation about its topic, relevant to preceding utterances, alert to those about to follow, and clear about its own contribution.

In these terms, an inauthentic voice would be "out of it"—unresponsive to what had been said or what might be said on its topic, dead to possibilities that others who share the language and the world could hear and expect responses to.

Ah, there's the rub. A paper perfectly responsive to what has been said by *some* others is suddenly "out of it" in a field of *other* others. An introduction will not do where the parties are already acquainted, and a point worth making in response to a strong opponent leaves us out of it when we make it among allies who take the point for granted. And what is worse, we can commit such faux pas without leaving a single discourse community or leaving its system of commonplaces or breaching its decorum of genres.

It is not enough, it seems, to learn to mind our academic manners, for we can still make fools of ourselves by not knowing to whom or after whom we are speaking. A student who writes a critical essay on "My Last Duchess" without mentioning a book the teacher has written on it may not impress that teacher no matter how well the essay otherwise reflects the decorum of the opening review of the literature, and the professional critic who submits a book or article for publication always takes the same risk of having ignored the major work of some anonymous referee. Knowing the conventions is indispensable, but it also helps to know who's out there.

It may appear, however, that in undergraduate instruction the conventions will suffice without the specific knowledge of prior voices. After all, one way the discourse of undergraduate instruction differs from the discourses of more advanced study and of professional academic writing is that we do not require undergraduate writers to situate their writing in the history or current published discussion of their topic. (Indeed we sometimes do not expect our graduate students or ourselves to do so.) What this distinction means in practice, however, is not that the undergraduate student adopts conventions and exploits commonplaces without regard to specific prior uses of them but that we or our class discussions or our sets of readings establish such specific prior uses for the working purposes of the class. We define a field of the "already said" and the "might be said" in our classes, and we trust our students to recognize the conventions of our discourse and to discover the opportunities and limitations set by the specific voices we take on or admit into those classrooms. Our students' writing depends not just on their learning the ropes but on their coming into contact with some representative voices from the field whose examples suggest projects to pursue and whose differences reveal problems to address. Their writing relies, in short, on whom they have heard of and whom they have heard out.

Dialogics differs from other social theories of discourse in its vision of ideologically situated persons involved in struggles over the meanings of things and the ownership of words. It de-emphasizes rhetorical common-places, calling attention instead to the appropriated, if not always proper, places of persons who have identified themselves with certain words, ideas, ways of talking, and social positions. And it envisions what Bakhtin calls "an individual's ideological becoming" not just as the learning of "infor-mation, directions, rules, models" or conventions but as the individual's struggle to make other people's language his or her own and to resist being owned completely by alien languages. As Bakhtin puts it, "the struggle and dialogic interrelationship of [authoritative and internally persuasive discourse] are what usually determine the history of an individual ideological conscious-ness" (342).

In that struggle, the voice that speaks the authoritative word is set apart in what Bakhtin describes as a distanced zone; the authoritative word can be received and repeated but is not to be responded to, modified, or questioned. It is the voice of the textbook or the lecturer that students learn to parrot back on tests, the voice of the instructor's summary judgment, the voice of given rules and conventions that must be observed but that do not have to account for themselves. The internally persuasive word is not, however, a word belonging solely to the inner world of the student, a dialectical coun-terpart to a wholly external authoritative word. Bakhtin writes that

> the internally persuasive word is half-ours, half-someone else's. Its creativity and productivity consist precisely in the fact that such a word awakens new and independent words, that it organizes masses of our words from within, and does not remain in an isolated and static condition. It is not so much interpreted by us as it is further, that is, freely, developed, applied to new material, new conditions; it enters into interanimating relationships with new contexts.
>
> (345–46)

Just as the authoritative word is set apart in the distanced zone, the internally persuasive word is in the "zone of contact" in which its receiver is also its user (345). This word differs from the authoritative word not so much as inner to outer, though Bakhtin uses these misleading terms, but as prox-imate to distanced, touchable to untouchable, answerable to unanswerable language. It is not inert and undigestible, nor does it dominate from within as the authoritative word appears to dominate from without. Rather, Bakhtin writes, "it enters into an intense interaction, a *struggle* with other internally persuasive discourses" (346). The internally persuasive word does not settle things and take over the voice but engages actively with other such words in vital dialogue that marks the authentically situated voice. The authoritative word remains aloof from that dialogue, co-opts it, or even silences it. The voice under the influence of the authoritative word repeats it thoughtlessly or imitates it confusedly or cites it passively or complies with it formally or defers to it silently.

Although the participants in the Chicago conference who emphasized teaching students the conventions of scholarly writing may also have intended to demystify the norms of authoritative discourse, I feared and still fear that their primary emphasis risks teaching no more than formal compliance with those norms. Many disciplinary courses already aim no higher than enforcing such conformity, and I would be sorry to see the writing course, whether in English or across the disciplines, confine itself to explaining the conventions that the disciplinary courses mutely impose.

As I see it, the writing class opens up a space in which individual ideological development can become not just the accidental outcome of encounters with the disciplinary languages but the deliberate goal of a reflective practice. Such a class can modify the terms of disciplinary education in the students' favor by letting them in on the secrets of genre and convention that the disciplines silently observe, by sharing with students the power produced by switching genres and defying conventions, and by suspending for the sake of students' development some of the conditions of disciplinary discourse itself. Though we would not want to train students in inappropriate genres and behaviors that would hinder their success in history or biology or even other English classes, we are free to engage them in intellectual struggles from which they learn to hold their own and choose their own genres, not just to behave themselves.

The special conditions we set up in our writing classrooms depend on how we understand new college writers and the specific problems of developing their individual ideological consciousnesses. Such students are beginning to encounter a number of disciplinary languages that claim, in their domains of expertise, to be more precise and comprehensive than the languages students bring with them. To master these disciplines, students are expected to assimilate disciplinary languages and to write them in preference to the languages they ordinarily speak. There is a powerful pressure to adopt these authoritative languages, even though students do not find them internally persuasive and feel alienated when they use them in written discourse. The vocabulary and tone of these disciplines seem remote to students and their form of presentation seems complicated. Developed arguments, articulated parts, and elaborate tropes replace the face-to-face exchange of words or opinions or tones. Finally, the classical texts or textbooks of some of these disciplines are set apart in time, in language, and in authority. Students are invited to defer to the language of such texts instead of engaging it.

As part of a college education designed to initiate students into reflexive use of these authoritative languages, the study of college writing should not permit students to retreat from the challenges presented by these demanding languages to languages with which they are already comfortable or to conform without struggle to the new academic languages. It is more important to cultivate students' understanding of their ambivalent situations and to validate their struggles to remake themselves and the languages imposed on them. If they see that they do not already possess a finished authentic identity and an authentic language, which the new alien languages threaten from without, they may also see that the new languages do not promise to provide such an identity but only offer new resources for seeing and saying.

Recognizing languages as languages and exploring the worldviews inherent in them allows us to engage languages in a new way: responsibly, self-consciously, and openly, or—for it amounts to the same thing—authentically. To know our minds as the site of dialogue among languages is to discover both the relevance of other people's words to our predicaments and the relevance of our contributions to others with whom we share the world and the ongoing dialogue about it. It is to take up membership not just in the community defined by the authority of a given discipline or religion or class and its language but in the whole community where those languages are in contention within and among the voices of writers and speakers for whom they are internally persuasive.

Two practices to cultivate authentically situated voice follow from the goals I have described—objectifying students' words and having them retell others' words in their own. Students need to examine the words they arrive with and take for granted, whether those words are the prose of *Reader's Digest* and *Time* or the unexamined languages of class, party, religion, age group, gender group, or region. We need to encourage students to characterize these languages and to respond to what they have characterized. Paul Cardacci of Georgetown University reported at the Chicago conference that he uses George Lakoff and Mark Johnson's *Metaphors We Live By* to help basic-writing students recognize the metaphors that orient their thought and to help them make those metaphors available for criticism. Bakhtin suggests that inventing characters who speak a particular social-ideological idiom is a good way to objectify those idioms and liberate ourselves from their authority. Here the genre in question is ultimately that of the novelist, not the professional academic, but the function of such portraiture in individual ideological development is important enough to give it a place in the writing classroom.

The professional and high-cultural languages that intimidate students from without need to be demystified and rewritten in terms available to students. Assignments in which students retell or even parody these authoritative voices and styles can bring these languages into the zone of contact. While a disciplinary course encourages students to appropriate its languages and conventions accurately and completely, a writing course can put students in a position to answer those languages by minimizing their authority and finality. We should authorize our students to reaccent, not just reproduce, the disciplinary languages we and our colleagues impose on them.

For Bakhtin, retelling in one's own words is not a sterile exercise in paraphrasing but a working-out of evaluative relations between the reporting and the reported discourse—a necessarily double-voiced practice that "includes within it the entire series of forms for the appropriation while transmitting of another's words" (342). This range of forms includes the journal that copies out a quotation on the left page and responds to it on the right, the marginal annotation, the admiring or parodic reformulation, the quoted passage preceded by the writer's point in quoting and followed by the writer's interpretation, and many others. These forms are of interest not just as conventions to be learned but as sites where productive verbal-ideological work goes on. Most handbooks on argumentation treat the quotation as a technical citation in support of the author's claims in genres like the research paper, but I suggest that quotation is the very act in which one voice creatively absorbs another and defines itself in relation to that second voice. When we interrupt the quoted text, interrogate it, clarify its point, or expose its ambiguities, we make an opening for our own utterances and give shape to our own roles in the conversation. The point of this exercise is to practice aligning what we are saying with other voices, whether we affirm, redefine, differ with, or develop them. The exercise should avoid confronting students with too many voices or with overelaborated voices, concentrating instead on making significant contact between the student writer's words and the words he or she reproduces.

I have been urging that we engage our writing students not just with disciplinary conventions, genres, and commonplaces but with specific other voices in relation to which they may define their own voices, but I should note that we may imagine those other voices in several ways. David Bartholomae's essay "Inventing the University," which accords with my position here in many respects, contains the striking image of " 'off-stage voices,' the oversound of all that has been said." He continues:

> These voices, the presence of the "already written," stand in defiance of a writer's desire for originality and determine what might be said. A writer does not write (and this is Barthes's famous paradox) but is, himself, written by the languages available to him.

> (143)

In this passage, previous voices merge first into the "already written" and then into available "languages," losing their individual profiles and characteristic limitations as they acquire the power to defy efforts of origination and to write the writer who would write in them. As this passage transforms them, they are no longer individual voices but Foucauldian discourses that contain within themselves all the possibilities of utterance. They do not situate and provoke our own utterances as specific other voices do but anticipate and contain them. Our only choice, if we wish to participate in the writing they empower, is to move inside them and assume the position of privilege they grant us. Their authority, in this formulation, is absolute and does not allow for our taking them as "half-ours and half-someone else's," as Bakhtin says we take the internally persuasive word (345).

But Bartholomae's essay suggests elsewhere a position closer to Bakhtin's, for Bartholomae admires the student essay that Bakhtin would call double-voiced, the essay that Bartholomae says displays "two gestures . . . one imitative and one critical" (157). Furthermore, Bartholomae repeatedly opens the alternative between a single code or discourse and competing codes or discourses that might question and debate any single claim to authority. But the drama he points to "in a student's essay, as he or she struggles with and against the languages of our contemporary life" (162) or "against competing discourses" (158) would be even more dramatic if the characters in it were permitted to assume their identities as specific dramatis personae, other persons whose use of the languages of our contemporary life provokes the students to respond. The languages or discourses themselves as disembodied systems of inescapable terms and commonplaces have too much power to make the struggle with them dramatic, unless they are the gods of a Foucauldian universe whose power reveals the tragic drama of our own and our students' futile struggles.

Elaine P. Maimon's essay "Maps and Genres" also offers an image of other voices as the student writer encounters them:

> The lonely beginner condemned to the linearity of ink on the blank page hears all the wrong voices. As he tries to imagine those absent strangers to whom he must write, he hears the voices of doubt and despair: "You don't belong here. This paper will show your smart English teacher how stupid you are. You never could write anyway." We want students to drown out these voices with other voices—voices that impersonate the missing readers. Nancy Sommers' research in revision makes clear that experienced writers know how to imagine a reader who is "partially a reflection of themselves and functions as a critical and productive collaborator—a collaborator who has yet to love their work."
>
> (124)

The voices in this drama are all voices from the pedagogical situation itself, the discouraging voice of the teacher who will unmask the student writer's masquerade as an academic writer and the encouraging voices of the student's collaborative colleagues whose criticism does not threaten ostracism from their community. But in this image neither the teacher's voice nor the voices of other students shape the lonely beginner's utterance or provoke it; they only judge it, either harshly or kindly. Acknowledgment of others' help remains a ritual in this community because no one in it has discovered the other voices whose prior writing provides the language and the provocation for the beginner's utterance. Its members are innocent of the kind of debt with which Bartholomae's writers are all too burdened.

Bakhtin's prose writers enjoy no such innocence, but neither do they meet other voices as embodiments of all-powerful intimidating discourses. For them other voices are writers like themselves who are already on the scene and already having their say about the world:

> Any concrete discourse . . . finds the object at which it was directed already as it were overlain with qualifications, open to dispute, charged with value, already enveloped in an obscuring mist—or, on the contrary, by the "light" of alien words that have already been spoken about it. It is entangled, shot through with shared thoughts, points of view, alien value judgments and accents. The word, directed toward its object, enters a dialogically agitated and tension-filled environment of alien words, value judgments and accents, weaves in and out of complex interrelationships, merges with some, recoils from others, intersects with yet a third group: all this may crucially shape the discourse, may leave a trace in all its semantic layers, may complicate its expression and influence its entire stylistic profile. . . . For the prose writer, the object is a focal point for heteroglot voices among which his own voice must also sound; these voices create the background necessary for his own voice, outside which his artistic prose nuances cannot be perceived, and without which they "do not sound."
>
> (276–78)

Other voices for Bakhtin give our voices their occasions and provocations, their reasons for saying one thing rather than another, their differences that make them distinguishable and audible among the many voices in the forum.

Bakhtin's open forum that excludes no prior or contemporary voices is the ultimate forum in which the voices we learn in our disciplinary and pedagogical communities get their hearings and find their meanings. Its manners are rough-and-tumble, its genres are mixed, its commonplaces are always getting appropriated, and its only convention is the taking of turns by all the voices it has convened, though there is no guarantee they will not interrupt one another. Specialized discourses branch off from the forum but cannot entirely separate themselves from it into purified universes of discourse invulnerable to parodic revoicing from some other language's point of view.

Classrooms protect the young from its full cacophony to cultivate students' capacities to speak up and be heard in it, but they offer no permanent refuge from it; indeed they cannot even do without some sample of its voices, selected to provoke students without overwhelming them. Even the communities of our national languages and our cultural groups give us only partial shelter from translated voices from outside and their barbarous neologisms (like *heteroglossia* and *dialogics*).

Bakhtin suggests that novelists make this entire heteroglot forum the object of their discourse, while scholars and teachers confine themselves to their specialized objects and their more decorous genres. But if we aim for individual ideological development we cannot leave this forum to the novelists. In the final analysis what Bakhtin calls the "linguistic consciousness of the educated person" resembles the novelist's language:

> [W]ithin it, intentional diversity of speech . . . is transformed into diversity of language . . . ; what results is not a single language but a dialogue of languages. . . . a highly specific unity of several "languages" that have established mutual contact and mutual recognition with each other.
>
> (294–95)

To clarify the character of this consciousness, I offer one last long quotation from Bakhtin:

> Concrete socio-ideological consciousness, as it becomes creative . . . discovers itself already surrounded by heteroglossia and not at all a single, unitary language, inviolable and indisputable. The actively literary linguistic consciousness at all times and everywhere . . . comes upon "languages," and not language. Consciousness finds itself inevitably facing the necessity of *having to choose a language*. . . . Only by remaining in a closed environment, one without writing or thought, completely off the maps of socio-ideological becoming, could a man fail to sense this activity of selecting a language and rest assured in the inviolability of his own language, the conviction that his language is predetermined.
>
> Even such a man, however, deals not in fact with a single language but with languages—except that the place occupied by each of these languages is fixed and indisputable, the movement from one to the other is predetermined and not a thought process; it is as if these languages were in different chambers. They do not collide with each other in his consciousness, there is no attempt to coordinate them, to look at one of these languages through the eyes of another language.
>
> (295)

Those different chambers are not unlike different knowledge communities, each insulated from the others in its own department and each enterable by those who adopt its taken-for-granted conventions and learn its language. The students' movement from one such community to another is, as Bakhtin says, often predetermined and not decided by a thought process—a fact of requirements and schedules that separate communities. Students can learn the conventions and language of each community without undergoing any "socio-ideological becoming" at all as long as they learn the manners appropriate in each department and never see one from the point of view of any other. Bakhtin illustrates such insulation of verbal domains in the life of a peasant who moves from the language of church to the language of family to the language of official transactions without giving the differences among them a second thought.

But in the forum and the consciousness where all these languages meet and compete to be chosen, no such blithe passage from one to another is possible, and the participation in diverse knowledge communities opens a struggle among them that knowledge of conventions and mannerly behavior cannot resolve. For Bakhtin, self-conscious participation in that struggle marks the free and educated consciousness—the dialogic self. The writing course, like the novel and the public square, may be one of the forums in which that consciousness comes into being.

Magic, Literacy, and *the* National Enquirer

❖

William A. Covino

> You can get rid of negative thoughts—and get on with your
> life—by following an expert's simple four-step program. . . .
> Admit that you don't know what's causing your problem.
> . . . Accept responsibility for your problem, but don't blame
> yourself for it. . . . Gain a fresh perspective. . . . Think
> positive.
>
> —*National Enquirer*

THIS quotation from the *National Enquirer* is one example among many of that publication's coercive incantations, language that seeks to control and transform readers by declaring that they can overcome difficulties through patterned behavior. Discussing the *Enquirer* as a specimen text of such pronouncements allows us to distinguish between "good" and "bad" magic and advances a lexicon for evaluating coercive rhetorics and the literacies they enfranchise. More generally, I propose that magic and magic consciousness are foundations of rhetoric and literacy, and, as they are exploited in language, magic formulas and magic consciousness define mass culture.

Magic as Rhetoric

It is possible to distinguish between magic in the strict, or real, sense and magic in the weak, or metaphorical, sense; we might restate this distinction as one between magic as such and magical rhetoric. Magic as such includes medical magic (e.g., the curative spells of the "medicine man"), black magic (witchcraft, sorcery), ceremonial magic (rainmaking), religious magic (exorcism), occultism (fortune-telling), and the paranormal (ESP, flying saucers). Daniel O'Keefe, who has written the most comprehensive recent social theory of magic, distinguishes magic in the strict sense from magical rhetoric by pointing out that, in real magic, "speeches are not extemporaneous or composed, but entirely traditional; and audience response is preordained." Further, real magic "does not try to 'persuade' [as does rhetoric], but to compel." O'Keefe does admit, however, with reference to Plato and Aristotle, that the function of rhetoric (as persuasion) may be "wrenching the consensus and foreclosing it" and that "there is some resemblance to magic in this operation—in the attempt to suspend communal dialogue, in the first person singular speaking as the first person plural ['we believe'], in the partialism of the viewpoint." But "magic itself" is rigidly scripted, while rhetoric is "much freer and more plastic." Strictly speaking, rhetoric "reminds us of magic" (O'Keefe 82–83).

I suggest that we may borrow terms from magic to illuminate rhetoric and, in particular, to understand the workings of coercive discourse. Although my subject is the rhetoric of coercion, addressed in the terms of magic, you should understand that when I use the word *magic* I mean *rhetoric*. I argue here for the synonymy of magic and rhetoric; after sketching that argument, I leave off any mention of rhetoric, with the hope that magic will sound like rhetoric to you as well.

Consider, for instance, that illusion is the common goal of both magic and rhetoric. Jacqueline de Romilly emphasizes this point in *Magic and Rhetoric in Ancient Greece*, holding the Sophists responsible for illusions of truth achieved through the incantatory spell of language and reminding us that Plato's Socrates often charged his opponents with bad magic, while also weaving his own spells (see esp. 26–27, 36). The Sophists made a world of multiple forms appear and disappear, while Plato's Socrates kept rehearsing one trick—making dialogue disappear into essence but continually admitting that it can't be done because the essence of language is illusion.[1]

While Aristotelian and Ciceronian rhetorics contributed to the establishment of rhetoric as *techne* without magic, as a pursuit associated with political and institutional control and stability, the link between magic and rhetoric persisted. Through the Middle Ages and into the Renaissance, many prominent humanists were also occultists, and while the emphasis on technical rhetoric continued, "a revival of the Greek sophistic notion of rhetoric as magic" also occurred (Ward 109). From John O. Ward's recent study of magic and rhetoric, we learn that teachers such as Isidore of Seville wrote textbooks on both rhetoric and magic, and a typical government adviser in the Middle Ages was a "practicioner of magic and rhetoric, a supplier of skills to ruler and crown—administrative, ideological, rhetorical, historical, liturgical, and architectural skills" (101; note the analogy between this characterization of government advisers and the astrologer Joan Quigley's role in the Reagan administration).

The need for magic, which Susanne Langer posits as part of the "inventory of human needs" (38), seems to coincide with the need for technical rhetoric; as Ward points out, "high points in the history of rhetoric are also high points in devotion to the occult" (87). In particular, the proliferation of new facts, the "steady increase of certain knowledge" (Ward 115) that accounts for the beginning of each traditional epoch of progress in Western history, provokes doubt about what is "really" true and drives those who manage a newly more complex world to magic and to magic rhetoric. Thus the overtly magical sophistry of early antiquity, the renewed reliance on both magic and technical rhetoric in the late Middle Ages and the Renaissance (Ward 107–109), the appropriation of magic to empirical methodology in the Enlightenment (O'Keefe 557), and the growth of both New Age occultism and data-management systems in our own "information age" may all reflect the appeal of both magic and rhetoric, or of magic as rhetoric, at times when the influx of new knowledge and of new living patterns makes us search for a spell to control the demons of change. Recent best-sellers include both Shirley MacLaine's *Out on a Limb*, which offers a reactionary mysticism that looks backward for selfhood and constructs identity by invoking past lives, and E. D. Hirsch's *Cultural Literacy: What Every American Needs to Know*, a reactionary pedagogy that looks backward for a common language of established facts and constructs identity through a dictionary of cultural literacy, a list of terms we must memorize and speak to transmigrate into the mainstream, a virtual lexicon of incantations.

Insofar as programs such as Hirsch's provide schemata for public discourse, they constitute a technical rhetoric. The congeniality of magic and technical rhetoric results from the real power of rhetoric to design and alter reality: the mastery of institutional discourse makes one an insider who can, in turn, invoke and impose facts and formulas. As Kenneth Burke writes, this power exists because "the magical decree is implicit in all language; for the mere act of naming an object or situation decrees that it is to be singled out as such-and-such rather than as something-other." Magic is a "coercive command," the "establishment or management by decree," and insofar as it is intrinsic to language, it is unavoidable. Further, all magic is a strategy calculated to address a situation "in the name of" a certain power (*Philosophy* 3–5). For Burke, strategy, situation, and power are the elements of magic and (I would add) the elements of rhetoric, when embodied in discourse: "Stop in the name of the law." Herbert Marcuse emphasizes the force of these elements as they operate on mass culture:

> At the nodal points of the universe of public discourse, self-validating, ana-
> lytical propositions appear which function like magic-ritual formulas. Ham-
> mered and rehammered into the recipient's mind, they produce the effect of
> enclosing it within the circle of the conditions prescribed by the formula.
>
> (88)

For Marcuse, "the closing of the universe of discourse" is effected by "magical, authoritarian and ritual elements [that] permeate speech and language. . . . It is the word that orders and organizes, that induces people to do, to buy, and to accept" (84–86). Abbreviated thought and thoughtless behavior are the consequences of the tendency in media and government institutions to prefer the abridgment of information: "In its immediacy and directness, [media language] impedes conceptual thinking; thus, it impedes thinking" (95). A popular and obvious current magic-ritual formula is "just say no," which at once makes the victims of the drug problem responsible for elim-inating it and prescribes an incantation that will make it disappear, all in the name of (again) the law. (As I propose more fully later, victims who don't use magic words effectively are typically left to blame themselves.)

True Magic and False Magic

Burke sketches the conditions for a true magic, a correct magic, and a false or incorrect magic. True magic is the result not of formulaic incantation that attempts to suspend or control "the laws of motion" but of action that creates action, words that create words. It is consequential, producing "something out of nothing," and it is generative (*Grammar* 66). Writers are assistants to the magic of words causing words, to the play of language

> where the act of the writing brings up problems and discoveries intrinsic to
> the act, leading to developments that derive not from the scene, or agent, or
> agency, or extrinsic purposes, but purely from the foregoing aspects of the act
> itself. . . . Our act itself alters the conditions of action, as "one thing leads
> to another" in an order that would not have occurred had we not acted.
>
> (67)

The power that generates true magic is novelty.

Like true magic, correct magic also entails revelation and change, but instead of the "pure" magic of words causing words, correct magic is social, a decree that is least coercive and most inclusive, approachable through the "collective revelation of testing and discussion," that is, dialectically and dialogically. Thus, correct magic entails what Burke calls "scope" (*Grammar* 59); it accounts more fully for facts by subjecting them to the broadest inquiry. (The ideal practice of correct magic is "possible only to an infinite, omniscient mind" [*Philosophy* 4, 7].)

With Burke as a guide, I propose that while all magic is always coercive because it constitutes reality by decree, true-correct magic is practiced as *constitutive inquiry* or the *coercive expansion of the possibilities for action*, while false-incorrect magic—distinct from both the pure novelty of true magic and the shared creativity of correct magic—is practiced as *enforced doctrine* or the *coercive reduction of the possibilities for action*: "Stop in the name of the law."[2] Other distinctions between true-correct and false-incorrect magic (listed below) extend the definitions I have presented for each and point us toward further explanation and illustration with reference to that widely read American medium for false-incorrect magic, the *National Enquirer*.

True-Correct Magic
generative
enlarges the grounds for action by the creation of choices
originates on the margins of mass culture, as critique
practiced as dialogue
results in integration

False-Incorrect Magic
reductive
exploits the laws of motion by the restriction of choices
originates in the center of mass culture, as technique
practiced as inculcation
results in adaptation

I abbreviate true-correct magic as true magic and false-incorrect magic as false magic—collapsing correctness into truth and incorrectness into falsehood—partly for stylistic economy and partly to stress the moral distinction between one magic and another.

Magic and the National Enquirer

Magic power appeals, on the one hand, to aspiring insiders who want to be part of the intellectual or political or economic establishment that issues decrees. On the other hand, the more marginalized and oppressed one is, the more susceptible to magic and to technical rhetoric (Ward 69). Roland Barthes and Jacques Ellul complain that the burden of "facts" accounts for this susceptibility; a world that seems to contain too much knowledge and too many associations makes us more inclined to accept magical solutions (O'Keefe 476). Paulo Freire contrasts "critical consciousness" with this "magic consciousness," associating the latter with the oppressed classes. Magic consciousness "apprehends facts and attributes them to a superior power, [leading people to] fold their arms, resigned to the impossibility of resisting the power of facts" (*Education* 44). Such resignation finds its common expression in "that's the way it is," which is an acceptance not of truth examined but of circumstance enforced.

Widely circulated and widely read by the American working class, the *National Enquirer* may represent a habit of false inquiry rooted in magic consciousness. Advertising the "largest circulation of any paper in America," the *Enquirer* (established in 1926) sells over 4 million copies of each issue, reaching a total adult audience of nearly 19 million. Its closest newspaper rival is *USA Today*, which advertises a national readership of 5.3 million (on every front page) and whose audience is probably in a different class than that of the *Enquirer* audience.

While *USA Today* devotes a good deal of space to news about financial markets and yuppie trends, thus appealing to the upwardly mobile, the typical *Enquirer* reader is a working-class woman who has not attended college. According to a profile of the 1987 *Enquirer* audience, 77% of all readers have not attended college, and annual household income for nearly 64% is under $30,000. Female readers outnumber male readers 2 to 1. They are older (36.7 is the median age for women, 33.6 for men), they are less well-educated (80% of the women have no college, compared with 73% of the men), and they earn less (65% of the female respondents have annual household incomes of less than $30,000, compared with 60% of the male respondents).[3]

While proposing that such numbers indicate a majority of working-class women readers, I must also admit the difficulty of defining *working class*. The color of one's collar on the job and the possession of a job outside the home are questionable determinants; beliefs and feelings about one's status and group identity may be the significant factors (Jackman and Jackman 38). Identifying class with the power and authority enjoyed by its members, we might, at least, distinguish the working class from the middle class by adopting O'Keefe's definition that middle-class people are "those who do not run things, but are treated well in return for their loyalty" (O'Keefe 467); consequently, working-class people are those treated less well, those Paul Fussell calls "people things are done to" (44). According to the 1980 census, this definition certainly applies to working-class women, who "suffer disproportionately from economic marginality, unsatisfying jobs, poor working conditions, inadequate social and municipal services, deteriorating neighborhoods, and alienation from the American mainstream" (Hunter and Harman 388). In general, *Enquirer* readers lack the resources and experience that make upward mobility possible, and thus they are relegated to the status that Fussell describes. *Enquirer* readers need magic, and the *Enquirer* provides it, with all the characteristics of false magic that I proposed above.

False Magic Is Reductive

Most *Enquirer* stories are tethered—often explicitly—to governing maxims: the same ones, repeated in similar stories from issue to issue, are "hammered and rehammered into the recipient's mind," so that they become "proverbial" examples of Marcuse's magic-ritual formulas (88). A handful of "proverbs" recurs in each issue:[4]

Self-Improvement Is Simple. "Simply Eating Certain Foods Will Make You Smarter" (2 Aug. 1988; 23); "Living a Long, Happy Life Is Easier Than You Think" (12 Apr. 1988; 9); "52 Simple Tips That Will Put Thousands in Your Pocket" ("Bone your own chicken breasts. . . . Don't let the water run while you're brushing your teeth. . . . Don't buy premium paper towels" [10 Jan. 1989; 6–7]). Articles such as these are virtual extensions of the proverbial wisdom that defined *Poor Richard's Almanack*, which set aside complexity and difficulty and advertised discipline.

Success Techniques Apply to Everyone. The *Enquirer* sets aside individuality along with complexity and difficulty. Generalized schematic advice—advertising better living through sameness—aligns success with following universal rules. There are five rules for handling mistakes on the job (22 Dec. 1987; 12), seven rules for saving time in the kitchen, seven rules for getting a promotion (27 Sept. 1988; 15, 20), ten ingredients in the "recipe for a happy marriage," and three steps to falling asleep (23 Aug. 1988; 13, 48). In a world where individual differences are homogenized into generalized behaviors, individual psychology is understood only as an instance of universal categories. For example, "The Way You Celebrate Your Birthday Reveals Your Personality" (23 Aug. 1988; 12), but you have just nine personalities to choose from; similarly, the way you take compliments, give gifts, and smile, along with your favorite ice-cream flavor, allow you to type yourself.

Failure Is an Attitude Problem. Success results from the imposition of mind—equipped with the prescribed rules and principles—over matter. And the proper mind-set is a positive attitude, a Reaganesque image of "morning in America," in which sniveling about pains and problems is taboo (a regular *Enquirer* feature is "$10 for Happy Thoughts"). The sky diver whose chutes don't open saves himself by refusing to imagine his imminent death and instead picturing his family:

> "We're so happy!" I thought. "Our future looks so bright!" I saw a mental picture of my mischievous little son Ben, a fantastic little 4-year-old who's everything a father could want. I saw his 18-month-old brother Matt, with that dribbly chin that melts my heart whenever I see it. Nope, no way would death meet up with me at this point in my life.
>
> (30 Aug. 1988; 3)

Determined not to die, he meditates himself into "a ball of fat, a rubber ball. I won't get hurt. I'll just melt into the earth or bounce off it," and bounce he does, surviving a two-mile fall. This is an extreme instance of the "you can be anything you wanna be" attitude that the *Enquirer* insists on continually, through the very frequency of its success prescriptions.

Medical Technology Can Fix Anything. The power of attitude and technique to make life better is rivaled by the power of technology, mainly medical technology. New machines, drugs, and surgical procedures can make blood clots disappear, eliminate hemorrhoids, remove fat, grow hair, smooth wrinkles, cure arthritis. While numerous *Enquirer* articles reveal such breakthroughs, *Enquirer* advertising, with its decided emphasis on fixing one's body, represents the most strident and substantial appeal to those who want to make pain, age, and mortality disappear. Typically, nearly half the ads in each issue are selling skin treatments, body beautifiers, reducing programs, indigestion and pain relievers, or ambulatory aids.

Nobody's Safe. Although technique, attitude, and technology ensure personal and professional success, anyone can become a victim or a freak. *Enquirer* articles describe Australians who are violently allergic to plastic and chemical additives, little girls who are dying from exposure to light, a boy who won't grow, a boy who can't stop eating, women who have been unable to stop having babies, a house possessed by demons. Celebrities, the culture heroes of the *Enquirer*, are just as vulnerable: Liz Taylor fights back pain, alcoholism, and suicide; television star Alan Thicke is pursued by a terrifying, lovesick fan; Ringo Starr fights drug addiction. From issue to issue, the diseases, deaths, and divorces of the rich and famous illustrate a world of misfortune and tragedy from which no one is protected.

Implicitly, we are all already victims of technical and technological advances; they reduce the latitude of human behavior and individuality. The threat that technology will overcome humanity is occasionally explicit, in articles about machines taking over human labor:

> "Robots will take over the Earth!" declares a university robotics expert [Hans Moravec, director of the Mobile Robot Laboratory at Carnegie Mellon Uni-

versity]. . . . "They won't need us. They will be knowledgeable enough to handle their own maintenance, reproduction and self-improvement. It seems that the takeover by robots is almost inevitable."

(3 Jan. 1989; 4)

While mimicking science fiction, this piece is also the logical extension of the *Enquirer* view that facts and formulas exert more control in the world than people do.

Survival Is in the Hands of Providence. A grizzly bear and a "man-eating crocodile" number among the murderous animals who miraculously end their attacks, to sighs of "thank God" from their victims. Renegade machines— airplanes, tanks, cars—level property but leave inhabitants unhurt, each survivor repeating the sentiments of Stephen Bright, whose car was sliced in half by a runaway airplane: "I'll thank God every day for the miracle that saved my life" (18 Oct. 1988; 3). Escapes from a monstrous death get providential credit from issue to issue, reinforcing both the traditional belief that life-saving reversals of fortune are ordained by heavenly forces and the idea that individuals are powerless; Stephen Bright joins the other *Enquirer* survivors who remind readers "how easily life can be lost."

The *Enquirer* joins God as an agent of good luck, advertising its power as an amulet for the suffering. Reading the *Enquirer* is itself featured as the way to survival and happiness. Once or twice a month, the paper prints testimony from grateful readers; Petta Bourdreault writes, "Thank God for the *National Enquirer*—it saved me from a lifetime of agony!" and explains that her seven years of "living in hell" with the pain of shingles ended with an *Enquirer* story about a new cream that "cleared up her pain completely" (2 Aug. 1988; 17).

Altogether, the *Enquirer* names the world as, on the one hand, a threatening realm of inexplicable forces and, on the other, a realm where formulas and technology and a subscription to the *Enquirer* can overcome human pain and poverty. Its maxims define a "circle of . . . conditions" (Marcuse 88) that reduces the possibilities for human action, by prescribing devotion to the magic of technique, attitude, and technology while also saying that they are no insurance against disaster. Participating in the contradictory worlds of the *Enquirer* has its domesticating effect: one must meet each day with happy thoughts, discipline, and fear.

False Magic Exploits the Laws of Motion by the Restriction of Choices

Any behavior that occurs as an unwitting reduction of complexities may be classed as motion rather than action. Burke makes the distinction by saying that insofar as a vote is cast without adequate knowledge of its consequences, one might even question whether it should be classed as an activity at all; one might rather call it passive, or perhaps sheer motion (what the behaviorists would call Response to a Stimulus).

(Grammar xx)

And insofar as false magicians create "simple" solutions to complex problems, they appeal to motion rather than action; a closer look at one typical *Enquirer* formula for overcoming personal problems, *"Enquirer's* No. 1 Plan to Conquer Shyness," reveals the magicians' work:

> Top experts have worked with us in developing this special plan—which will enable you to greatly reduce this crippling problem within a matter of weeks. . . . Accept the fact that you are shy. . . . Realize that you have nothing to be afraid of. . . . Observe how confident people behave. Watch people who do well in social situations. You'll see that during conversations, they: Smile frequently. Stand and act naturally instead of folding their arms defensively across their chest. Speak loudly enough to be clearly heard. Lean forward to demonstrate interest in the person they're talking to. Make frequent eye contact. Occasionally touch the other person on the arm or shoulder. Nod often to show interest. . . .
>
> Don't try to be the life of the party. . . . Set realistic goals for situations that make you shy. . . . Make your conversation totally positive—don't criticize. . . . Meet other people through your hobbies. . . . Practice in simple "safe" situations. . . . Review your social successes—and congratulate yourself.
> Dr. Danilo Ponce, professor of psychiatry at the University of Hawaii School of Medicine and one of the experts who helped devise the plan, told the *Enquirer*: "Shyness is far from being incurable. By following the advice of this plan you can greatly reduce your problem within a matter of weeks.". . . And Dr. Gordon Deckert, professor of psychiatry at the University of Oklahoma Health Sciences Center in Oklahoma City, added, "By consistently following the advice in this plan, you'll be able to overcome your shyness—no matter what degree—and become happier, more popular and more successful."
>
> (22 Nov. 1988; 2)

The emphasis here on watching and imitating, and the focus on symptoms rather than causes, is the typical *Enquirer* attempt to prescribe motion rather than action, patterned behavior rather than critical understanding or reflection.

False Magic Originates in the Centers of Mass Culture, as Technique

Significantly, the "experts" who advertise magic formulas are almost always university professors (mainly in social sciences and medicine), that class which inhabits an academic otherworld unknown to the typical *Enquirer* reader who has not been to college. The magicians of culture—those who either invent magic formulas for success (the professors) or are themselves transformed by the magic of determination, discipline, and luck (the celebrities)—are called, respectively, experts and insiders. These secular oracles speak to a working class on the margins of the happiness, popularity, and success that Dr. Deckert promises.

False Magic Is Practiced as Inculcation

The chant of maxims and prescriptions that recurs in each *Enquirer* identifies knowledge with the invariable, suggests that learning about the world means remembering facts and procedures, and proposes that any fact is worth knowing. The bimonthly feature that lists miscellaneous statistics, "What Happened since You Last Read the *Enquirer*," joins the other numerical facts that make headlines in each issue, all restating the importance of simplistic empiricism:

> Video rentals soar 1900% in five years . . . 8 in 10 grocery shoppers bring along coupons . . . 1 in 4 students is a college grad . . . last week Americans spent almost $2 million on maps and atlases . . . last week Americans bought 24,000 guitars, mandolins, banjos and ukeleles . . . there are over 41,000 pizzerias in the U.S. . . . gasoline costs $4.24 a gallon on the Ivory Coast . . . 6 to 12 iron tablets can kill a child . . . 2,760 American teens become pregnant daily. . . . Between 10 billion and 12 billion pennies are minted every year. . . .
>
> (3 Jan. 1989; 11, 12, 13, 40, 42, 46, 60)

This is the *Enquirer* narrative of American life: if it can't be quantified and memorized, it didn't happen; if it can be quantified, it's worth knowing. It's not that some things count more than others; whatever can be counted counts.

False Magic Results in Adaptation

Freire distinguishes integration from adaptation, associating adaptation with magic consciousness:

> *Integration* with one's context, as distinguished from *adaptation*, is a distinctively human activity. Integration results from the capacity to adapt oneself to reality *plus* the critical capacity to make choices and to transform that reality. To the extent that man loses his ability to make choices and is subjected to the choices of others, to the extent that his decisions are no longer his own because they

result from external prescriptions, he is no longer integrated. Rather, he has
adapted. He has "adjusted." Unpliant men, with a revolutionary spirit, are
often termed "maladjusted."

(Education 4)

Enquirer magic appeals to the desire for normalcy. Shyness, weakness, anxiety,
anger, disaffection, and infidelity are debilitating maladjustments. They make
happiness, popularity, and success less likely; they make a person more like
the *Enquirer* freaks of nature, who represent what it means to be abnormal.
Nobody's safe, but adaptation, with its attendant docility, is a hedge against
adversity.

Magic and Literacy

Other, less established and less glossy "prole weeklies" (Fussell's term) such
as the *National Examiner* and the *Weekly World News* appeal to incredulity by
featuring blatantly weird phenomena like two-headed babies and repeated
Elvis sightings. The *Enquirer*, with its emphasis on normalcy rather than the
paranormal and its avoidance of the extremely lurid and grotesque, asks to
be taken seriously. (A colleague of mine recently cut the *Enquirer* from a
popular culture course because "it isn't sleazy enough"—its pseudojournalism
is too subtle, too factual, too difficult to dismiss.) Regular *Enquirer* readers
may be aware of its negative reputation, but the paper's straight-faced appeal
to conservative mainstream values, the apparent veracity of its prescriptions
and statistics, and its disdain for complexity and confusion ensure it a good
measure of credibility. A middle-aged married couple who have read the
Enquirer regularly and thoroughly for several years told me recently that (while
they seldom admit it) the *Enquirer* helps them feel well-informed. Such
anecdotal evidence aside, the *Enquirer* appeals to—and accounts for the leisure
reading of—a substantial number of working-class people and may be used
as an index to working-class literacy. Taking the *Enquirer* seriously and reading
it uncritically demonstrates a literacy limited by the information, beliefs,
and attitudes that the paper enfranchises. It is a literacy limited by the dictates
of false magic, a literate susceptibility to the coercive reduction of the possibilities for action. I say this not to continue castigating the *Enquirer* per se
but to propose that uncritical literacy—the ability to read and write unreflectively that is often called functional literacy—invites and sustains false
magic. To the extent that mass media generally advertise a reductive, technocratic ideology of adaptation, they are the agents of false magic. More
important, to the extent that education and educators generally advertise a
reductive, technocratic ideology of adaptation, *they* are the agents of false
magic.

Recall that the *Enquirer* magicians are usually professors whose work contributes to both the formulaic management of abnormality and the ideology of career success. Their characterization as *Enquirer* experts alerts us to the ambiguous position of the academy and academics; the more proximate the academy's mission and the work of academics are to the center of mass culture, the more likely they are to entail false magic. The professors attacked by the *Enquirer* are those who get government grants for projects that offer no practical benefits for mainstream Americans; a typical attack, "Should You Foot the Bill to Dig Up Ancient Mexico?" responds with outrage to a $73,000 National Science Foundation grant for studying "Prehistoric Political Economy in Mesoamerica's Northern Periphery" (24 Jan. 1989; 30).

True magic, because it is a dialogic critique that seeks novelty, originates at a remove from the mass culture it would interrogate. Efforts to identify literacy with true magic have not become popular in American education, which is, paradoxically, as it should be; such popularity would entail the transmutation of dialogic critique into slogans, the disappearance of one magic into another. And so, true magic remains the work of radicals: Freire's literacy program—with Ira Shor as its American publicist—is a striking revolution against false magic, founded in generative language, reflection and action, and continual dialogue and critique (see Freire's *Education for Critical Consciousness* and Shor's *Freire for the Classroom*). Freire's opposition of a mechanistic, servile literacy to a dialogic, critical literacy parallels the opposition of false magic to true magic, so that we may think of his insistence on a liberatory literacy as his magic remedy for magic consciousness. Literacy is itself the offer of a new magic:

> We wanted to offer the people the means by which they could supersede their magic or naive perception of reality by one that was predominantly critical, so that they could assume positions appropriate to the dynamic climate of the transition.
>
> (*Education* 44)

Grounded in an "active, *dialogical*, critical and criticism-stimulating *method*," literacy brings with it "an attitude of creation and re-creation, a self-transformation producing a stance of intervention in one's context" (*Education* 45, 48). Noting Freire's emphasis on the transformative magic of dialogue, I stress that a Freirean educator's task is precisely the coercive expansion of the possibilities for action, that constitutive inquiry I have posited as the true magic method.[5]

Grounded in false magic, literacy becomes, effectively, the perpetuation of the *National Enquirer*; grounded in true magic, literacy enlarges both exploration and community. The very identification of literacy with magic asks that we define our roles as teacher-magicians and makes it more difficult for us to measure progress in our students in terms of adaptation and career success; to do so may contribute to the world of *Enquire*ry rather than inquiry.

NOTES

[1]For recent discussions of the play of essence and illusion in the *Phaedrus*, see Covino 10–21 and Neel 1–29.

[2]My distinction here between true and correct and false or incorrect magic is an elaboration of hints by Burke, especially in *Grammar* 59, 66, and in *Philosophy* 3–4.

[3]To get a profile of *Enquirer* readers, I first wrote to the senior editor, Iain Calder, explaining,

> I am currently conducting a scholarly study of the reading habits of working-class Americans and have concluded that the *National Enquirer* is the publication they read most often. I am asking your help to verify this conclusion. Might you supply me with (1) the circulation figures for the *Enquirer* and (2) any information regarding the types of readers who tend to buy and read the *Enquirer* (socioeconomic level, sex, race, etc.)?

Calder responded with a courteous refusal, saying, "We receive hundreds of requests like yours for assistance, and we simply do not have the time or the staff to help everyone who asks" (6 Oct. 1988).

However, when I phoned the *Enquirer* advertising department and said that I wanted to buy ad space but needed demographic information first, they immediately sent me a state-by-state breakdown of paid circulation and a profile of the 1987 *Enquirer* audience, with breakdowns according to age, education, and household income.

I offer this tale as a contribution to scholarly research methods and leave its further implications to you.

[4]For the analysis that follows, I examined *Enquirer* issues from 29 September 1987 through 31 January 1989.

[5]Jonathan Kozol, with his insistence that literacy is more than the incorporation of "adult nonreaders into the accepted mainstream of noncritical America" (182), has also identified "fundamental humane literacy" with characteristics that would disallow false magic; they are:

1. informed irreverence
2. tolerating indecision
3. political sophistication
4. respect for history
5. counteraction of violence
6. wise anger
7. taste ("the willingness to state that some things count a lot, others much less, and some things not at all")

8. global literacy (as against "geographical myopia")
9. ability to decode doublespeak (174–82)

Brian V. Street reminds us that

> what governments and companies want from literacy is primarily technological competence and improvement. The relationship between this and "intellectual competence" is problematic. . . . Literacy programmes will still be justified on the grounds of "productivity."
>
> (185)

By defining the literate individual as broadly informed, critical, participatory, and skeptical, Kozol realizes that he "portends some danger for the social system as a whole" (133), as he counteracts the public emphasis on literacy as unreflective and obedient behavior.

The Subject in Discourse

John Clifford

T HE most basic inquiries are often the most perplexing: What do we teachers of composition hope to accomplish? Are we intent on developing in our students the literacy skills and attitudes necessary to succeed in college and beyond, or do we hope to empower them with critical habits of mind, with a skeptical intelligence, with an awareness of themselves as potential actors in a sociopolitical context? Or, more pointedly, do we want to fulfill our contractual obligations to the university and the state by focusing primarily on rhetorical competence, syntactic clarity, and other communicative conventions highly valued in business, industry, and government; or do we dare to encourage oppositional thinkers, social activists, and resistant readers and writers? Are these two goals incompatible? Must we choose, or could we or should we do a little of both? Can we be politically responsible in traditional institutions? With whom do we want to be aligned? The implications are significant, as Kenneth Burke chillingly implies in his not so enigmatic analogy: "The shepherd, *qua* shepherd, acts for the good of the sheep, to protect them from discomfiture and harm. But he may be 'identified' with a project that is raising the sheep for market" (*Rhetoric* 27).

Somehow, for writing theorists and instructors this burden of political responsibility seems more acute. Perhaps the Romantic suspicion of rhetoric for the "palpable designs" it has on us is still an anxious influence in the profession. The Marxist critics Mas'ud Zavarzadeh and Donald Morton recently characterized the increasing demand for writing courses as nothing but "career and vocational training" (12). But even among more traditional humanists, composition is usually the minor term in the literature-rhetoric polarity, disparaged as utilitarian, marginalized as an editorial service to other departments. It would not be too difficult to deconstruct these false oppositions, to demonstrate how reading literature in certain formalist ways can also be seen as training for careers in the establishment and, conversely, how recent essays by, say, Alice Walker or Adrienne Rich challenge dominant ideas. But I want to take a different and somewhat paradoxical tact: I want to think hard about the plausibility of the charge that in educational institutions writing is, in quite subtle ways, a servant to the dominant ideology. I do not, however, want to suggest that writing instruction is somehow more politically complicit than literature is or that literature in general is in any way more subversive or more filled with liberating possibilities than rhetoric is. Even if, as Julia Kristeva and other radical feminists contend, avant-garde texts disturb the patriarchal order, it matters little within the constraints of educational institutions and all their pedagogical apparatuses whether the class reads Percy Shelley or Denise Levertov or writes a descriptive essay. Differences are incidental to the larger function of education in contemporary American culture. This is the theme I want to explore, that the teaching of writing is inevitably an ideological act and thereby one part of any culture's attempt to reproduce itself, both intellectually and economically, by creating accommodating students who are eager to fill designated positions of influence within various institutional landscapes.

One way to put into focus the perhaps insoluble contradictions facing politically conscious instructors is to consider the struggle over the meaning and status of the writer, or the writing subject, in English studies, especially in rhetoric and composition. For the traditional humanist, the writer has always been seen as a creative individual, the locus of significance, the originator of meaning, an autonomous being, aware of ends and means, of authorial intentions and motivations. In other intellectual contexts, the unconscious or the political is certainly admitted, but rarely is the writer thought of as the site of contradiction, as being written by social or psychological forces that might diminish the clarity of consciousness or the singularity of individual intentions. Traditional and expressive rhetorical theory, in fact, unproblematically assumes that the individual writer is free, beyond the contingencies of history and language, to be an authentic and unique consciousness. Since the theory boom of the sixties, however, the centuries-old tradition affirming the power of the unfettered individual writer has come under increasing pressure, first from structuralists and later from Marxists, feminists, poststructuralists, and motley social constructionists.

The structuralist projects of Claude Lévi-Strauss and Roland Barthes cast doubt on the autonomy of the freely choosing individual by positing instead a subject created or written by linguistic, sociological, and anthropological codes. Writers do not simply express themselves or reflect unique social realities, the structuralists asserted, but rather mirror a general and systematic pattern of oppositions common to all narratives, myths, or languages. Writing does not directly express an individual's ideas; it transmits universal codes. The poststructural (re)vision, however, was more historically aware of the specificity of the contingencies of power and struggle; consequently, this movement was and still is skeptical of general transhistorical systems of meaning. Discourse, for example, is now thought to achieve meaning only in "the concrete forms of different social and institutional practices" (Macdonell 12). Meaning is thereby made situational and relational. Everything depends on the specific institution where the discourse takes place; in varying contexts the same words are radically transformed to mean one thing and then another. Poststructuralism, then, decenters writing as well as the self, seeing both not only as the effect of language patterns but as the result of multiple discourses already in place, already overdetermined by historical and social meanings in constant internal struggle. In the writings of Jacques Lacan, Michel Foucault, and Jacques Derrida, as well as of the neo-Marxist philosophers Louis Althusser and Antonio Gramsci, the stability of writing and the fixity and coherence of the writer have been relentlessly challenged.

Lacan, for example, develops a materialist theory of the speaker, or the speaking subject, where the "I" that enunciates differs from the ego that employs the "I." The "I" is split between the imaginary and the symbolic, between desire and the social order, between the signifier and the signified. The subject position one enters through language never fully reveals itself since the unconscious always displaces and condenses through such linguistic masks as metaphor and metonymy. The subject thus becomes positioned through language. Derrida similarly displaces the subject from the center, for example, in his notion of *differance* where attempts to define linguistic signifiers create an endless postponement of presence, an endless play of signification. For Derrida, one signifier gives way to another so that meaning is always relational, always changing. From another perspective, Foucault asserts similar decentering ideas, denying the possibility of objective knowledge by claiming that only discourses exist, some more powerful than others. Our knowledge of the subtle rules of these specific discourses lies beyond our consciousness, beyond our ability to know accurately why we write and think as we do. As a result, the independent and private consciousness formerly endowed with plenitude and presence, with a timeless and transcultural essence, becomes in postmodern thought a decentered subject constantly being called on to inhabit overdetermined positions, the implications of which can be only dimly grasped by a consciousness written by multiple, shifting codes.

These postmodern themes—especially the decentering insights that subjects who write are also written, that all discursive signs are unstable and institutionally specific, that the truth is negotiated only within the conventions of various disciplinary discourses at specific historical moments—are all developed in Althusser's 1971 essay "Ideology and Ideological State Apparatuses." Althusser makes an important contribution to our understanding of ideology and discourse by revising the negative connotations of traditional Marxian notions of ideology as pure illusion. Marx, like other humanists, believed that insight into the exploitative class struggle would eventually allow individuals to locate the real through the distorting fog of ideology. Althusser, however, destigmatizes ideology as natural and inevitable, as ineluctably woven into everything we do; consequently, it cannot simply be expunged. The dominant ideas, assumptions, expectations, and behaviors of this ubiquitous ideology are transmitted from a centerless web of educational, legal, and cultural institutions where, in Richard Ohmann's Gramscian terms, "domination filters through a thousand capillaries of transmission, a million habitual meanings" (*Politics* xii).

Critics often see Althusser's rather rigid structuralist approach as antihumanist because he so relentlessly downplays the subject's power of cognition in favor of the constraining force our disciplinary subject positions carve out for us in institutions. Although his system does not leave room for much resistance to dominant ideas, Althusser is not antihuman, nor is he content to accept the status quo. His work is insightful and useful, and his later work hints that he might reconsider his gloomy Foucauldian perception about the seamless efficiency of the ideological state apparatuses. He might have eventually seen, like contemporary theorists Raymond Williams and Edward Said, that inevitable contradictions within subject positions can be a catalyst for resistance and counterhegemonic thinking. Nevertheless, as it stands, Althusser's conception of the ideological state apparatuses offers a powerful heuristic for looking at the ways composition and the political intersect.

Althusser begins his influential essay with what is now a post-Marxian commonplace: that schools, families, the arts, sports, and churches are more subtle but more powerful conveyors of ruling-class ideas than are the agents of state power—the police, army, courts, and penal institutions. Control is maintained not by brute force but through an internalized ideology embedded in practical knowledge, such as law or writing. Two levels of ideology exist, then: general and local, with the general level embedded in all language and the more local variety situated in specific disciplines. Although diversity thrives among university discourses, they are unified "beneath the ruling ideology, which is the ideology of the ruling class" ("Ideology" 146). Since these discourses are not formally connected except through language in their unified replicative goal, the crucial ground of ideological socialization and resistance is, as Frank Lentricchia reminds us, "the specific institutional site" where we find ourselves, "in [our] specific, detailed, everyday functioning" (*Criticism* 6, 7). Local and specific resistance and not global struggle makes the best sense in Althusser's conception, since each discourse has the same teleological aim: to "construct subjects for a particular social formation" (P. Smith, *Discerning* 14). Althusser's distinction between ideology and ideologies dramatically raises the importance of the apparently trivial conventions and rituals of teaching composition, for these same disciplinary behaviors help to install us as subjects within society.

Playing off Freud's notion of the eternal unconscious, Althusser asserts that these ideologies last forever. Although his conception differs sharply from the false consciousness traditional Marxists hope to dissolve, Althusser still insists that ideology represents "the imaginary relationship of individuals to their real conditions of existence." Within disciplines, for example, rhetoricians, literary theorists, and sociologists all have "world outlooks" that Althusser judges to be "largely imaginary, i.e., [that] do not correspond to reality" ("Ideology" 162). In responding to the obvious question of why, say, composition instructors would represent reality to themselves in an imaginary form, Althusser first dismisses conspiracy and alienation as possibilities: "Cynical men who base their domination and exploitation of the people on a falsified representation of the world" have not enslaved the unwary. He also dismisses Ludwig Feuerbach's answer: "The material alienation which reigns in the conditions of existence" (163, 164). Unlike many traditional Marxists, however, Althusser does not really talk about how accurately the factual world is being represented. He is mostly concerned with the illusionary relation we have to social and political reality; or, to cite a more specifically Marxist idiom, disciplinary ideologies distort the actual relation we have to the conditions of production and reproduction. Since in Marxian economic theory the superstructure allows the base to reproduce class distinctions and asymmetrical distributions of wealth, Althusser suggests a provocative analogy between economic reproduction and the ways knowledge gets reproduced through academic discourse.

Dismissing the paranoid notion that a devious clique of ideologues have obfuscated our real political situation, Althusser claims that ideology always has a material existence in whatever discourses we use, "assured by their subjection to the ruling ideology" (166). But the writing subjects usually feel that they can adopt a range of discourse options. For instance, in writing across the curriculum they might decide whether to write feminist history,

Marxist economics, ecological biology, or existentialist philosophy. The internal range of options depends on the degree of hegemony within each discipline. In the fifties, for example, compositionists and literary critics were largely univocal; in the nineties we appear to have more alternatives. According to Althusser, however, these choices matter little; more germane, the subjects believe that these are the only reasonable choices, that these norms are already firmly in place, that the personas, values, and expectations saturating the discourse and classroom behavior reflect the allowable parameters of disciplinary reality. Hundreds of minor and arbitrary truths are taken for granted, unchallenged, accepted as inevitable. Thus the governing conventions, rules, and rituals of a particular discipline become naturalized and institutionalized.

The "good" subject who comes to internalize the ideology of academic success, individual achievement, and rhetorical competence "decides," because it is the normal course, to write appropriately and to have appropriate attitudes about the discipline of work, about evidence, syntax, form, and so on. Althusser, however, claims that these positions have already been constructed to create just this seductive illusion of choice. Conventions about form, for example, "still appear in our rhetorics and handbooks as merely a problem in organizing our thinking" (Clifford 35). But form is also an attitude toward reality; it is rhetorical power, a way to shape experience, and as such it constructs subjects who assume that knowledge can be demonstrated merely by asserting a strong thesis and supporting it with three concrete points. But rarely is knowledge or truth the issue. Writing subjects learn that the panoply of discourse conventions are, in fact, the sine qua non, that adherence to ritual is the real ideological drama being enacted. This lesson serves them well in other institutional and public spheres. The myriad ways in which writing subjects can make the world intelligible have already been carefully proscribed so that the dutiful subject, true to ideals already internalized, believes it is possible to "inscribe his own ideas as a free subject in the action of his material practice. If he does not do so, 'that is wicked' " (168).

Writing subjects are, for instance, allowed to feel that the rhetorical stance they are encouraged to take is the only credible one, really the only possible one. In *English in America*, a critique of our profession, Ohmann cites numerous writing textbooks that almost universally affirm the need for a balanced, judicious, and authoritatively informed persona for the writer to argue effectively. That position still holds in the recent, best-selling *St. Martin's Guide to Writing* (Axelrod and Cooper), perhaps the most well received of the new process rhetorics. Ohmann expresses disappointment that the rhetorics from the seventies privileged the middle way while denigrating strong positions, conflict, and a committed sociopolitical agenda. In "How to Argue in Liberal" (182), a section of *English in America*, Ohmann claims that these seemingly progressive rhetorics blur and distance the flesh-and-blood writer, offering instead a restrained mask of moderation. A decade later little has changed.

The St. Martin's Guide claims that arguing "means presenting a carefully reasoned, well-supported argument . . . in a thoughtful and convincing way" (494). In this view, writers base their positions on reasons (also facts, statistics, authorities, and textual evidence), which can be "thought of as the main points supporting a claim" (498). The primary purpose of "argumentative writing is to influence readers. Therefore, careful writers seek to influence their readers with each choice of a word, each choice of a sentence" (509). Although *St. Martin's* does mention that a writer might want to build "a bridge of shared concerns" (509), it makes no attempt to put writers or readers in a concrete social situation, considers none of the overdetermined complexity governing the motivations of a writer trying to persuade, and pays no attention at all to how race, class, gender, sexuality, religion, nationality, or material interests might prevent readers from objectively following a logical sequence of facts and reasons. I can just imagine my students using cogent reasons and cold facts to persuade Jesse Helms to support abortion rights or funding for AIDS patients, or perhaps students could use logic and statistics to persuade their professors to give up tenure or to convince the tobacco industry to make the ethical gesture of switching its crops to bean sprouts. Like almost all contemporary rhetorics, *St. Martin's* creates the illusion that we can transcend ideology with three well-developed paragraphs of evidence, that we can somehow change the minds of others in a rhetorical vacuum freed from the pollutants of prior social alignments. This thinking is more than naive; it denies identity, represses class conflict, negates the way ideas originate in specific social configurations. It asks writers to believe that by adopting and carefully orchestrating an objective, rational argument, they can win the day and bring Jesse Helms to his senses.

The subject position constructed for the student writer in this seemingly pluralist rhetoric leaves out resistance, excluding radical feminism, Marxism, and other committed political agendas. Masked as reasonable pragmatism, it seeks to ignore and therefore disparage dissent, discontinuity, and confrontational discourse. Our felt experiences, our various subjectivities, and our specific social situatedness as readers and writers is obviated under the guise of disinterestedness, as if race, class, and gender were messy accidents. Wayne Booth, for instance, in an apparent attempt to exclude these same irrelevant, confounding subjectivities, asserts that foregrounding them is "reductive vilification" (259). Obviously he feels that something important is being threatened. Ellen Rooney suggests that Booth wants to vindicate the hegemony of a pluralist polemic, which she sees as inescapably partisan (14).

Although the kind of pluralist rhetoric that *St. Martin's* exemplifies asserts an "ethic of tolerance and intellectual openness" (21), Rooney holds that such a discourse is interested in domination. It claims to be antitheoretical and nonideological, but its exclusion of writers considered antipluralist suggests its hegemonic intentions. Rooney notes that "the subject of pluralism assumes an infinitely persuadable audience" (53), one that is willing to enter a dialogue, one that is open to reason, all the while ignoring the social contingencies, forgetting the intricate web of ideology. Rooney believes that what these rhetorics leave out is not random; gender, race, and class are not simply overlooked. They are, in Althusser and Etienne Balibar's terms, pluralism's "invisible . . . forbidden vision" (26). An analysis of the ideological stance of contemporary rhetorics that focuses on the outside, on what is excluded, reveals as much as an examination of actual content. In Althusser's symptomatic reading, absence is as revealing as presence. He refuses innocent readings that take the immediate transparency of the text at face value, holding instead that Marx created a radically new mode of reading, opposed to "the myth of the voice (the Logos) speaking" (*Reading* 17). From this perspective, what *St. Martin's* does not say validates what Ohmann asserted in 1976, "that the educational system will support the tacit ideas of the dominant groups in the society" (*English* 159). A critique of writing theory and practice can only be fully understood when it is situated in a sociopolitical context. Teachers who ask students to rehearse particular composing rituals in the classroom impose an ideological agenda, admitted or not.

By constantly enacting these discursive rituals, the subject imperceptibly begins to identify with an appealing image reflected in a particular position. Individuals, enthralled by this image, soon subject themselves to it (Eagleton 172). Althusser thus uses the Pascalian dialectic—that belief follows from the ritual of kneeling down in church and moving one's lips—to conflate and dissolve our traditional notions of how ideology is created: "Ideology interpellates individuals as subjects" ("Ideology" 170); that is, ideology exists only by subjects and for subjects, constituting their subjectivity in language imbued with ideological overtones. Without a strong commitment from subjects to fulfill the tasks of their positions, an ideology would not be easily replicated. Tasks must, therefore, seem unavoidably obvious. "Yes," we must say, "this is what needs to be done; this is the only way." Teachers must recognize the need to punish the unwilling and reward the dutiful, eventually coming to see themselves in subject positions of unquestionable authority because others constantly refer to them as occupying such positions. This phenomenon, known as the recognition function, is exemplified by the familiar answer "It's me" to the question "Who's there?" Even though we are "always already subjects," already fathers or daughters, managers or workers, humanists in an English department or executives at IBM, we are constantly required to rehearse such rituals of ideological recognition. Teachers, for example, always call on specific students, require them to sign their names, and grade essays that guarantee that they are indeed "concrete, individual, distinguishable and (naturally) irreplaceable subjects" ("Ideology" 172–73).

Encouraging writers to develop prose styles that reflect their individuality, for example, is one technique among hundreds that ensures our positions as teachers and grade givers, the writer's position as student and supplicant, and both as unequal subjects in a constructed hierarchy. At the same time, such rituals foster the illusion of individuality and choice, as if the student writers created the possible styles of a given discursive genre. The pellucid naturalness of heading an essay with one's own unique name; the endless routines of assignments written to exacting specifications; the quizzes, grades, and discussions; and all the disappointments and failures, successes and rewards of school life become absolutely recognizable through repetition, not logic. As we successfully find our place, our position in the hierarchy of "merit," we also learn not to wonder if this rather particular and arbitrary way of teaching people to write is the only way. And, of course, since ideology thrives on anonymity, we think of our appointed tasks as commonsensical, not ideological.

Because we so thoroughly inhabit academic discourse, we often reify its arbitrary and contradictory conventions into inevitable organizational patterns that seem to have evolved through judicious, apolitical consensus. This tendency is especially true for students, many of whom lack both a historical perspective on rhetoric and a skeptical turn of mind, particularly when they are eager to become willing participants in the university's discursive mystifications. Gramsci's idea of struggling working-class students' giving "spontaneous consent" to values that are inimical to their best interests certainly applies to the almost blissfully naive attitude with which composition instructors and their students approach their assigned roles, as if the whole point of becoming a writer could be limited to the learning of certain skills and the acquisition of abstract rhetorical principles.

Students want to become writers not because they have mastered syntax but because they are convinced they have something to say and, more important, somebody to say it to. They want an audience they can trust, one that encourages (even expects) them to interrogate dominant values as part of their composing process, to look carefully at the social contingencies of family, religion, gender, and class that have shaped their unique histories. Writers do not want to rehash what is already known; they are propelled forward by the quest to clarify their identities, order their existence, and understand their values and the world's. Instructors can help students become inquisitive writers by avoiding rigid rules, constant evaluation, and an obsession with socializing students into the conventions of "normal" academic writing. They can, instead, develop interactive writing workshops imbued with a sense of the writing process as multifaceted, evolving, and exploratory. Readings that foreground the ideological and cultural also encourage the critical consciousness necessary for committed writing.

Since writing is always much more than a technique, students need to understand explicitly that defying normative discourse, attempting to stretch the parameters of traditional thought, and not agreeing with all our purposes and procedures will not put them at a disadvantage. A climate conducive to good writing often strikes a delicate balance between acceptance and support and the pressure to produce. Although such an environment is not easy to create or sustain, it is possible and, in our present institutional context, necessary for psychological and political survival. Those who know the pleasures and excitement of discovering and writing a truth not in concert with institutional norms are difficult to silence or mystify. Perhaps more than other students, writers seem better poised to understand their intellectual and psychological possibilities in institutions. Writing, when studied and practiced in a rich sociopolitical context, can open spaces for the kind of informed resistance that can actually affect hegemonic structures. Although most students decide not to inhabit these oppositional spaces, dissonance and conflict simulate the complex mix of contending forces out of which all discourse evolves. Without the awareness of ideological struggle that comes from trying to intervene into academic conversations, students remain confused about the purpose of composition studies.

In graduate school I can remember being perplexed by the negligible effect early composition research had on classroom practice. In 1929, a review of empirical studies compiled by Rollo Lyman overwhelmingly demonstrated that direct instruction in grammar did not have a significant effect on the student's actual writing. Needless to say, this research was not acted on in the schools and colleges. But I was looking in the wrong direction. Grammar was taught not because it was effective but because it was good discipline. It was rigorous and arcane, and it privileged upper- and middle-class language conventions against those of the working class and the poor. Teaching grammar, like teaching math or science, clearly installs the instructor as the Subject who knows against those subjects who clearly cannot know, unless they apply themselves diligently and, of course, without wondering why. As a metonymy for a host of other disciplines, grammar successfully interpellates subjects into clear relations of power and authority. Students submit, teachers dominate. Ironically, students have very little to show for their great effort. One might argue that such submissiveness should have a payoff in mastery of some kind, but as Paul Diederich used to say, grammar instruction is probably harmful to writing since it takes the place of direct writing instruction. Although traditional grammar instruction functions as an almost pure ritual of control and domination, it also serves as an effective sorting mechanism for race and class discrimination, with poorer students always already speaking and writing incorrectly—a blunt reminder that school life often seems alien and hostile and offers no stairway upward for those on the wrong end of the class struggle.

Of the many other methods used to make students occupy submissive subject positions, perhaps the most familiar—and the one most adults remember about their writing instruction—is the way teachers seem overly concerned with error, misspellings, syntactic lapses, and usage distinctions of the most subtle dimensions. If we include rhetorical shortcomings in structure, development, focus, and logic, the stage is set for an elaborate drama in which the Subject cannot be challenged and in which subjects must always be wanting, must always be in fear of offending conventions and codes beyond counting. The good student who can negotiate this minefield intuitively knows that little depends on the ideas in the essay, that the discursive shell matters more than the ideation inside. As a result, the status of the "I" that "writes" the essay is so decentered, so alienated from actual experience that many students have as much emotional identification with their school writing as they do with geometry. That identification is absent because students sense that only their submission to a task is required. Those who enthusiastically embrace the positions typically available in the composition classroom are accepting the inevitability and strength of the dominant ideology. If they fail, they often blame themselves, seeing their deficiencies as personal rather than systemic. They are learning how academic discourse and institutional reality proceed: one is assigned tasks to be completed on time and according to the Subject's wishes; those who comply succeed, those who don't deserve to be excluded.

It seems to matter little if these tasks are modified by pedagogical innovations. The process approach to writing, for example, is easily appropriated by the ideological state apparatuses. An instructor down the hall from me has turned composing into such a labyrinthine sequence of prewriting heuristics, drafts, revisions, and peer-editing sessions that she has probably truncated years of bureaucratic socialization into three months. With dozens of discrete steps and scores of self-interrogating, self-purifying questions about coherence devices and structuring techniques that M. A. K. Halliday and Rugaiya Hasan would be proud of, she has validated the darkest epiphanies of Foucault and Althusser. Quite naturally she has been praised and rewarded for her commitment to improving her students' writing. And her supporters are right: she has forged a truly constructed subject, committed primarily to reinscribing the obvious and the known in hypercorrect and bloodless prose. However perverse she might be professionally, she is emblematic of the ways dominant ideologies resist change and replicate inequality through rituals of ideological interpellation.

Although many specific and obvious correlations exist between subject positions and educational institutions, Althusser holds that the structure of ideology changes little from one institution to another: a voice of authority addresses individuals, assigning them tasks to be completed according to indisputable criteria. Take, for example, religion—specifically Catholicism: a God (another Subject with a capital letter) speaks through a pope to the faithful, requiring them, if they are to be saved, to reproduce the model of the virtuous subject by adherence to numerous rituals and commandments, thereby becoming "his mirrors, his reflections" ("Ideology" 179). Only thus can they be interpellated as Catholic subjects. Similarly, traditional writing instructors speak and judge from a position of authority, bolstered by the sacred rules of handbooks and rhetorics whose precepts are repeatedly reproduced in essays carefully orchestrated to instill respect for academic writing as it is now and will be hereafter. And because most good subjects are believers, excessive punishment is not needed to compel obedience. Schools and churches do use "suitable methods of punishment and expulsion," but the good subject wants to do what is required; thus, ironically, this "individual is interpellated as a (free) subject in order that he shall submit freely to the commandments of the Subject, i.e., in order that he shall (freely) accept his subjection, i.e., in order that he shall make the gestures and actions of his subjection all by himself" (Althusser, "Ideology" 145, 182).

The guarantee of salvation, academic success, or worldly advancement given by the Subject to his or her subjects produces the appropriate mirror recognition, a power that ultimately allows the relations of production and reproduction of knowledge to be replicated. When subjects eventually complete their training and receive their new posts in society, the internalized mechanism of ideology begins once again in a new institutional situation. And so it goes.

Althusser, however, wants to remind us that ideological state apparatuses entail more than this technical, mutual recognition of Subjects and subjects. Relations of production within the class struggles of advanced capitalism typically involve exploitation. It follows, then, that these struggles between the dominant and the exploited are inevitably reenacted within the ideological conflicts of educational institutions. This confrontation has two dimensions: one struggle is directed against the former ruling class, as for example in the expressive revolt against the dominance of traditional handbooks in the sixties; the other struggle is against the exploited class itself, as in the conservative backlash in the seventies against nonstandard dialects. The discursive conflicts in composition classrooms, then, derive their form and function from the specific conditions of existence that govern class conflicts beyond the educational institution. The ideologies of the state apparatuses we find enmeshed in our discourse are internalized versions of those ongoing confrontations between the dominant and the other. As instructors we can never fully transcend these struggles or our role in them as Subjects of hegemony. We must learn to live with this contradiction if we work in institutions. We are Subjects who do the sorting work of an unequal society. And although we may also hope to be oppositional agents, we cannot fully escape the institutional interpellation.

The implications of this crucial Althusserian insight need to be developed. If we can accurately speak of a "source" of ideology, we usually try to locate it in the consciousness of a particular group, as in Marx's famous dictum from *The German Ideology* that the ruling ideas of a given time are ruling-class ideas. But Althusser situates ideology's origin instead in the continuous struggle between antagonistic classes, in the "simultaneity of these relations within a particular context" (Dowling 67). Ideology is not simply a mirror of the values of the dominant class but rather those ideas modified through bitter, contentious struggles with one another, a compromise, a trade-off, a melding of opposing discourses. So too does the struggle for dominance within English departments, between historians and deconstructionists or empiricists and cultural critics, determine the shape of the ideas that survive. As a result, no pure ideas or conventions develop in an ahistorical, apolitical vacuum. As Diane Macdonell notes, "No ideology takes shape outside a struggle with some opposing ideology" (33). Of course, although opposing discourses such as epistemic and expressive rhetorics exhibit many differences, they still operate beneath a powerful ideology with its inevitable dialectic of domination and resistance. Yet, even the most carceral Foucauldian discourse, which college rhetorics clearly are not, always has room for dissent, for resistance. For oppositional critics, the parameters of this opposition must then become the contestatory sites of political possibility as ideas are relationally reshaped, never fully constructed, always marked by that which they oppose, always carrying traces of that which they would flee, always brimming with contradictions, constraints, and openings. The discursive subject positions available to students and indeed to all of us within these ideologies are also constructed by conflicting, partial, interesting codes, not by the coherent and stable consciousness posited by traditional humanists or by the completely decentered subject of poststructuralism. Terry Eagleton notes that he does not feel he is "a mere function of a social structure" (172). Part of that belief, of course, comes from ideology's ability to disguise itself, but we are so written by contradictory discourses that we think there is space for "dialectical self-consciousness" (Goleman 113). When we finally perceive how hegemonic rituals construct us in ways we would like to oppose, we want to be agents instead of subjects. This self-consciousness can assist us in the academy with the "project of respeaking both our own subjectivity and the symbolic order" (Silverman 283). Paradoxically, this undertaking seems both trivial and ambitious. It is trivial because much of the work would have to be carried out on a local level in our classrooms, in conversations with colleagues, in committee and departmental meetings, and in journals and texts and at conferences, where we profess a more sociopolitically aware rhetoric to a wider audience. Gramsci believes that only through such a "minute, molecular process" (194) can a transformational collective will be born. The results probably seem modest indeed. But we seem to have no other plausible strategy. True, our work with students can often be exciting and rewarding, but no matter how effective we are in raising their consciousness about the ideological dimensions of rhetoric, we receive little positive reinforcement from an essentially conservative academic culture. Gramsci and others certainly recognize this dilemma. Their alternative to professional paralysis is quite simple: since power is also decentered in our culture, finding its energy in properly socialized subjects, the most ambitious undertaking is not to storm the hegemonic barricades. Instead we should do the intellectual work we know best: helping students to read and write and think in ways that both resist domination and exploitation and encourage self-consciousness about who they are and can be in the social world. This is where our hope lies; even if, as James A. Berlin suggests, we are "lodged within a hermeneutic circle" ("Rhetoric and Ideology" 489), we can still change ourselves and others. When we achieve a distance from the inherited ideas of traditional rhetoric, multiple possibilities of "revising, synthesizing, or transforming ideas that had been merely passively accepted before" (Cocks 68) are opened for our intervention.

Our beliefs about rhetoric, finally, do not originate in an authentic, voiced consciousness; do not exist primarily in enlightened cognition; and are certainly not the cumulative result of consensual, transcendent scholarship, research, and intellectual will. For perhaps obvious political reasons, the discourse of rhetoric as conventionally constructed has ignored or repressed the ideological dimension developed in the work of neo-Marxist thinkers like Althusser. A critique of our rhetorical ideology, however, suggests that the struggles in our disciplinary discourses are not esoteric, ivory-tower theories without social impact; they just may be the primary areas where hegemony and democracy are contested, where subject positions are constructed, where power and resistance are enacted, where hope for a just society depends on our committed intervention.

Marxist Ideas in

Composition Studies

Patricia Bizzell

THE virtual absence of Marx from American intellectual life is a curious gap. Although we certainly acknowledge the importance of studying Darwin, Freud, Nietzsche, and other major thinkers, the need to know Marxist work may be even greater, since it forms part of the intellectual horizon of academically educated people the world over, not only in Europe.

It is curious, then, that Marxist ideas are scarcely mentioned in America —that is, outside the work of the handful of Marxist scholars in various disciplines, who seem to be talking mainly to one another. Frank Lentricchia's history of modern literary theory, *After the New Criticism*, provides one example of this de-emphasis. The work gives much more attention to the influence of Nietzsche than to that of Marx, even though Lentricchia deals extensively with European theorists such as Jacques Derrida and Michel Foucault, who have surely been influenced as much by Marx as by Nietzsche.

Lentricchia is not even especially hostile to Marxist thought; on the contrary, he has devoted a book, *Criticism and Social Change*, to Marxist literary theories. This book focuses on an aspect of the problem I address here, through

Lentricchia's analysis of the persistent tendency of other critics to read Marxist influence out of the work of Kenneth Burke. But, in general, the ignorance of Marxist ideas amounts almost to a superstitious fear. Most academics can recount horror stories of scholars whose careers were arrested by an interest in Marxism. These stories, though often infused with moral indignation, nevertheless serve as cautionary tales to warn others away from a taboo area of study.

Composition studies presents at least a partial counterexample to this trend. We often draw on European and Third World Marxist theories of literature, literacy, and education, citing Mikhail Bakhtin, Paulo Freire, and Lev Vygotsky, for example. As I have argued elsewhere ("Composing Processes"), we rhetoricians like to see ourselves as social reformers, if not revolutionaries. Simply because we teach writing, we often find that we are underdogs in the profession and that our struggling students are academic underdogs.

We do reflect the typical American willed blindness to Marxist thought, however, in our tendency to denature the Marxism of theorists whose work we use frequently, to assimilate the Marxist thinker into a more apolitical discourse that covers some of the same ground. For example, Beth Daniell shows that Walter Ong draws hasty conclusions from the work of A. R. Luria because Ong fails to note that Marxist ideology shapes the way Luria interprets his results. John Trimbur argues that we often "domesticate Vygotsky's Marxism" by conflating Piaget and Vygotsky ("Beyond Cognition" 220). Hence we tend to overlook some crucial differences between Vygotsky's understanding of language and Piaget's because these differences arise from Vygotsky's historicism, which is part of his Marxism.

Along the same lines, I argue that Ann E. Berthoff, the foremost American exponent of Freire's thought, consistently emphasizes the philosophical aspect of his work and thus downplays the projects of large-scale political change that always accompany Freire's practice, whether on behalf of revolutionary governments as in Guinea-Bissau or in defiance of authoritarian governments as in his native Brazil. For Berthoff, the most important aspect of Freire's pedagogy for "critical consciousness," as Freire calls it, is that he enables peasants to learn "*how* they make meaning and *that* they make meaning" through "the transformation of the familiar to the strange and the strange to the familiar" ("Recognition" 550). As long as the focus is on "interpreting their interpretations," it appears to make little difference to Berthoff what the students interpret; she sees no fundamental difference between her preference for asking students to look at seeds and bones and that of Ira Shor, another American follower of Freire, for showing them the contents of a wastebasket ("Recognition" 550).

Putting Freire back into a Marxist context does not mean that teachers should leave their classrooms for the revolutionary barricades. But it does mean attending to the content of critical consciousness. For Freire, studying one's meaning-making processes is not enough; one must study how these meaning-making processes are culturally constituted and, to be more precise, selectively constituted to maintain the social privileges of some groups and the disenfranchisement of others. Thus, Freire's literacy materials move quickly from natural objects to human artifacts. By comparing a picture of a cat hunting with a picture of a man hunting with a bow and arrow, Freire's Brazilian peasant students come to recognize the human power to create culture. But by comparing the bow-and-arrow hunter with a man hunting with a rifle, the peasants recognize the social power that distributes access to culture differentially, with unequal consequences for human life and freedom.

Berthoff, of course, has the right to create her own Freire through her reading of him: indeed, I agree with Berthoff that reading is necessarily a formative or creative act. But Berthoff's influential interpretation of Freire is consistent with the way American academics treat Marxist thinkers generally.

My purpose here is to suggest that rhetoricians have something to lose by continuing to avoid Marxist thought and something to gain by exploring it. I do not wish to debate what Marxism "really" means or who is "really" a Marxist. Such debates often constitute another strategy of avoidance or containment, discouraging the consideration of more general and potentially influential Marxist ideas. I think we need some less inhibited discussion of Marxism if we are to understand our intellectual and political situations as Western academics.

Two kinds of intellectual activity might be facilitated by attention to Marxist ideas. Fredric Jameson summarizes them at the end of *The Political Unconscious*, a book outlining a Marxist theory of literary criticism and interpretation generally. He writes that Marxism

> can no longer be content with its demystifying vocation to unmask and to demonstrate the ways in which a cultural artefact fulfills a specific ideological mission, in legitimating a given power structure. . . . [Marxism] must not cease to practice this essentially negative hermeneutic function . . . but must also seek, through and beyond this demonstration of the instrumental function of a given cultural object, to project its simultaneously Utopian power as the symbolic affirmation of a specific historical and class form of collective unity.
>
> (291)

The "demystifying vocation" or "negative hermeneutic" of Marxist analyses, as Michael Ryan has shown, contributed much to the development of deconstruction in Europe, and through deconstruction—albeit a typically American version that has forgotten or erased its Marxist roots—we may already be somewhat acquainted with ideological analysis. It is a postmodern commonplace that everything is ideological, that all meanings are interested or ideologically invested. Everything surely seemed ideological at the 1988 CCCC meeting, where half the session titles included the words *historical, ideological,* or *political,* and the politicizing trend has continued at subsequent conferences. We have yet to bring explicitly Marxist analyses into our de-mystifications of ideology, however; we have yet to talk much about power structures or social class.

Moreover, we have hardly even begun to explore the "Utopian" activity that Jameson outlines. In calling for a utopian side to analysis, Jameson may simply wish to ensure that his analysis is as comprehensive as possible, that it accounts for the fact that ideological constructs include as well as exclude, welcoming some ideas warmly. But I suggest a further point here, namely, that the Marxist critics must be constructive as well as destructive—must have dreams as well as nightmares about history. Presumably in these dreams the present, unjust social order moves toward justice.

Of course, to speak of justice and injustice is to define an ethical com-mitment. Nowadays we are uneasy about avowing such commitments, per-haps because our understanding of ideology has given ethical commitments a bad name. That is, I think we use the term *ideology* to demonstrate that no person has access to unfiltered reality. How we construe and value the world constitutes an interpretive process and, moreover, a process that is learned, culturally conditioned, and collectively developed. We do not really use *ideology* in Marx's sense, as an explanation that distorts reality, an expla-nation we could presumably escape from if we had a truer vision of reality. Rather, we tend to adhere more to Louis Althusser's notion of ideology as an interpretation that constitutes reality. This view offers no retreat from ideology into reality. We may indeed free ourselves from a particular ideology, but the lever that pries us loose can only be another ideology, which manages at that moment to be more persuasive for reasons, again, that are culturally conditioned.

Thus enmeshed in ideologies, we see ethical commitments as just another ideological construct, ratified by no transcendent authority or by no match with transcendent truth. The scholar who avows ethical commitments, then, risks looking foolishly ignorant of this postmodern understanding of ideology.

Here, however, is precisely where we need Marxist utopian thinking. In a way, our embarrassment about ethical commitments indicates a real nos-talgia for the transcendent ratification that we in theory reject. For if we were utterly convinced of the inevitability of ideology, we would not feel uneasy about seeing the world through ideological interpretations—including ethical commitments—any more than we feel embarrassed about needing to eat or drink.[1]

Some sort of ethical or utopian commitment to constructing a more just world seems not only a necessary part of the Marxist critical project but a precondition for being intrigued by it. Those who are not strongly motivated to pursue this goal in their scholarly work lose little by continuing to avoid Marxism. But, as I mentioned earlier, many rhetoricians would like to see themselves as social critics and reformers. The value of Marxist work lies in its ability to offer methodologically sophisticated and ethically informed modes of social analysis, especially analysis of language use in the construction and control of knowledge.[2]

In *The Political Unconscious*, Jameson presents a Marxist theory of literary criticism, or semiotic interpretation generally, that builds from Georg Lukács's concept of "totality." For Lukács, the totality of a given time and place is the sum of all the relations among people, culture, and the material world. Economic activity and cultural activities such as religion and the arts are included in the totality even though we may not be able to trace the older Marxist notion of a "base-superstructure" relation between the two types of activities. Moreover, for Lukács, the totality must be understood as constantly changing (see Jameson, *Political* 50–56).

Jameson wants to develop a Marxist theory of interpretation that encompasses all other theories, not one approach among many but the intellectual horizon of them all. Such a theory, or what I would call cultural criticism, needs the concept of totality to describe the domain it claims.

We can question Jameson's totalizing impulse on at least two grounds. First, he seems to place his version of Marxist interpretation on a plane beyond or "above" ideology. In other words, he claims that his theory alone offers escape from constitutive ideologies into a more unfiltered vision of reality. Jameson does indeed intend to privilege his method of interpretation, but he seeks to establish its authority through argument that is openly ideologically interested—rhetorical argument—and not through some presumed superior access to reality.

We could also object that the interpretive study of totality, given the comprehensiveness of Lukács's definition of the term, seems hopelessly enormous—or accessible only to a person who possesses a talent for symbol-reading equivalent to that of a person who can play fifty chess games simultaneously. For Jameson, however, the advantage of taking on a hopeless task is that it protects one from thinking that nothing but ideology exists in the world. Contemplating the complexity of the totality reminds us that while our understanding of the world may be constituted by ideologies, it is not absolutely determined by them, in the sense that people's impulses and their interactions with one another and with the material world impinge on ideologies and change them. Change is a crucial element in the Lukács-Jameson model of totality.

Jameson boldly suggests a way to begin the seemingly hopeless task through a three-part interpretive process. The first part, the "study of forms," reveals that works of literature (or any other symbolic configuration) grow out of changing social pressures as an attempt to solve the contradictions enacted in social relations. Another part, the "study of ideologies," views the text in question as an utterance in the discourse of a particular social class, which is seen in certain fixed relations to other social classes. The third part of the analysis emerges as we come to realize that the discourse of one social class exerts ideological control or "hegemony" over other discourses through a process of struggle. Jameson modifies earlier versions of the concept of hegemony. In some Marxist analyses, dominant classes exercise their ideological control so thoroughly that the very people they are oppressing assent to the oppression. The marginalized agree that they deserve to be marginalized and, instead of hating their exploiters, wish only to become like them. Jameson suggests that while this hegemonic process does indeed operate, its control is never effortless or total. People resist it, with varying degrees of success, and the hegemonic situation is never static. The dominant class maintains control only through constant struggle. In noting this process of ideological struggle, we direct our attention to large-scale and long-term changes in the totality. Jameson describes, in effect, a history of totalities in which one complex of social relations fades away, along with its hegemonic networks, while another comes into being. He uses the earlier Marxist term *mode of production* as a synonym for the totality, but to shift emphasis from economic to ideological relations he focuses on the production of meaning and the struggle over who controls it. Meaning is produced through forms, or, as Jameson says, "the production of aesthetic narrative form is to be seen as an ideological act" (*Political* 79). Hence, to study history, or the sequence of modes of production, is to study changes in the ideology of form.

Certain questions are raised by an analysis that, following Jameson, attempts to demystify the concept of community, an important concept in recent work in composition studies. In what Raymond Williams calls its "warmly persuasive" connotations of "common concern" and "common organization" (*Keywords* 66), community seems to stand against the pain and struggle evoked by the concept of resistance. I prefer an extended or evolutionary definition of *community*, as it has been used in composition studies by myself and others.

My interest in the concept of community began with an attempt to use it to solve a contradiction, a process in the study of literature that Jameson calls the study of forms. While the dominant ideology proclaims equal educational opportunity for all, the social reality is that academic success or failure relies as much on social-group membership as on individual ability. I have argued that Linda Flower and John R. Hayes take, in their early work at least, too individualistic a view of writers' difficulties by focusing exclusively on an acontextual model of composing processes ("Cognition"). This model places the burden of responsibility for failure on individual students and their presumed linguistic or cognitive deficits. By describing such students as initiates into an unfamiliar academic discourse community, I emphasized the contextual or social elements in composing, elements screened from view by the Flower-Hayes model. I saw student writing problems as affected not only by the students' social-group memberships but also by our own as academics.

This use of community seems to resolve the contradiction between supposedly equal access to education and unequal academic success based on social-group membership by suggesting that our awareness of the academy as a social group can help us remove barriers to access for students from diverse backgrounds. If the students' problem is unfamiliarity with a community, then we should facilitate students' initiation, both by teaching students in composition classes about academic discourse and by teaching their teachers in faculty seminars—for all disciplines—about writing instruction. We should make the academic community more welcoming and more flexible.

This line of argument led to an interest in writing across the curriculum. I advocated designing freshman composition as an initiation into the academic discourse community ("College Composition"). In an initiation ceremony or rite of passage a mentor typically guides the newcomers through the process and carefully manages their interactions with the judges who test their fitness to become community members. I imagined the writing teacher filling this mediator's role. This model for what happens when student writers come to college has many affinities, I believe, with Elaine Maimon's work in writing across the curriculum. Maimon describes newcomers to college writing as people who are "talking to strangers." The writing teacher thus becomes the friendly neighbor who introduces them around in the community—literally, by putting students in touch with institutional resources they may need, such as the peer tutors' writing workshop, and figuratively, by helping students to use language like natives of the academic discourse community, that is, in David Bartholomae's phrase, to successfully "invent the university" audience and so win a responsive reading whenever they sit down to write for us.

But this resolution of the contradiction, through a concept of the welcoming academic community, relies on a hegemonic function for the rhetorician. His or her professional expertise smooths the way for students and manages their introduction to academe, mediating for them with other professors. Hence the reliance on this expertise tends to conceal an important fact: the academic community possesses much more power than its incoming students do, especially if they display culturally determined "otherness" of social class, race, or gender. Our social positions allow us to influence students' intellectual habits, values, and future lives and livelihoods to a much greater degree than they can influence ours. In such unequal circumstances, students may have a strong tendency either to conform totally to community expectations or to withdraw from the community entirely.

Initially, then, rhetoricians have used the concept of community to attack injustice by removing the onus of failure from students, by treating failure as a systemic problem, and by seeking to involve all teachers more actively in circumventing educational inequality, on behalf of all students. But as Joseph Harris argues, the very invocation of community, which was meant to galvanize such efforts, then comes to seem like an oppressive affirmation of one—and only one—set of discursive practices. Community becomes a sort of cultural procrustean bed, as Jameson points out in his critique of the work of the sociologist Robert Bellah (*"Habits"*). The supposed resolution of social contradiction is thus shown to be untenable.

We can ask, then, which social-class affiliations adhere to the concept of community? In what sense is community the utterance of one social class in dialogue with other social classes? Community has entered the discourse of composition studies through the work of middle-class scholars such as myself. I suggest that individualism is a key feature of the concept of community considered as a middle-class utterance—however ironic this idea may seem when we remember that one important motive for introducing community into composition studies in the first place was to combat the individualism of early cognitivist work.

Think about the local quality of individualism as part of middle-class ideology—the notion that one person can make a difference if he or she really wants to. Early uses of the concept of community construe students' difficulties as lack of familiarity with the academic community. The task of introducing someone to a community, which this definition of the problem seems to call for, can be accomplished by an individual or a small group. Community as such fully develops its warm, cordial, convivial overtones—but at the risk of reducing social context to social graces. The very warmth of the word conceals the fact that the academic neighborhood does not welcome everyone equally. Just as in other communities, tacit exclusions obtain.

As a dialectical strategy, then, community seems to be an utterance that helps middle-class teachers fend off criticism from those both above and below them in the social order. To those below, it seems to promise that we're not excluding anyone. To those above, it seems to ensure that we're not admitting anyone truly disruptive of the status quo, either.

Yet our attempts to abrogate this self-serving dialectical strategy may very well be frustrated. We expect to find working-class students eager to embrace critical education and to revalue their own cultural capital (ethnic languages and literatures, work experience, and so on). Conversely we expect to find middle-class students quite comfortable with their greater proximity to the seats of hegemonic power. Our expectations of both groups are frequently dashed. Many disenfranchised students yearn only to be assimilated into the academic community, while many middle-class students resent an educational system that exacts greater and greater tribute for smaller and smaller securities. Our working-class students are all too ready to respect us, unless we fail to initiate them into the system of power; and our middle-class students are all too ready to fear our exactions, unless we show a cynical willingness to help them beat the system.

Thus the function of community as a protective utterance in middle-class discourse breaks down. As a result we direct our attention to the third part of Jameson's interpretive process. We realize that ideological interpretations of reality, such as that enforced by the concept of community, are implemented for reasons having to do with the struggles of social classes for power over one another. Such struggles work to constitute the character of the present or indeed any totality. Recall that Jameson renames totality the "mode of production," where the chief product is meaning. The notion of struggle also underlines change in the history of totalities; one struggle is always passing away as another is coming into being.

This vision of change may help us to understand why we have difficulty defining the social order in modern America and securely delineating the boundaries of the working, middle, and upper classes. A college-educated high school teacher may make considerably less money than a plumber who is a high school dropout; and both may be considerably less comfortable with left-oriented political ideas than the psychologist with a graduate degree and an income totaling more than theirs combined. The so-called American exception to typical Western patterns of social class and political development is well-known to historians and political theorists. Suffice it to say that we need a more diverse, less smoothly integrative notion of community to allow us to discuss these social disjunctions.

Henry Giroux's study of members of a community who work against the common concerns and organization helps us enlarge our definition of *community*. Giroux argues that such disruptive behavior should be interpreted politically; that is, it should be understood as "resistance." Giroux's analysis suggests not only that disruptive action is a normal and inevitable part of community life but that it can lead to profound changes in the community. His work expands on that of his mentor Paulo Freire, who wishes to see such change develop in radical or liberatory—that is, Marxist—political directions. Grasping the analytical possibilities offered by the work of Freire and Giroux, then, presents special challenges to the ethical commitments of American teachers of writing.

The term *resistance* commonly means an impediment to a smoothly operating process, some check in the flow. It usually focuses on transmissions of power—whether electrical, economic (as in resistance to a sales pitch), or political (as in resistance to the Nazis). Giroux brings the term *resistance* into an analysis of breaks in the educational process, moments when the school's socializing function does not proceed smoothly. He develops the meaning of *resistance* for Marxist educational theories by distinguishing it from the concept of opposition.

A break in the educational process happens when a student or teacher refuses to play by the rules and chooses instead to violate academic norms. For example, a student in a writing classroom submits a rambling personal narrative in place of the cogently argued essay the teacher asked for; or a teacher gives such a paper a high grade even though writing it may not have prepared the author for the impending multiple-choice grammar exit exam. When deliberate subversions of routine occur in isolation and without much reflection, they constitute what Giroux terms "opposition"—essentially futile, or even self-destructive, defiance. By contrast, acts of resistance encompass collective and self-reflective dimensions. Giroux states, "Resistance must have a revealing function" (109). What, then, does resistance reveal? As Giroux uses the word, *resistance* cannot be applied to any behavior intrinsically. Rather, behavior becomes resistance when the participants understand it in a certain way and when it can thus become the basis for further action. Most likely, in Giroux's analysis, behavior potentially understood as resistance springs initially from anger, boredom, despair, or other painful emotions aroused in students and teachers by institutional education. Giroux believes that when such oppositional behavior begins to be understood as resistance, it reveals the inequities in the educational system that first evoked the behavior.

Giroux assumes that these inequities comprise the dominations and exploitations inherent in the unjust order of our society, which the schools have an institutional duty to reproduce. Understanding behavior as resistance, then, means revealing social injustice. This assumption leads Giroux to call for "a semiotic reading of behavior" as resistance, inviting both students and teachers "to decipher how the modes of cultural production displayed by subordinate groups can be analyzed to reveal both their limits and their possibilities for enabling critical thinking, analytical discourse, and new modes of intellectual appropriation" (111).

By interpreting oppositional behavior as resistance, Giroux hopes to change its meaning from the ineffectual defiance of a monolithic process of reproducing social injustice to the intellectual basis for liberatory social change. One of Giroux's most important theoretical projects is simply to convince us to understand resistance in this enlarged political sense, to make us believe that such resistance is possible. He rejects the inevitability of reproduction. At the same time, Giroux recognizes that oppositional behavior itself may have limits because it is produced by someone who has been dominated and exploited. Reading behavior as resistance means respecting the behavior's reasonable origins in resentment of mistreatment while encouraging participants to distance themselves from the limiting aspects of the behavior.

Giroux cites an example, taken from the work of Peter McLaren, that concerns a class of fifth graders who disrupt their math lesson by calling for an art lesson instead, asking for a model with "great big tits," nominating one of their classmates for the job, and so on (93–94). Reading this behavior as resistance requires acknowledging not only the sources of defiance occasioned by a math lesson and the complex role of art as an alternative but also the sexism involved in the students' responses. All these responses may be understood as shaped by a dominant unjust social order that, perhaps, links math and science skills with the illusory possibility of rising in society, devalues the function of social criticism in art, and turns men and women against each other to deflect the rage that should be addressed to the social injustice.

Giroux makes clear, however, that it is not the teachers who provide students with the ability to read behavior as resistance. Students must learn to perform such interpretations for themselves. Giroux sees the function of writing as crucial to working out and sharing readings of resistance. This function emerges when he speaks of "critical literacy":

> Students must be given critical literacy skills that not only help them understand why they resist, but also allow them to recognize what this society has made of them and how it must, in part, be analyzed and reconstituted so that it can generate the conditions for critical reflection and action rather than passivity and indignation.
>
> (231)

Giroux is not talking about the imaginative awakening associated with the development of a "personal" writing style or "authentic voice," a reconstitution that begins and ends in the individual's mind. Instead, the content of critical literacy, as I have called it in connection with Freire's similar concept of critical consciousness, receives explicit treatment in Giroux's work:

> Literacy skills, in this case, become tools that enable working-class students to appropriate those dimensions of their history that have been suppressed, as well as those skills that will reveal and explode the false attractions and myths that hide the deep divisions and inequities of the capitalist state.
>
> (231)

In other words, critical literacy develops from engaging a negative herme-neutic with what the dominant ideology offers to students as models of success and reward and from encouraging a utopian recovery of cultural capital that has been excluded from academic canons. This process of cultural criticism looks beyond local instances of oppression to broader patterns of domination and especially to speculative futures in which domination is resisted.

Some American educators have attempted to implement the ideas of Giroux and Freire, in classrooms that are not only organized democratically but also focused critically on ideological oppression and how it can be resisted. Shor's pedagogy attacks "capitalist myths" that promote the consumption of worth-less commodities such as nutrition-free fast-food snacks. Kyle Fiore and Nan Elsasser help their adult Bahamian women students to a critical literacy that encourages resistance to the dominant depiction of marriage, an image con-cealing the "deep divisions and inequities" these women felt that the marriage relation imposed in their lives. Geoffrey Chase urges his student Karen to link her working-class life experiences with those of Meridel LeSueur to produce, in place of the traditional research paper, a report reflecting her own history that had been suppressed, unknown to her.

Like Giroux, Freire assumes that problems in education arise from edu-cation's institutional function to reproduce an unjust social order—and Freire hopes to help transform that social order. His primary concern involves introducing reading and writing to illiterates who are among the most po-litically and economically oppressed classes in Third World countries. Also like Giroux, Freire initially worked to demystify the dominant culture's definition of his students as marginal. At the very least, Freire argues, it makes no sense to define the majority of a country's population as somehow outside the social order in which all participate. The first step in acquiring literacy, Freire believes, is to understand how one's supposed marginality actually functions to maintain an unjust social order—one must acquire, that is, a new understanding of the world. One must self-reflectively "read and write the world" before reading and writing the word. This redefinition of marginality into a critical understanding of oneself as dominated and exploited resembles Giroux's reinterpretation of oppositional behavior as resistance. For both Giroux and Freire, the effective discourse for learners is criticism of social injustice.

But how does large-scale political action issue from this discourse? Giroux and Freire refuse to see their educational mission as contained within the classroom, as merely placing an ideological tool in people's hands without attempting to influence how they will use that tool outside the institution. Giroux hopes to inspire us all with "the possibility of galvanizing collective political struggle around the issues of power and social determination" (111). Freire has been employed by revolutionary governments, as I noted earlier.

Indeed, Freire and Giroux have debated the question of how directive the
teacher should be, with Giroux criticizing Freire's approach as too phenomenological. Giroux thinks that Freire treats ideology in Marx's sense, as a
distortion of reality, rather than in Althusser's more interpretively sophisticated sense, as constitutive of reality. Giroux thus fears that Freire tends
to assume that pedagogy for critical consciousness simply removes distortions,
allowing language transparently to reveal oppressive social conditions, which
the students will then be automatically moved to correct.

Yet many American teachers find even the phenomenological version of
Freire too directive, especially with middle-class students who are not part
of Freire's most obvious constituency. Howard B. Tinburg, who works with
"First World" students—"white, middle class students in an urban university" [2]—feels uncomfortable with the emphasis on the directive political
action he sees in Freire's most recent work. Tinburg's concern is that a
supposedly liberatory discourse whose politicization students find threatening
may smother their self-defined needs.

The problem here seems to be a failure of imagination, a failure to join
with Freire and Giroux in a utopian Marxist analysis that projects beyond
struggle to an achieved collective unity embodying social justice. Teachers
often pose the issue thus: Should we define ethical goals for our students or
let them set their own goals? Most humanists would answer that students
should set their own goals—yet with a Marxist negative hermeneutic in
mind, we should realize that no such "offering of choices" can be ideologically
neutral.

Michael Holzman's recent work reflects this delicate tension between a
desire not to be intrusively or hegemonically directive and a desire to effect
liberatory social change (see "Post-Freirean"). He describes with approval the
widespread acceptance in Third World literacy programs of a post-Freirean
pedagogy that seeks only to "accompany" the poor and minister to their self-
defined needs, for literacy or other capabilities. This pedagogy certainly
seems to eschew the directive. Yet Holzman draws his model of this
pedagogy from the work of the Maryknoll Sisters, a Roman Catholic order
that presumably defines itself not as ideologically or morally neutral but
rather as actively combating injustice. The problem is one of conflicting
ethical commitments—to the learners' personal integrity and interpretive
power on the one hand, and, on the other, to the teacher's need to feel
active in a liberatory vocation.

Freire suggests that politically aware education should not—indeed,
cannot—resolve ethical contradictions. Rather, critical education should urge
us to continue struggling with such contradictions, because they necessarily
arise from the deepened awareness of an unjust social order that critical
education also seeks to arouse. By projecting a classless utopia, an analysis

of injustice informed with Marxist ideas suggests precisely the kind of struggle with contradictions that will cease in this unattainable end time. Meanwhile, I fear that if we abandon all our authority in the classroom, internalizing the marginality the dominant ideology seeks to impose on intellectuals, we simply avoid a contradiction we must learn to live with—that between acknowledging our class allegiances and imagining a larger social vision.

Donaldo Macedo has asked Freire whether critical consciousness creates enormous conflicts within the individual's subjective experience:

> On the one hand, students have to become literate about their histories, experiences, and the culture of their immediate environments. On the other hand, they must also appropriate those codes and cultures of the dominant spheres so they can transcend their own environments. . . . How can emancipatory literacy deal effectively with this tension so as not to suffocate either dimension?
>
> (Freire and Macedo 47)

Freire replies:

> The role of critical pedagogy is not to extinguish tensions. The prime role of critical pedagogy is to lead students to recognize various tensions and enable them to deal effectively with them. Trying to deny these tensions ends up negating the very role of subjectivity. The negation of tension amounts to the illusion of overcoming these tensions when they are really just hidden.
>
> (Freire and Macedo 49)

In other words, the individual subjectivity or consciousness that becomes critical also becomes more cognizant of tensions, contradictions that the dominant society has tried to conceal. Becoming critical means studying these tensions. They cannot be resolved autonomously because they arise from the social order; they can only be coped with in such a way as to generate energy for working collectively to change the social order. Cultural criticism should work to reveal the inequities in the social world around us—beginning, I think, with the most immediate site, the school itself—and also to help students imagine liberatory alternatives to the unjust status quo by drawing on the knowledge they possess from their membership in groups at some remove from those who enforce this status quo. I suspect that even the most privileged students are enmeshed in contradictions that could generate this knowledge, such as clashes between the dominant economic ideology and religious beliefs or gender.

Marxist thought can help us learn to live with contradictions. As Freire and Giroux suggest, contradictions should not be understood simply as hard choices between conflicting values or actions. Rather, contradictions seem to present impossible choices, where neither A nor B can actually be selected or where choosing A over B ends up destroying A and B. Freire and Giroux allude to several kinds of subjective contradictions—those arising from a perceived conflict among an individual's values and those arising from a perceived conflict among an individual's actions—as a function of membership in various social groups. For example, students may experience subjective contradictions between their home culture's values of deference to authority and the academy's valorization of intellectual independence and questioning. One of my students recently pointed out that if he questioned a text the way I wanted him to do, he would be giving up his intellectual independence to me, and after all, his father was paying good money for him to attend this fancy liberal arts college so he could learn to think for himself. Similarly, consider the teacher who tries to act on a commitment to egalitarian politics within an authoritarian institution. Marilyn M. Cooper provides a paradigmatic example of such contradictions in an account of her dealings with a student she calls Bartleby.

Obviously, we can't neatly separate these kinds of contradictions, for our actions perforce influence our values just as our values influence our actions. In other words, our subjective experience is socially constructed—our values and the conditions that create perceptions of conflicts among them arise from our participation in society. At the same time, our attempts to act on those values or to escape the pain of internal contradictions can affect society, can change it.

Living with contradictions means viewing these inner and outer tensions as opportunities to imagine liberatory change, not as problems we must either solve once and for all or accommodate. Marxist analysis can help us take this more complicated and generative view of contradictions; it can teach us to understand their origins in ideology and to imagine alternatives that break the rules of the current social game. Thus, we gain richer possibilities for studying the cultural elements in language-using processes, and we enlarge our theoretical perspective from the social units of classroom and business office to the political structures of class and capitalism. I believe that Marxist ideas are also valuable because they can challenge individualism, challenge our American tendency to see ourselves as autonomous intellects like the Walden resident, Ahab, or Huckleberry Finn. We should not strive each to become, as Emerson has it, a transparent eyeball. Instead we should complicate our communal relations with one another, share more, reveal more. We must not only acknowledge and express our ethical commitments but also acknowledge the intellectual fathers and mothers against whom we collectively define ourselves. We must be prepared to discover that we belong to feuding families, that while we can share a desire to explore contradictions, we may not share the same contradictions.

Sharing perceptions of our contradictions and the ethical issues they raise is perhaps the most taboo subject of all—even more sensitive than sharing salary figures. I hesitate in calling for such communal work, like the analysand who senses the therapeutic conversation moving in a dangerous direction and responds by refusing to use any personal language at all. In Jameson's phrase, we are verging on uncovering the "political unconscious," precisely that explosive realm of major contradictions in our national life that we seek to escape by avoiding Marxist ways of thinking. How can we subject such sensitive, self-implicating issues to the piercing light of Freirean critical consciousness? Perhaps only in the hope that it is, indeed, time now to speak of our dreams.

NOTES

[1] In *The Political Unconscious*, Jameson uses the term *ethical* to refer to an analysis of human relations that purports to be based on universal human nature but that actually enforces the interests of dominant social classes. This ethical analysis sets up a "binary opposition" of good and evil (114). Jameson agrees with Nietzsche that, in this opposition,

> what is really meant by "the good" is simply my own position as an unassailable power center, in terms of which the position of the Other, or of the weak, is repudiated and marginalized in practices which are then ultimately themselves formalized in the concept of evil.
>
> (117)

Marxist analysis, Jameson implies, can resist the ethical binary opposition by exposing it in operation as it oppresses women, racial minorities, and other groups that have traditionally been marginalized in the West.

Jameson also attempts to resist the ethical binary opposition by refusing to cast his thought in binary terms. He tries to hold both poles of an opposition in a dialectical tension, instead of totally valorizing one and rejecting the other. In effect, he names the "evil" pole of the opposition the "ideological" and the "good" pole the "utopian." The ideological in human relations may be exemplified by the unexamined operation of the ethical binary opposition, whereas the utopian strives to imagine and bring about more equitable, collectively oriented social relations. The two poles are intertwined in that analyzing the ideological clears the ground for the utopian and generates if only by contrast what the nearly unimaginable utopian might be like.

Jameson realizes, however, that his dialectical tension still requires two poles for its own operation. He notes that his "terminology of 'positive' and 'negative' remains unavoidably imprisoned" in "the ethical code of good and evil," not only because his terminology has a binary structure but also because he cannot help but value one half of the pair and devalue the other (*Political* 286). He cannot help but long for the utopian and attack the ideological. A truly "collective dialectic" that would dissolve all oppositions, Jameson implies, cannot become fully operational until Western social relations become more collective (*Political* 287).

When I speak of ethical commitment, then, I do not endorse the traditional structure of oppression Jameson initially names the ethical binary opposition. Rather, I urge American intellectuals to abandon their postures of frozen horror at the operations of the ethical binary, to accept a dialectical movement such as Jameson envisions, even if it involves the risk of not escaping binary categories. Like Jameson, I am skeptical of Nietzsche's claims, which Jameson characterizes as Romantic, that binary categories can be escaped. But I'm trying to find a better way to use them in aid of a potential "collective dialectics" and collective social relations. In the process I attempt to turn the term *ethical* toward a more classical rhetorical sense, the position, as we say, that a person stands for or represents in his or her body. This position is culturally defined, not transcendently ratified, but not totally determined either—with social and political ramifications and susceptible to social and political change.

[2]I thank Bruce Herzberg and John Trimbur for their detailed assistance with this paper.

Michel Foucault's Rhetorical Theory

❖

Bruce Herzberg

"I T IS in discourse," says Michel Foucault in *The History of Sexuality*, "that power and knowledge are joined together" (100). In his theory of discourse, Foucault posits an intimate relation between discourse and knowledge; he describes in detail the functions of disciplines, institutions, and other discourse communities in producing discourse, knowledge, and power; he examines the ways that particular statements come to have truth-value, the material constraints on the production of discourse about objects of knowledge, the effects of discursive practices on social action, and the uses of discourse to exercise power. Foucault's work thus addresses some of the deepest concerns of modern rhetoric and composition theory. Foucault also locates the central dilemma of discourse at a point in history that reveals the connection between what he calls "discourse" and what we may wish to call "rhetoric."

In "The Order of Discourse," a lecture first published in English as an appendix to *The Archaeology of Knowledge*, Michel Foucault tells this fable about the origins of philosophy and the division it drew between truth and discourse:

For the Greek poets of the sixth century BC, the true discourse (in the strong and valorised sense of the word), the discourse which inspired respect and terror, and to which one had to submit because it ruled, was the one pronounced by men who spoke as of right and according to the required ritual; the discourse which dispensed justice and gave everyone his share; the discourse which in prophesying the future not only announced what was going to happen but helped to make it happen, carrying men's minds along with it and thus weaving itself into the fabric of destiny. Yet already a century later the highest truth no longer resided in what discourse was or did, but in what it said: a day came when truth was displaced from the ritualised, efficacious and just act of enunciation towards the utterance itself, its meaning, its form, its object and its relation to its reference. Between Hesiod and Plato a certain division was established, separating true discourse from false discourse: a new division because henceforth the true discourse is no longer precious and desirable, since it is no longer the one linked to the exercise of power. The sophist is banished.

(54)

In his earlier book, *The Order of Things*, Foucault locates the decisive change in the nature of "true" discourse in the eighteenth century. It was then, he says, that the magical quality of language was dispelled and the essential similitude between signs and their referents was disrupted (32–34). Discourse began to disappear or become invisible, its workings hidden by new relations of knowledge that placed the truth outside language. In "The Order of Discourse," Foucault places the decisive moment earlier, in the defeat of the Sophists by the model of philosophy associated with Plato. The eighteenth-century event now seems to be one of many "new forms of the will to truth": "From the great Platonic division," Foucault now says, "the will to truth had its own history" (54–55). The will to truth is manifest in attempts to define truth in such a way as to make it knowable but not linguistic.

I take it that what Foucault means by "true discourse" in the time of the Sophists is what the Sophists themselves called rhetoric (I explore Foucault's avoidance of this word in a moment). This discourse embodies and creates truth because the truth it speaks is social, a truth of persuasion, decision, political power, justice, and cultural cohesion. It is "efficacious and just." But after Plato, after philosophy defeated sophistry, truth is "displaced" from the social to the ideal. The proper role of discourse in Plato's scheme is to represent truth. The truth is to be found, not created. Truth in this non-discursive sense can be known without being said; statements are linguistic phenomena (they have form and meaning, as Foucault says), but it is what they express (their object or reference) that may be judged as true or false. Discourse always conveys something other than itself in this new view: it is not the act of discourse but the signified object of discourse that determines whether the discourse is true. What Foucault calls "the will to truth" is the effort to define and secure the boundaries of a truth that can be found and kept. And one consequence of this effort, as all historians of rhetoric know, has been the isolation of rhetoric (and its realm of probability, argument, and persuasion) to keep it from contaminating the truth.

Foucault makes the point in "The Order of Discourse" that the truth-making work of discourse did not cease in the time of Plato or in the eighteenth century. What changed was not the power of discourse; rather, its power was hidden by a will to truth whose object was conceived to be absolute and immutable, not social, not contingent, not conventional, not affected by language. The philosophical ideal, since the demise of the Sophists, has been to seek an identity of thought and language, to deny "the specific reality of discourse" (65), and to think of discourse as the dress of thought or the conveyor of meaning. The desire to locate truth in something other than discourse itself has supported the belief that the author or speaker is the source of discourse: the speaker's task (in this view) is "animating the empty forms of language" (65). Or discourse is imagined as simply a naming of things in the world, whose meaning is to be extracted by a careful reading, as if of a prior true discourse. Finally, disciplines and institutions (including, notably, schools), founded on this will to truth, reinforce the idea that the rules of discourse are subsidiary to the expression of thought. The idea that true discourse reflects, conveys, expresses, or represents something outside discourse acts as a constraint on what counts as truth (think of how Descartes—or Kant or Hegel—locates truth, to select a few bright figures in Foucault's genealogy). The will to truth hides the sociopolitical nature of discourse, something that the Greek true discourse presumably did not hide.

Hiding the power of discourse does not dispel that power. "It does not matter," says Foucault, "that discourse appears to be of little account, because the prohibitions that surround it very soon reveal its link with desire and power."[1] Furthermore, he continues:

> [D]iscourse is not simply that which manifests (or hides) desire—it is also the object of desire; and since, as history constantly teaches us, discourse is not simply that which translates struggles or systems of domination, but is the thing for which and by which there is struggle, discourse is the power which is to be seized.
>
> ("Discourse" 52–53)

Edward Said glosses this discourse succinctly:

> [T]he will to exercise dominant control in society and history has also discovered a way to clothe, disguise, rarefy, and wrap itself systematically in the language of truth, discipline, rationality, utilitarian value, and knowledge. And this

language, in its naturalness, authority, professionalism, assertiveness, and antitheoretical directness, is what Foucault has called *discourse.*

(*World* 216)

Foucault is not simply repeating Nietzsche and arguing that truth is an
invention of the philosophers, though that is one of his concerns. In "On
Truth and Lies in a Nonmoral Sense," Nietzsche argues that truth is a social
arrangement necessitated by the powerful tendency to tell lies. Lying is clearly
an act of discourse: it is a misrepresentation of actual circumstances. But
truth telling is by no means simply the representation of actual circumstances.
Truth must be seen as a convention of discourse, for there is no way to convert
things directly into language. Language "designates the relations of things
to men," and these relations are expressed in "the boldest metaphors" (82).
But having evolved this means of communicating about things, we forget
that it is a conventional arrangement and come to "believe that we know
something about the things themselves . . . yet we possess nothing but
metaphors for things" (83). Social pressures reinforce the conventional ways
of speaking of things and of regarding that way of speaking as truth. Thus,
truth is a rhetorical construction, arising from the creative use of language
for the purpose of making an effective social arrangement.

My use of *rhetorical* in the previous sentence is not tendentious. Nietzsche
wrote his essay on truth and lying just after he gave a seminar on the history
of rhetoric at the University of Basel. In his lecture notes, he asserts that

> there is obviously no unrhetorical "naturalness" of language to which one could
> appeal; language itself is the result of purely rhetorical arts. The power to
> discover and to make operative that which works and impresses, with respect
> to each thing, a power which Aristotle calls rhetoric, is, at the same time, the
> essence of language; the latter is based just as little as rhetoric is upon that
> which is true, upon the essence of things.
>
> ("Ancient Rhetoric" 21)

Nietzsche grapples later with the problem of the existence of essences that
cannot be named. But here he makes more than a casual connection between
power and rhetoric in the production of a truth that is presumably—
ironically—outside language. Taking the psychological approach that characterizes his early work, Nietzsche notes that "our utterances by no means
wait until our perception and experience have provided us with a many-sided,
somehow respectable knowledge of things; they result immediately when the
impulse is perceived. Instead of the thing, the sensation takes in only a *sign*"
(23).

Foucault does more than echo or annotate Nietzsche—though we may
regard *discourse* as Foucault's gloss on Nietzsche's *rhetoric*. (The fate of *rhetoric*

as a useful and positive term in the hundred years between Nietzsche and Foucault is not my present concern—note, nevertheless, that Foucault takes *discourse* to be the more comprehensive term and that the two terms are evidently converging in the current development of rhetorical theory.) Foucault searches for the strategies by which discourse was supposedly effaced. In *The Order of Things*, he analyzes the way discourse was made to disappear, to appear transparent: The linguistic sign was treated as a counter, not as an event, as a means, not as a force, so that the sign itself became part of the strategy of the will to truth. In "The Order of Discourse," Foucault observes summarily that in a philosophy which replaces discourse with the relations of signifier and signified, "discourse is annulled in its reality and put at the disposal of the signifier" (66).

The goal that Foucault articulates for himself in response to this problem is "to question our will to truth, restore to discourse its character as an event, and finally throw off the sovereignty of the signifier" (66). To do so, he must *reverse* the order of relations between discourse and what is traditionally taken to be its source: that is, he must see the author as a function of discourse, not as its source. He must insist on the *discontinuity* of discourse, to show that it does not come either from some pure source of meaning or (as deconstruction supposes) from a limitless field of silent discourse, the great unsaid that must be restored to speech. He must examine what he calls the *specificity* of each discourse, treating discourse as a practice, a form of action, and not a reflection of the world. And finally, he must apply the principle of what he calls *exteriority*, which opposes the interpretation of the text and looks instead for the external conditions of its existence.

"The Order of Discourse" summarizes the themes of *The Archaeology of Knowledge*, where Foucault elaborates his ideas about the restoration of discourse as an event. After discussing historiography and the dangers of easy assumptions about the continuity of the development of ideas, *Archaeology* looks at the ways that knowledge emerges from discourse. What, Foucault asks, connects statements about an object of knowledge, such as mental illness? Not, he says, the phenomenon itself:

> [M]ental illness was constituted by all that was said in all the statements that named it, divided it up, described it, explained it, traced its developments, indicated its various correlations, judged it. . . . Moreover, this group of statements is far from referring to a single object, formed once and for all; the object presented . . . by medical statements . . . is not identical with the object that emerges in legal sentences or police action. . . . Each of these discourses in turn constituted its object and worked it to the point of transforming it altogether.
>
> (32)

Thus, to speak of madness is not to speak directly about a phenomenon, to name the qualities of an object of knowledge, but to enter into a particular kind of discourse:

> [I]t is not enough for us to open our eyes, to pay attention, or to be aware, for new objects suddenly to light up and emerge out of the ground. . . . [T]he object does not await in limbo the order that will free it and enable it to become embodied in a visible and prolix objectivity; it does not pre-exist itself.
>
> (*Archaeology* 44–45)

So knowledge is created, not by an act of will, but through "relations . . . between institutions, economic and social processes, behavioral patterns, systems of norms, techniques, types of classification, modes of characterizations; and these relations are not present in the object" (*Archaeology* 45). This assertion does not deny the existence of phenomena but says that what we know of them is a function of the needs or desires of society and institutions and of available methods (which may be different in different communities) of coming to know something. "The world is not the accomplice of our knowledge," Foucault says ("Discourse" 67).

By showing how the objects of knowledge emerge from discourse, Foucault rejects the traditional assumption that objects account for the unity of a discourse. He examines three more such possibilities: the speaker, the formation of concepts, and the formation of strategies.

When discourse about knowledge is produced, Foucault asks, who is speaking? What institutional role, legal status, social privilege, educational certification, and so on determines who may claim the right to speak authoritatively? Not all statements about an object of knowledge count as knowledge—to be acted on, passed on through education, collected, and cited. Who speaks with authority, and from what institutional settings are effective statements made? Only after we have established the institutional perspective that authorizes such speakers and settings, Foucault says, is it possible to look at the forms of reasoning that may have been used in the statements. To do otherwise would be "to see discourse as a phenomenon of expression—the verbal translation of a previously established synthesis." The authority of the speaker, the authorizing power, and the mode of expression are mutually defining, and each is part of the larger discursive formation that makes it possible to speak of certain objects at all. "Thus conceived, discourse is not the majestically unfolding manifestation of a thinking, knowing, speaking subject, but, on the contrary, a totality, in which the dispersion of the subject and his discontinuity with himself may be determined" (*Archaeology* 55).

Thus we see that discourse does not emerge from its objects or from the autonomous thinking and speaking subject. The third possibility Foucault looks at is whether a discourse can be organized around a consistent use of concepts, as accounts of the history of ideas often suppose. Certainly not, he answers, for that would return us either to the independent rational existence of the concepts or to their residence inside individuals. Foucault's alternative account posits a (rather unsatisfactory) "preconceptual level" at which statements operate and from which they rise by various discursive means to the status of concepts. Here, though Foucault seems eager to avoid traditional rhetorical categories, we find the apparatus of conventions that disciplines and other discourse communities provide for defining, comparing, and proving concepts—"the various rhetorical schemata according to which groups of statements may be combined (how descriptions, deductions, definitions, whose succession characterizes the architecture of a text, are linked together)" (*Archaeology* 57)—as well as standards of reasonableness and judgment, standards of reference to common knowledge and the history of the community, and rules for the construction of texts. Foucault also wishes to avoid describing concepts in "their progressive and individual genesis in the mind of man" and to focus on "their anonymous dispersion through texts, books, and *oeuvres*" (*Archaeology* 60). Here, nonetheless, is where we find argument and persuasion in the quotidian sense, the interactions of speakers, audiences, texts, and readers.

By strategies, the fourth unifying scheme, Foucault means to refer to theories and themes, which might again be defined as the underlying sources of the coherence of a discourse. Foucault is, of course, concerned to show that themes are not simple continuities but are, precisely, strategies that serve different functions in different periods or communities. Under this heading, Foucault discusses the "function that the discourse under study must carry out in a field of non-discursive practices" (*Archaeology* 68). The description of discursive practices, for Foucault, must include the effect of discourse in society and the means by which such effects are brought to bear, through teaching or in the formation of laws or in the creation of disciplines. Discourse is a material property that may be appropriated for use and that has effects, as he has shown consistently in all his books. Theories of madness, for example, were strategies for domesticating an alien discourse, and each had its effect on those who were defined as mad, subjecting them to religious or legal or medical authority. Foucault admits, in *The Archaeology of Knowledge*, that this analysis of strategies is the most difficult aspect of discursive formations, and he takes up the idea in later books under the rubric of "power," which questions the relation of discourse to objects of observation, judgment, analysis, legal control, physical control, naming, management, regulation, and modification.

Having outlined the discursive practices, Foucault turns to the "state-

ment," which fills out the material existence of the discourse. A statement
is virtually identical to a speech act, although Foucault insists that they are
not the same. The speech acts that interest Foucault are those that have truth-
value in a community, and perhaps this quality explains why he wants to
separate his statements from mundane speech acts. More important, he carefully distinguishes the statement from its linguistic formulation as a sentence
and from its possible misapprehension as a logical proposition. The statement,
he concludes, is a function that operates in and constitutes discourse. It entails
a number of discursive phenomena. First, a referential—"not exactly a fact,
a state of things, or even an object, but a principle of differentiation." Next,
a subject—"not the speaking consciousness, not the author of the formulation, but a position that may be filled in certain conditions by various
individuals." Next, an associated field—"not the real context of the formulation . . . but a domain of coexistence for other statements." And
last, a material existence—"not only the substance or support of the
articulation, but a status, rules of transcription, possibilities of use and
re-use" (*Archaeology* 115). This definition thus includes very nearly the
same categories of existence within the statement as were outlined for the
discursive formation as a whole. Discursive formations are made up of
statements, but the statements do not have the status of statements outside
the discursive formation.

Foucault refers to the four elements that govern discursive formations as
"rules"—*conventions* would seem a better word, given Foucault's application
of the term. These rules determine what can be said at a given moment in
that formation or, more precisely, what can be said that has truth-value,
what can be said that has consequences for social practices, what can be said
that counts as meaningful. The rules determine objects of discourse (hence,
of knowledge); they determine the authority of speakers and the situations
in which discourse may take place, the conventions for producing discourse,
and the conventional forms in which concepts take shape. Foucault treats
these rules as descriptive, intended for use as research guides in his later
books. But he also treats them as prescriptive, in the sense of being regularities
that on the one hand honor discontinuity by fending off the traditional sources
of transcendental continuity and on the other hand explain the coherence of
effective knowledge as a function of discourse itself. In *The Archaeology of
Knowledge*, these rules serve as the forces that hold together statements, verbal
context, institutional support, disciplinary knowledge, and social effects, all
of which make possible the appearance of objects of knowledge, and the
discourse that constitutes them.

Foucault is now able to define knowledge as "that of which one can speak
in a discursive practice. . . . There is no knowledge," he says, "without a
particular discursive practice; and any discursive practice may be defined by

the knowledge that it forms" (*Archaeology* 182–83). Knowledge has no transcendental continuity, in misty origins, in experience, or in the subject. It is the function of a material discourse in a social order. Foucault urges that these rules

> must not be understood as a set of determinations imposed from the outside on the thought of individuals, or inhabiting it from the inside, in advance as it were; they constitute rather the set of conditions in accordance with which a practice is exercised, in accordance with which that practice gives rise to partially or totally new statements, and in accordance with which it can be modified. These positivities are not so much limitations imposed on the initiative of subjects as the field in which that initiative is articulated. . . . It is an attempt to reveal discursive practices in their complexity and density; to show that to speak is to do something—something other than to express what one thinks; to translate what one knows, and something other than to play with the structures of a language (langue); to show that to add a statement to a pre-existing series of statements is to perform a complicated and costly gesture, which involves conditions (and not only a situation, a context, and motives), and rules (not the logical and linguistic rules of construction); to show that a change in the order of discourse does not presuppose "new ideas," a little invention and creativity, a different mentality, but transformations in a practice, perhaps also in neighboring practices, and in their common articulation.
> (*Archaeology* 208–09)

This idea is not easy to grasp or apply. It opposes the familiar and comfortable notion that knowledge is discovery. It challenges the dominant epistemological religion whose credo asserts that truth is to be found by naming, counting, calculating, analyzing, and sorting. It challenges the sanctity of the laboratory and the priesthood of the monastic researcher. It also embarrasses the notion that writing is the mastery of a skill, albeit a skill that may be applied to the work of knowledge. It must lead us, therefore, to question many of the available ways for representing the source and purpose of writing to students—that the source of writing is the self, one's voice, experience, or observations; that writing represents truth, describes reality, or communicates ideas.

Foucault's theory of discourse contributes much-needed elaboration to the idea of rhetoric as a function of discourse communities, to the notion that rhetoric is epistemic, and to the concern for access to knowledge that informs modern critical theories of composition. It states in compelling terms that rhetoric is bound up with power and social action, by showing the ways that seemingly diverse discourses come together in formations that affect social practices and social controls. Foucault traces the routes of power through the interstices of statements and the fields of their support to their relations of appropriation and use.

Foucault seeks to explain cultural phenomena by historical analysis, treating texts not as the trace left by other actions or by knowledge itself but rather as actions (we can only call them rhetorical actions) that represent one kind of node in the networks of power that shape culture and experience. Texts tell us what was taken to be knowledge, what was worthy of examination, what was subject to control. They show how objects of knowledge came into existence, how they were divided, scrutinized, questioned. These knowledge acts, Foucault shows, were possible because they had a disciplinary space in which to act, and they generally if not universally contribute to social acts of regulation or production, sometimes to moral principles, self-concepts, and experience (as he shows in *The Use of Pleasure*). Foucault does not deny the existence or effectiveness of actions that are not in discourse (as Derrida seems to claim when he says *il n'y a pas dehors texte* 'there is nothing outside the text' [*Grammatology* 158]).[2]

To reveal the operations of power and discourse is a critical act, one in which criticism is "both knowledge and a modification of what it knows, reflection and a transformation of the mode of being of that on which it reflects" (*Order* 327). How is such criticism embodied in a critical pedagogy of rhetoric and composition? Rhetoric has for millennia been taught and studied in Plato's shadow, as a victim and servant of the will to truth. Hence rhetoric's bad name, its association with decoration and emptiness. But rhetoric in the twentieth century has increasingly been seen as a critical theory, as in the work of Kenneth Burke and Chaim Perelman and in Terry Eagleton's powerful challenge that literary theory should accept the breadth and responsibility of rhetoric as a basis of analysis. Rhetoric should be a source of critical insight precisely because it is an approach to discourse as contentious, effective, socially relevant, and epistemologically active. Rhetoric is already a science of discursive forms, intentions, methods, contexts, and effects. A critical rhetoric must account for these discursive practices with reference to canons of truth and propriety and to the powers of institutional alliances and pressures.

Foucault's ideas vastly expand the perspectives that are already part of modern critical rhetoric. For epistemic rhetoric, for example, the basis of knowledge is argument and persuasion. Foucault makes it clear that the notion of argument and persuasion must be contextualized within discursive formations supported by systems of authority and control. Context itself has been a key term in the development of critical rhetoric. Foucault vastly enriches and complicates the concept of rhetorical context with a network of archives, disciplines, institutions, and social practices that account for the production of discourse. Critical rhetoric must be concerned about the consequences of knowledge and the ethics of rhetoric, which Foucault enlarges by examining the microphysics of power that resides in the knowledge of detail; that is disseminated in discourses, appropriated by institutions, embodied in laws, regulations, texts, the very architecture of hospitals and schools; that shapes experiences, moral standards, and self-concepts.

In the context of composition in particular, one implication of accepting Foucault's ideas is that we must reevaluate the several types of local contexts for rhetorical analysis—author, audience, oeuvre, even general historical knowledge. We must begin to include, as well, those broader studies that analyze social institutions and other systems that support the development of significant discourse. On this issue, Foucault sides with those who insist on the social production of discourse in opposition to universal, personal, or psychological theorists. But this position does not automatically endorse socially oriented pedagogies. Students collaborate not with one another so much as with the educational system, the disciplines, and the social forces they reproduce. The collaborative writing group as a pedagogical technique has been theorized as a means of making the social construction of knowledge part of the explicit learning process. Clearly, critics and critical teachers must make visible that which is hidden. But a number of questions have arisen about this technique and the degree to which it has been contextualized in the school as a social institution. Does the social-constructionist approach amount to an attempt (a "foundationalist" attempt, some would say) to capture in the collaborative technique a closer approximation to the way that knowledge is *really* formed? Is it an expression, to use Foucault's terms, of the will to truth?

There is much justice in this charge, I believe. And we could reasonably ask similar questions about the writing-across-the-curriculum or academic-discourse approaches. The initial critical or demystifying impulse that produces these techniques is laudable, but the techniques themselves do not carry the critical agenda or guarantee critical action. Indeed, the success of these pedagogical techniques is more likely due to their efficiency than their critical results. One question, repeated by several critics, suggests the kind of difficulty I am thinking of: What is the source, in the collaborative group, of the conventions of discourse that the group or the class enforces on its members? In other words, when the group agrees on standards for sufficient evidence or adequate organization or coherent argument, what is the source of its authority? The danger is that the group may take credit for its rules (claiming that the rules express the experience of conviction); that it may point to rational principles for its choices (they are logical); even that those choices are distilled from assimilated experience of conventions (they are contractual). All these (quite typical) answers evade Foucault's critique.

Foucault is useful to us not only because he raises explicit questions about the effects of relying on experience, concepts, and so on as premises about the source of knowledge but also because he warns of the dangers of technique.

Said brings out this quality of Foucault's work in his discussion of critical consciousness and the need for critics "to place themselves skeptically between culture as a massive body of self-congratulating ideas and [on the other side] system or method . . . a sovereign technique that claims to be free of history, subjectivity, circumstance" ("Criticism" 202). The critical teacher has precisely the same concern. If a technique becomes a means of normalizing the very relations of knowledge that need to be investigated, then it has in effect collapsed the demystified procedure into its mystified outwork. A critical agenda comes not from technique but from the continually renewed critical impetus: a desire to oppose negative and oppressive power, a desire to mend the world.

Collaboration, as a technique, does open the possibility of questioning the sources of conventions about writing and constraints—productive and repressive—on knowledge. It does not of itself insist on those questions. And the same may be said for other techniques. The difficulty for the composition teacher is to negotiate between the need to reach the closure of performance—the practical goal of producing writing, a goal not to be abandoned—and the openness of an inquiry that may go far afield. Here we question, quite appropriately, the basic goals of education. As Foucault says:

> Although education may well be, by right, the instrument thanks to which any individual in a society like ours can have access to any kind of discourse whatever, this does not prevent it from following, as is well-known, in its distribution, in what it allows and what it prevents, the lines marked out by social distances, oppositions, and struggles. Any system of education is a political way of maintaining or modifying the appropriation of discourses, along with the knowledges and powers which they carry.
>
> ("Discourse" 64)

The familiar contradiction between reproduction of and access to knowledge expressed so strikingly by Foucault may suggest two related projects for teachers. One is to analyze more closely the role of our institutions and disciplines in producing discourse, knowledge, and power (a process many have advanced by heeding the extant analyses of critical educationists). The other is, of course, to find a place for a critical agenda in the classroom.

Foucault's message for rhetoric and composition may seem disturbingly diffuse. Composition scholars have cited Foucault dutifully as a powerful influence on modern epistemological skepticism, but he seems to have had little place in the classroom. One valuable exception is Carol Snyder's "Analyzing Classifications: Foucault for Advanced Writers," in which Snyder describes her classroom use of Foucault's observations about taxonomies and the material effects of disciplinary discourse. Her goal is to help students see that classification systems are not just intellectual inventions: they direct our thinking and have material consequences. Using examples from Foucault to model a kind of research and to stimulate critical questions, Snyder asks her students to investigate the classification schemes that divide up the objects of knowledge in their major disciplines. Students identify the object of classification and ask, at a minimum, What is excluded? Who devises or uses the system? When was the system put into place? Where is it applied? This use of Foucault may seem very distant from the purposes of freshman composition, but a commitment to critical consciousness means combining critical reflection with writing practice. Composition has long been dominated by a view of language that Foucault rejects. If, with Foucault, we reject the theory that language is the servant of knowledge in favor of the theory that discourse constitutes knowledge and its powers, we may be able to reconstitute our composition courses under the rubric of a new rhetoric. Snyder has adopted this strategy and so can we, by insistently placing the construction of discourse, as Foucault does, in the space between coercion, on the one hand, and consent, on the other. Here, says Foucault, we see discourse in its relation to power, and "where there is power, there is resistance" (*History* 95).

NOTES

[1]In "The Order of Discourse" as well as in earlier works, Foucault speaks of power as negative and repressive. In his later works, he rejects this view as inadequate and proposes instead the theory that power is productively dispersed through institutions and disciplines. "There is no power relation without the correlative constitution of a field of knowledge," he says in *Discipline and Punish*, "nor any knowledge that does not presuppose and constitute at the same time power relations" (27). And, in *The History of Sexuality,* he argues that the real problem of power and knowledge is not how the state appropriates knowledge or how domination is served by knowledge; rather, the questions to ask are how local power relations make discourses possible and how discourse supports power relations (97). In "The Subject and Power," Foucault distinguishes three types of power relations: (1) physical modification of things for use (that is, labor); (2) communication, which is "always a way of acting on another person"; and (3) relations of inequality between individuals and groups (217–18). See also "The History of Sexuality" and other pieces in *Power/Knowledge*.

[2]Edward Said compares Foucault's and Derrida's views on this issue in "Criticism between Culture and System." See also Peter Dews, *Logics of Disintegration*, for a lucid account of the development of French poststructuralist thought on the questions of language, knowledge, and power.

Writing against Writing: The Predicament of Ecriture Féminine in Composition Studies

❖

Lynn Worsham

> . . . to get to the point of writing a paper, I had to combat the writing in me.
>
> —Hélène Cixous

> Academic discourse, and perhaps American university discourse in particular, possesses an extraordinary ability to absorb, digest, and neutralize all of the key, radical, or dramatic moments of thought, particularly, a fortiori, of contemporary thought.
>
> —Julia Kristeva

POLITICS makes strange bedfellows indeed—and composition studies and *écriture féminine* provide an excellent example.[1] On the one hand, we have a discipline that defines itself largely as a discourse community whose positive task it is to teach academic discourse(s); on the other, we have a language "event" that, in its more accessible moments, unleashes a damning critique and denunciation of academic discourse as the instrument par excellence of phallocentrism. What the French might say about an entire discipline that would reinvent the university in every student requires little speculation. Still open for consideration, however, is an effort by composition theorists to bring together two discourses that will surely lock in mortal combat—a battle royal—over the issue of academic language. Curiously, this antagonism does not seem to pose any serious obstacle for the handful of essays importing *écriture féminine* into the institutional discussion of writing (see Caywood and Overing for a limited treatment of French feminism). Perhaps the hostility does not run as deeply as it first appears, making détente conceivable through a profitable exchange of terms and methods. Or perhaps composition simply seeks to display its cultural capital by contending with the newest of the new intellectual fashions, and French feminism is certainly haute couture. This explanation is simultaneously too cynical and too reductive; *écriture féminine* is one of the most dramatic developments in recent writing theory and pedagogy, not only because it may reformulate our notion of literacy and its consequences but also because it could produce a crisis in composition's self-understanding. The hostility, in other words, is deep and abiding, as the epigraphs opening this essay are meant to suggest. What difference, then, do their differences make?

Before considering that question, I want to address another one, which concerns the way we read *écriture féminine*. Especially useful in the task of discriminating our hermeneutical options is a distinction, developed by Julia Kristeva, between two styles of reading: the political and the postmodern.[2] These two styles of reading articulate and open up two rather different fates for *écriture féminine* in American university discourse. While it can be read either way, the dominant tendency, both in composition studies and elsewhere in the academy, has been to read it politically, as political discourse.

In the notion of political interpretation, Kristeva links everyday language and the so-called specialized discourses of the university. Political interpretation, which is truly "political" in the ancient Greek sense of "popular" (of the people), is "only the ultimate consequence of the epistemological attitude which consists, simply, of the desire *to give meaning*"; hence, it seems so natural, so fundamental that it is beyond partisan interests (Kristeva, "Psychoanalysis" 303–04). The desire to give meaning, to explain, to interpret certainly plays a fundamental role in human experience and characterizes our ordinary relation to the world, but it is never innocent. It is rooted in our need for meaning when confronted by meaninglessness, our need for mastery when confronted by what we fear most: the enigmatic other that exceeds and threatens every system of meaning, including individual identity. Although the desire for meaning appears to be the least personal (both transpersonal and objective), it is based on subjective needs and desires. When the epistemological attitude encounters the unknowable, it becomes resourceful. It takes a stance vis-à-vis the other as an object of knowledge and thereby draws the other into its circle of desire, reducing otherness to sameness, trading a relation of difference for a regime of domination. Political interpretation begins as a quest for a meaning and ends as phallocentric obsession with one meaning. Its most paranoid form occurs in the totalitarian demand of the Enlightenment for one truth, one mind.[3] Even when political interpretation openly acknowledges its status as fiction, a gesture typifying poststructuralist philosophy and literary criticism, it does so without abandoning its goal of stating the true meaning of the discourse it interprets ("Psychoanalysis" 314). If meaning is the obsession of political interpretation, then total consensus is its deepest fantasy.

When French feminists say that *écriture féminine* is a new language, epistemologists in several disciplines quite predictably set to work trying to identify and isolate its distinctive features and the source of its coherence as a system of discourse. They expect to find, if not a theory, then a loosely related group of theories or propositions about language, "woman," "the feminine," or "female experience," including the nature of "feminine" textual practice. They assume an interpretive stance toward *écriture féminine* as an object of knowledge and a repository of truth. Submitted to the discursive obligations of political interpretation, however, *écriture féminine* is typically found lacking, fraught with contradictions, riddled with (theoretical) inconsistencies, and short on concrete strategies for changing the material conditions of everyday women's lives (see, e.g., Jones; Rabine; Spivak; Plaza). Since the feminine has been defined as lack within patriarchy, the fact that *écriture féminine* is found lacking may not come as a surprise, though we should be profoundly suspicious of an approach reaching specifically this conclusion. The challenge now is to read *écriture féminine* politically but as a form of postmodern discourse, which arises not from the desire to give meaning but from the desire to go beyond meaning to a topos of pure invention where discourse becomes more radically political to the extent that it approaches the heterogeneous in meaning.

This approach conserves the differences between composition and *écriture féminine* and hence makes possible an examination of the specific way in which French feminism has been read into composition as a form of political discourse. In the second part of this essay, I show how previous attempts to give meaning to French feminism within composition (1) neutralize its radical potential and (2) tell us something about the ideological investments of writing theory and pedagogy. The second part of my discussion, then, rests on an explanation, undertaken in the first part, of the specific way in which *écriture féminine* should be considered "radical," a term that perhaps has too much commerce in this most postmodern age. Thus, before turning to the way that *écriture féminine* has been read by composition theorists, I want to explore the way it might be read, assuming that the decision can be, as it should be, made again. The appropriate term for such a revision is Lillian Hellman's *pentimento*, which she describes as a form of repentance that occurs when a painter changes his or her mind and redraws the lines expressing an artistic conception. When the paint ages and becomes transparent, it is sometimes possible to see the original lines and the initial conception still etched in the memory of paint and canvas. Pentimento is "a way of seeing," Hellman writes, "and then seeing again" (1). It is still possible to repent, to redraw the lines determining our approach to *écriture féminine* and, in this context, see something of its truly radical potential.

What's Radical about Radical French Feminism?

Dick Hebdige's *Subculture: The Meaning of Style* is an indispensable read for anyone who has been fascinated, repelled, or amused by any of the spectacular youth subcultures emerging onto the cultural scene since World War II. Beatniks, rockers, punks, skinheads—all receive a semiotic analysis, inspired primarily by Roland Barthes, in which Hebdige argues that these music-centered subcultures begin as a movement away from consensus and take shape as symbolic challenges to the inevitability and the unquestioned status of the meanings and values governing a society. They are a form of resistance to hegemony but a resistance that is indirect. The deepest objections to the prevailing ideology are obliquely represented at the level of appearance and the cultivation of a style (17). Clothes, dance, music, and a special idiom work together to produce a subcultural style that communicates a "refusal" of a way of life, a refusal that also affirms identity for a subordinate group. What participants in a subculture seek, to echo Sartre, is a way to "make something of what has been made of [them]" (qtd. in Hebdige 139).

I want to explore *écriture féminine* more fully in terms of Hebdige's analysis of subcultures, as a new language and a form of postmodern expression. Specifically, I suggest a functional analogy between dominant culture and spectacular subcultures, on the one hand, and, on the other, political discourse and *écriture féminine* as a spectacular discourse subculture.[4] Functioning within and against political interpretation in a manner analogous to other spectacular subcultures, *écriture féminine* also arises in response to particular historical conditions and constitutes a style and an identity for a subordinate group, the members of which seek ways to make something of what has been made of them, directly and indirectly, by phallocentrism.[5] "Woman must write her self," Hélène Cixous says, and thereby put herself "into the world and into history" ("Laugh" 279). *Ecriture féminine* becomes "*the very possibility of change, . . .* a springboard for subversive thought," refusing every reduction of difference to sameness; thus it is destined to become an exile within (and a hostage to) a political economy of meaning ("Laugh" 283).

Ecriture féminine may be considered radical precisely in the same sense that punk subculture, for example, is radical. Both are essentially phenomena of style, disrupting the dominant order of meanings by expressing forbidden content—specifically, consciousness of difference—in forbidden terms (Hebdige 91). Spectacular subcultures, in general, serve as vehicles of semantic disorder by inscribing within the dominant order what it cannot immediately account for, what it cannot easily interpret and explain: safety pins through the cheek or lip, hair dyed bright yellow or lime green with pink polka dots or bleached-in question marks, and, of course, the swastika—to name only a few of the ways in which punk style fractures the syntax of everyday life. Violations of the accepted codes through which the social world is organized and experienced have the power to disorient and disturb. In their most extreme forms, they may even signify what mainstream culture fears most—nihilism and anarchy. Yet a subculture relies on what it resists for the elements of its style, taking the objects, values, and attitudes of dominant culture and using them in a way that perverts their "straight" meaning (e.g., a safety pin becomes a form of facial ornamentation; jewelry, a form of self-mutilation) (Hebdige 102–06). Through parody and pastiche, subcultural styles block the system of representation—that is, the apparatus of political interpretation that tames every enigma by assimilating it to an existing framework of meanings—and expose arbitrary social codes to open up the world to new oppositional readings.

The "object" French feminists do their subversive work on is language— in particular, the discursive operation of phallocentrism in academic language. This focus explains, in part, why French feminism elicits from its American audience responses that are not entirely unlike responses to the outrages of subcultural styles. Phallocrats and feminists alike have been fascinated, repelled, and perplexed by the very idea of "writing the body," which, in the guise of philosophy or criticism, parades before its readers every feature of female anatomy and physiology, every sexual and textual taboo. Cixous's insistent refrain, "I want vulva!" is emblematic of the kind of profane articulation that violates the authorized codes across which we typically construct and disseminate knowledge, and it raises the specter of epistemological, if not cultural, anarchy. Spectacular in its rhetoric, *écriture féminine* is shocking and outrageous, alienating, and, for others, exhilarating. It is the latest scandal wrought by a postmodern temperament. *Style* becomes the critical term—not a style of writing but writing as style, style as a form of cultural critique.[6] If *écriture féminine* is a social and political struggle waged at the level of style, then how does it dress itself, so to speak, to resist the desire to give meaning?

Luce Irigaray writes that the issue is one not "of elaborating a new theory of which woman would be the subject or the object, but of jamming the theoretical machinery itself, of suspending its pretension to the production of a truth and of a meaning that are excessively univocal" (*This Sex* 78). In her books *Speculum of the Other Woman* and *This Sex Which Is Not One*, Irigaray stages a rereading of Western philosophical discourse "inasmuch as this discourse sets forth the law for all others, inasmuch as it constitutes the discourse on discourse" (*This Sex* 74). She calls for "an examination of the operation of the 'grammar' of each figure of discourse, its syntactic laws or requirements, its imaginary configurations, its metaphoric networks, what it does not articulate at the level of utterance: its silences" (75). Only this work—a work on the figurations of the fathers—will jam the theoretical machinery and block the system of representation that defines the feminine as lack and deficiency and that ultimately controls the material conditions of women's lives.

Irigaray thus sets to work on dominant university discourses (such as philosophy and psychoanalysis) through a stylistic strategy she calls "mimicry." It is the only path, she says, in the initial phase of *écriture féminine*, which must articulate itself in terms of the historical conditions it resists so that feminism does not simply set itself up as another exclusionary practice. Mimicry works indirectly to hollow out the structures of a discourse from within those structures and therefore is a form of infidelity that, like marital infidelity, operates within an institution to ruin it (see Gallop, *Daughter's Seduction* 48). Mimicry requires that women assume the feminine role deliberately and thereby convert a form of subordination into an affirmation and then into a process of subversion. For a woman to play with mimesis

> means to resubmit herself—inasmuch as she is on the side of the "perceptible," of "matter,"—to "ideas," in particular to ideas about herself, that are elaborated in/by a masculine logic, but so as to make "visible," by an effect of playful repetition, what was supposed to remain invisible: the cover-up of a possible operation of the feminine in language.
>
> (*This Sex* 76)

Irigaray rejects "a direct feminine challenge" to phallocentrism because it demands that women speak as masculine subjects and hence maintain the sexual indifference of political discourse. A practice of self-exile, mimicry repeats and parodies phallocentric modes of argument to exaggerate their effects and expose their arbitrary privilege.

Working as a mime artist, then, Irigaray resubmits woman to the idea that she is "body." Her critics understand this literally to mean that the female body is the source for *écriture féminine*. They ask: In going back to female sexuality to describe or foresee a feminine textual practice, isn't Irigaray, like Freud, "falling back upon anatomy as an irrefutable criterion of truth" (*This Sex* 70)? Irigaray responds that she goes back "to the question not of the anatomy but of the morphology of female sex" ("Women's Exile" 64). The structure of political discourse possesses an isomorphism with the masculine sex; that is, working through an unstated correspondence—a "morphologic"—of sexuality and textuality, it privileges unity, form, coherence, oneness, the visible. Yet this morphologic has nothing to do with the female sex; it does not correspond to the feminine, because there is not *a* female sex. Irigaray uses the morphology of female sexuality—the logic of the female form, its multiplicity of erogenous places—to show that "it is possible to exceed and disturb this [masculine] logic" ("Women's Exile" 64).

In Irigaray's construction of *écriture féminine*, which may appear to be a positive effort to theorize a feminine style, the mime artist is still at work, disturbing masculine logic by refusing to theorize *écriture féminine*. She reminds us again and again that no objective or objectifying account of this syntax, this other mode of writing, exists or can exist. "It is spoken," Irigaray says, "but not in metalanguage" (*This Sex* 144). It cannot be theorized because *écriture féminine* is not, precisely speaking, an inscription of a specific content (e.g., the essence of woman) but an inscription of heterogeneity. Thus, her comments do not represent or refer to *écriture féminine* but only obliquely indicate a direction in which to think its operation. The mime artist reverses phallocentrism and puts *écriture féminine* into discourse as its opposite to resist and disrupt the dominant semantic order. Inasmuch as phallocentric discourse privileges the logic of noncontradiction, Irigaray therefore says: "Hers are contradictory words, somewhat mad from the standpoint of reason, inaudible for whoever listens to them with ready-made grids, with a fully elaborated code in hand" (*This Sex* 29). Since phallocentrism involves an obsession with property, propriety, proper names, proper terms, Irigaray says that *écriture féminine* "tends to put the torch to fetish words, proper terms, well-constructed forms" (*This Sex* 79). Since phallocentric discourse relies on the logic of the clear and the distinct through which identities are established and proprieties maintained, the mime artist says that a feminine "syntax" involves "nearness, proximity, but in such an extreme form that it would preclude any distinction of identities, any establishment of ownership, thus any form of appropriation" (*This Sex* 134). If *écriture féminine* can be said to have a "propriety," Irigaray suggests we locate it in a dynamics of "proximity" and "simultaneity" to refuse the linearity of phallocentric discourse and its tendency toward stasis and systematization through opposition and hierarchy.

Spinning possibilities from an analogy with fluid mechanics, Irigaray suggests that *écriture féminine* is "continuous, compressible, dilatable, viscous, conductive, diffusible" and therefore never remains within "the same type of utterance as the one that guarantees discursive coherence" (*This Sex* 78, 109).

It breaks up the orderly arrangement of discourse and the dominant framework of meanings: "There would no longer be either a right or a wrong side of discourse, or even of texts, but each passing from the one to the other would make audible and comprehensible even what resists the recto-versal structure that shores up common sense" (*This Sex* 80). Because phallocentric discourse, through the strategies of representation, posits the full presence of meaning and a relation of reference between signifier and signified, Irigaray says that *écriture féminine* sets the signifier free from the signified, and the imagination free from words:

> One would have to listen with another ear, as if hearing an "other meaning" always in the process of weaving itself, of embracing itself with words, but also of getting rid of words in order not to become fixed, congealed in them. For if "she" says something, it is not, it is already no longer, identical with what she means. What she says is never identical with anything, moreover; rather it is contiguous. It touches (upon).
>
> (*This Sex* 29)

Irigaray may stand phallocentric logic on its head, but her style becomes more flagrantly subversive with her refusal to take seriously her construction of *écriture féminine*.[7] "To escape from a pure and simple reversal of the masculine logic," she says, "means in any case not to forget to laugh." She laughs at the "seriousness" of any discourse (including her own) that, in claiming to state its meaning, forgets that what moves discourse, what moves through meaning is untranslatable, unrepresentable, irrecuperable within discourse (*This Sex* 163). She warns her readers, therefore, that even the motif of proximity, "isolated as such or reduced to utterances, could effectively pass for an attempt to appropriate the feminine to discourse"—that is, to the status of an object of epistemological speculation (*This Sex* 79). In all our efforts to construct from Irigaray's musings a metalanguage whose object is *écriture féminine*, we should hear her laughing, as if to say: "That is not it at all. That is not what I meant, at all."

Laughter is also a key figure and practice of resistance for Cixous. "The Laugh of the Medusa," for example, reclaims the myth of the Medusa as a positive figure of the feminine, and this time she is not deadly: "She's beautiful and she's laughing" (289). *Ecriture féminine* laughs at the philosopher's obsession with meaning, taking pleasure in breaking up "the truth" with laughter, "in jumbling the order of space, in disorienting it, in changing around the furniture, dislocating things and values, breaking them all up, emptying structures, and turning propriety upside down" ("Laugh" 291). Such violations of the semantic order are the discursive equivalent of laughter, the principal form of which is a refusal to theorize *écriture féminine*. What could be more subversive to the epistemologist than to assert the existence of something that is not defined, that always exceeds every instrument of theorization? *Ecriture féminine* is an outlaw, a fugitive from epistemological justification, taking place in "areas other than those subordinated to philosophic-theoretical domination." Cixous knows that by daring to create *écriture féminine* outside the theoretical, she will be "called in by the cops of the signifier, fingerprinted, remonstrated, and brought into the line of order [she is] supposed to know" ("Laugh" 287, 296). She will, in effect, be required to be systematic, theoretically consistent, and politically transparent.

Cixous refuses the epistemological stance, and, like Irigaray, she also rejects the economy of proper meaning, proper nouns, and common nouns because they "disparage . . . singularity by classifying it into species" ("Laugh" 296). She takes on the very concept of concept and the mode of thought that constantly produces concepts in order to take possession of the world.[8] In the etymology of *concept*, Cixous identifies the basic unit of thought in philosophical discourse or in what I call, following Kristeva, "political interpretation": "concept: etymologically, means something that seizes. Violent grip, rape, abduction. A concept has something of the seducer about it" ("Rethinking" 73). Academic language is also, in a sense, specialized: It is a way of speaking and thinking that captures and appropriates an external reality through models and concepts. "What organize, imprison, censure, are models," she charges; "the fact that there are modes of thought, models, ready-made structures into which one pours all that is still fermenting in order to congeal it" ("Rethinking" 71). Models immobilize; that is their purpose, and that is the pleasure they provide (cf. Lyotard, "Pseudo-Theory").

If what immobilizes us is the medusa of academic language, then Cixous projects *écriture féminine* as a force that steals into language to make it fly ("Laugh" 291; cf. Lyotard, "Pseudo-Theory"). Whatever is coded as profane or "other" by the phallocentric order therefore offers the terms for thinking *écriture féminine* as a practice of resistance and an inscription of heterogeneity that "doesn't annul differences but stirs them up, pursues them, increases their number" ("Laugh" 288). Since academic language immobilizes thought through the limits imposed by concepts, models, and methods, *écriture féminine* is a "spreading-overflowing. It spills out, it is limitless, it has nothing to do with limits" ("Rethinking" 74). Because academic language seizes, captures, and appropriates, thinking *écriture féminine* through the metaphor of gift giving provides terms for thinking another practice and another relation to the world: *Ecriture féminine* gives. It allows departures, breaks, partings, separations in meaning, the effect of which is to make meaning infinite and, like desire, nontotalizable. While the epistemologist maintains the propriety of thesis and position, origin and closure, *écriture féminine* works on the beginning but not on the origin, "for the origin is a masculine myth and it does not haunt the feminine unconscious." A feminine text starts on all sides at once, refusing to move logically, lineally, from beginning to end: "a feminine text can't be predicted, isn't predictable, isn't knowable and is therefore very disturbing" (Cixous, "Castration" 53). In particular, *écriture féminine* disturbs the logic of academic language, which depends on a scission between oral speech and written text, by working with the oral otherness of discourse, the nondiscursive possibilities of voice and rhythm that, in discussions of orality, Walter Ong rather abstractly calls "the somatic component" (*Orality* 67). Cixous calls these possibilities "the flesh of language," which is not a meaning—*écriture féminine* does not rush into meaning—"but [is] straightway at the threshold of feeling. There's tactility in the feminine text, there's touch, and this touch passes through the ear" ("Castration" 53).

Cixous places *écriture féminine* close to the voice—"writing and voice . . . are woven together"—but she does not do what Toril Moi claims she does, namely, produce "a full-blown metaphysical account of writing as voice, presence and origin" (*Sexual/Textual Politics* 119). Her account of a writing close to the voice does not posit a relation between meaning and sound; it does not make meaning(s) its obsession. It is concerned instead with writing and touch. The rhythms of the voice do not have the effect of socialization but simply move us to move with rhythm and sound (cf. Sloterdijk xviv). This intimacy between language and the body once again puts into discourse the sense that our deepest relation to language is concrete, material, existential—and rhetorical—not epistemic.

Kristeva, more than Irigaray or Cixous, directly theorizes our material relation to language in terms that generally coincide with the notion that *écriture féminine* functions as a spectacular discourse subculture.[9] She argues that *écriture féminine* is not a new and distinct language as such (see "Women's Time" 202–11). Rather, the feminine is a subversive operation within language and the distinctive trait of postmodern discourse, which Kristeva also describes as a transgressive practice of laughter (see "Postmodernism"). Postmodern discourse is produced by a specific *positioning* within language, offered by the "semiotic disposition." Heterogeneous to meaning and its ideology, the semiotic is "pre-meaning" and "pre-sign" or "trans-meaning" and "transsign." It is the otherness within language identified with the body and with what traditionally has been coded as the feminine. The semiotic manifests itself in transgressions from the grammatical rules of language that ensure meaning and communication and achieves its effects through contradiction, rhythm, disruption of syntax, and absences or gaps of meaning that are nonetheless significant—in short, through the effects we have traditionally associated with style. Yet postmodern style is interpretation, Kristeva writes; its unobjectifiable, unnameable "non-object" is emotion, drive, instinct, desire—in particular, the emotion experienced when a writer confronts the meaninglessness existing in spite of, in the midst of, all systems of meaning that are created precisely to hide this existential fact ("Psychoanalysis" 310 –17). Face to face with the void—the irreducible otherness—across which all our meanings are stretched like iridescent skin, postmodern "interpreters" do not pretend to communicate a meaning directly. They "musicate" to keep from being frightened to death and in so doing "individuate" themselves and their experiences, not as subjects or objects of knowledge, but in the creation of a style ("Postmodernism"; *Powers of Horror* 1–32).

Kristeva names that which is heterogeneous to meaning "desire" or "emotion" and thus suggests that our deepest relation to language and to the world is not epistemic but emotional and material. She also acknowledges that the semiotic always exceeds every effort to name it and therefore to place it within any system of meanings. Although we can observe important differences among Kristeva, Cixous, and Irigaray, they share some common concerns, not the least of which is their refusal of the epistemological attitude. In their effort to put into discourse what dominant discourse has relegated to meaninglessness—the feminine, the body, desire, emotion, sound, voice, rhythm, contradiction—they are not simply theorizing *écriture féminine* as the opposite of phallocentrism, simply reversing its hierarchical structure and creating a new language. Such objectives would confirm the charge that they are epistemologically inept essentialists who attack philosophical essentialism while creating a new language of "woman" (see Moi, *Sexual/Textual Politics*; Plaza). Instead, they reverse phallocentric logic to draw attention to its arbitrary privilege, its historical contingency. Furthermore, they put *écriture féminine* into discourse as the opposite of phallocentric discourse to resist the notion that it is a separate language cut off from the language and the historical conditions it arises to oppose. *Ecriture féminine* is a practice of self-exile within the dominant order of meaning. This is its "meaning." Yet *écriture féminine* is a moving phenomenon, a language event with a sense of its own historical specificity, and as such its contours will change as the material conditions of women's lives change.

Ecriture féminine (more precisely, for Kristeva, postmodern discourse) functions now as an inscription of heterogeneity that, in refusing to become an object of knowledge, seeks always to subvert our ordinary relation to the world. A spectacular discourse subculture, *écriture féminine* is spectacular in its effects, but it is not "specularizable"—in other words, it resists every effort to make it an object of knowledge and a spectacle for the gaze of the epistemologist. It insists on passage *out* of the system, any system, every system, toward what is "'other,' which if it is truly 'other,' there is nothing to say, it cannot be theorized" (Cixous and Clément 71). If it refuses to be objectified, if it exceeds any system's power of recuperation, then it cannot be brought within the university as we know it. It cannot become the object of research and scholarship; it cannot become the basis for a pedagogy. Indeed, *écriture féminine* does not want to be brought, from its position on the margin of official culture, into the university. It is more likely to decimate, not invent or reinvent, the university and its discourses, because it is in places like the university that people are crushed "by highly repressive operation of metalanguage, the operations, that is, of the commentary on commentary, the code" (Cixous, "Castration" 51). "Let's get out of here," Cixous says. "Not another minute to lose" ("Laugh" 289). In spite of our efforts to "know" it, *écriture féminine* is "somewhere else entirely," "conceived of [and performed] only by subjects who are breakers of automatisms, by peripheral figures that no authority can ever subjugate" (Cixous and Clément 137; Cixous, "Laugh" 287).

Because of these predispositions, *écriture féminine* cannot be freely imported into the writing classroom to work alongside academic discourse toward the goal of literacy—that is, to the extent that literacy and the literate mind are governed by the epistemological attitude and its positioning of the speaker or writer in a phallic position of mastery over discourse. To the extent that literacy is aligned with the ideology of the clear and distinct, the transparency of communication, the overriding need for consensus and communication, *écriture féminine* laughs in defiance of this narrowly political project for improving the human condition. This laughter is not that of an anarchist or nihilist. It should suggest instead that literacy itself is a regime of meaning to be interrogated regarding its power to recuperate the power of those already in a position to order and give meaning to the social world. While E. D. Hirsch's "cultural literacy" project seems to be the ultimate consequence of political interpretation, we must consider the possibility that multicultural literacy also arises from the need to bring the other within the circle of epistemological desire. As Alice Jardine observes, "There is, after all, a difference between really attempting to think differently and thinking the Same through the manipulation of difference" (*Gynesis* 17). *Ecriture féminine*, in contrast to both these literacy projects, inscribes an effort to think differently, to repent and repossess writing as an experience of the limits of meaning. It indirectly inscribes, within and against the dominant discourse, an experience in which writing does not contain, possess, or appropriate but steals into language to make it fly, to make it move, to make *us* move without our ever knowing what worked or works on us and toward what end. *Ecriture féminine* is a raid on the articulate.

This discussion, however, has moved inexorably toward the following articulation of the predicament: If composition studies were to make any sustained contact with *écriture féminine*, one of two things would happen. Either composition would neutralize the radical potential of *écriture féminine* in an effort to appropriate it to serve the current aims of the profession and, beyond this, the university, or *écriture féminine* would cast such suspicion on the whole enterprise of composition studies as an accomplice of phallocentrism that composition would be transformed beyond recognition. It would not be entirely inaccurate to say that composition would cease to exist as we know it, and by implication the university, along with its constituent discourses, would come tumbling down.

How to Take Out a Radical

The dilemma posed above becomes moot because every spectacular subculture is destined to be brought back in line, incorporated, and located within the dominant framework of meanings. Social order can only be maintained through the appropriation and definition—hence, the neutralization—of subcultures of resistance (cf. Hebdige 85). Dominant culture develops and depends on elaborate strategies of containment and incorporation to bring all competing definitions and interests within its range of influence, so that subcultures are, if not controlled, then at least contained within an ideological space that does not seem ideological, that appears instead to be neutral, nonaligned, and beyond particular interests (see Hebdige 16). Thus, subcultural styles, which begin as symbolic challenges to the dominant ideology, inevitably end by creating new conventions of meaning, new commodities, new industries or by renewing old ones (Hebdige 96). What begins as a practice of resistance gets incorporated and ultimately trivialized as "fashion."

Two essays—Robert de Beaugrande's "In Search of Feminist Discourse: The 'Difficult' Case of Luce Irigaray" and Clara Juncker's "Writing (with) Cixous"—offer an opportunity to observe the machine of hegemony working to neutralize the radical potential of *écriture féminine*. Neither essay, it should be noted, expressly intends to defuse what Juncker calls the "political dynamite" of French feminism (432). Both are meticulous, even masterful readings that offer much insight, including the sense that French feminism could produce "a genuine renewal of language and all that rides upon it" (de Beaugrande 272). Yet apart from any conscious intention or expressed hope, we must also be concerned with what happens above and beyond our willing and doing. And these essays, in their desire to give French feminism meaning within composition, unwittingly contain and neutralize it within an ideological space that it resists and refuses.

Neither essay reaches the impasse that requires either the neutralization of *écriture féminine* or the evacuation of composition theory and teaching. Neither essay addresses, through French feminism, the ideological investments of the profession. These remain unthought and unspoken. Neither asks questions, in short, that would focus attention at a metatheoretical level of analysis. Both writers are concerned instead with showing how *écriture féminine* works so that they can make it work in the interest of current writing theory and pedagogy. This strategy—"know how it works" in order "to make it work"—is part of the habitual gesture of scholarship in composition and is symptomatic of a dominant mode of political interpretation within the university.[10] Cixous indicates that this strategy is fundamental to the logic of mastery characterizing phallocentrism ("Laugh" 291). Pursued in these terms, French feminism cannot make a serious critique of composition but finds its potential indentured to serve the present system's equilibrium. The following discussion not only considers two specific cases in which *écriture féminine* is incorporated and neutralized but also exposes some of the values, rituals of appeal, and habits of mind characterizing the ethos of composition studies.

The first form of incorporation is already familiar to us as political interpretation, for which the fundamental move is a denial of difference. Juncker's title—"Writing (with) Cixous"—indicates her awareness of the process by which otherness is reduced to sameness, that is, assimilated to an existing regime of meaning. It suggests that she knows her essay both rewrites—and therefore distorts—Cixous and attempts to (re)model theory and practice in terms of Cixous's brand of *écriture féminine*. The object of interpretation, in other words, exists and it does not exist as such; it is both opaque and transparent (see Jardine, "Opaque Texts"). In the body of her essay, Juncker calls attention to the strangeness, the foreignness of French feminist thought and then enters into the circle of epistemological desire, assuming the task of making *écriture féminine* less strange, less threatening, and more palatable to a specific audience composed of those who are least likely to see anything useful in the often wildly obscure statements of French feminists. It is no accident, then, that Juncker explains *écriture féminine* by suggesting ways in which it "parallels" empirical studies of gender and writing. Certainly, the unknown becomes known through a hermeneutical operation in which existing structures of thought translate the unknown into the domain of the known. Yet it is impossible to understand how French feminism, which regards empiricism and humanism as part of the logic of masculine privilege, could have much to say that *parallels* any empiricist and humanist investments in composition studies.[11]

Juncker further naturalizes and domesticates *écriture féminine* by seeing it as a source for new textual and pedagogical models and strategies. If *écriture féminine* operates against models, concepts, ready-made modes of thought, then it is just as likely to operate against strategies, routines, plans, procedures—against techniques of any kind that, because they can be applied generally across different writing situations and by different writers, deny differences and annul singularities. Yet Juncker wants to inscribe a place for *écriture féminine* in the writing classroom because, as she says, "by opening ourselves to French (feminist) theories of writing, we teachers of composition,

male and female, might actually engender new textual and pedagogical strategies within our field and beyond" (424). This single statement reveals a
determining force in Juncker's essay, which I call a "pedagogical imperative"
or the "will to pedagogy." This imperative is at the heart of a discipline
requiring every theory of writing to translate into a pedagogical practice or
at least some specific advice for teachers. (To be sure, the burden of my own
discussion is to articulate if and how French feminism makes a difference
ultimately in the way I teaching writing.) The pedagogical imperative receives
its most recent justification from the critical-pedagogy movement, which
reinvigorates the study of pedagogy as concrete political practice, but a more
visceral commitment to the notion that theories and techniques serve as
instruments for the control and prediction of "writing behavior" still operates
within the field of composition. And even when writing "specialists" refrain
from demanding that theory operate in such mechanistic terms, they nonetheless demand that theoretical questions receive explicit answers that are
theoretical or practical or both. Such specialization excludes the possibility
that questions in some provinces of thought refuse to be answered and instead
lead to further questions in the spirit of radical invention. French feminists,
in short, do not offer a theory or even a set of theories of writing—that is,
if *theory* is understood as a systematic explanation of some phenomenon. They
are not interested in formalizing *écriture féminine* to offer us what we think
we need—a nugget of pure truth about writing.

Under pressure from the profession's pedagogical imperative, however,
Juncker seems to have little choice but to outline new strategies suggested
by *écriture féminine* and to recontextualize old ones already familiar to writing
teachers. These strategies are what we might expect: Students should be
allowed, even assigned, to write "experimental texts"; students should be
allowed to take possession of their own voices; writing assignments should
focus on invention, emphasizing beginnings rather than closure; students
should read noncanonical, even outrageous, literature in a nonaggressive,
nonmastering mode; teachers should assume a nonmastering pedagogical
stance. While Juncker's appropriation of *écriture féminine* simply confirms much
of what is already considered standard practice in the field, thus neutralizing
the very real differences between French feminist and American discourses
on writing, it does not successfully alter the deeply entrenched power relations
between student and teacher in the university system. Despite any pedagogical
posturing to the contrary, students know that power and knowledge flow
from the top down: teachers still determine assignments and still have the
power to give or deny students the right to their own voices.

What Juncker offers as the most radical innovation inspired by *écriture
féminine* turns out to be our oldest pedagogical model. She suggests that if
teachers assume the role of Kristeva's "phallic mother," they can "bring about

a quick revolution [in the classroom]—and not just in language" (434). Here Juncker eliminates a specific difference between Kristeva and Cixous and writes against Cixous, who argues that teachers who position themselves as phallic mothers actually have been "assigned by force of trickery to a precise place in the chain that's always formed for the benefit of a privileged signifier." The phallic mother, in other words, is only a new twist in the chain of significations that leads back to the "Name-of-the-Father" and to the logic of mastery ("Laugh" 296). The issue is not that Juncker's appropriation fails or that she fails to understand Cixous. Rather, any attempt to appropriate *écriture féminine* as a theory of writing or as a course for pedagogical strategies swallows up its specific force in the epistemological desires of a discipline that would rather not be questioned, for example, about the ways in which culture is reproduced through its theories and pedagogies, through its reliance on the ideas of theory and pedagogy.

The very process of political interpretation occurring in Juncker's essay cannot be meaningfully separated from a second form of incorporation—namely, commodification, which relies on the conversion of a subcultural style into mass-produced style. Once a subcultural style becomes generally available, it becomes frozen; it is emptied of its radical potential (see Hebdige 94–96). The process of political interpretation, which turns *écriture féminine* into an object of knowledge, is in effect a process of commodification. In other words, once objectified, it can be systematized, theorized, codified, and ultimately taught. By such means, it passes into fashion, a commodity generally available for consumption. The introduction and incorporation of this new intellectual commodity serves to rejuvenate or renew the industry of composition studies. That *écriture féminine* could (be made to) rejuvenate writing theory and pedagogy, without cracking its foundations, is a persuasive advertisement, but the power to rejuvenate belongs not to the specificity of *écriture féminine* but to the industriousness of composition. One can foresee a day, in the not too distant future, when a cottage industry of research and scholarship supplies textbooks on the production of so-called experimental texts; a day when summer seminars, conducted perhaps in the streets of Chicago rather than on Martha's Vineyard, are available for composition teachers who wish to "retool" themselves in the image of the phallic mother. We have seen this happen before with deconstruction and the decentered classroom.

I am not suggesting, however, that we ignore French feminism or regard it (or that it asks to be regarded) as a pure object, as irreducibly other, which would place it beyond analysis, beyond interpretation, and, most important, outside history. As I have said, I consider the conjunction of French feminism and composition studies a critical moment in the life of the profession. To regard *écriture féminine* as a pure object is simply another strategy of containment—one that works to defuse resistance by rendering heterogeneity meaningless as pure spectacle, pure exotica (see Barthes 152). *Ecriture féminine*, in effect, receives a tweek on the cheek for being cute (but useless) and gets sent back whence it came. If the process leading from resistance to incorporation and neutralization is inevitable, then perhaps we can exercise prudence about the level at which *écriture féminine* is introduced into and incorporated by composition studies. We may conserve some of its energy by realizing that it has less to contribute to the industry of composition—to the development of a new theory of writing or to the design of textual and pedagogical strategies—than it does to an examination of how composition conducts itself as a theoretical enterprise. It is relevant, in short, not as a critical model but as a force of resistance that indirectly calls into question the needs and desires governing the field. The epistemological attitude is one such need; the pedagogical imperative, another. Working at this level of analysis, I turn finally to "the difficult case" of Irigaray and the specific way de Beaugrande's essay works to neutralize *écriture féminine* by aligning it with the values of modernism, which are synonymous with those of the Enlightenment project. If de Beaugrande's essay represents the values and interests of the field, and I think it does, then composition is, at this point in its historical development, more nearly a modernist discipline than a postmodern intervention in the discourse on knowledge. [12]

On the level of conscious intention, de Beaugrande makes a determined effort to refuse the operation of metalanguage by weaving into his essay a tremendous number of quotations from Irigaray's two principal books. He gets beyond his reactions to her discourse, he claims, "by not filtering it through . . . paraphrase" (258). His concern is to create the proper relation to her discourse, to get on the "right" side of it—her side. Yet he arranges and quotes her words without acknowledging that his selection and arrangement are already the culmination of a process of (in)filtration and political interpretation. Then, too, there is the matter of the essay's title. What are we to understand by the choice of the word *difficult*, the importance of which is further emphasized by quotation marks? Certainly, it calls to mind a negative (male) stereotype of women. More generously, perhaps the word *difficult*, thus emphasized, is meant to indicate the interpreter's sense of humor, if not of irony, about his relation to his object. While his title may problematize the hermeneutical relation, it nevertheless calls attention to the fact that the interpreter chooses to play the part of the analyst explaining (curing?) the case of the difficult, the enigmatic female (discourse).

Taking up the position of the subject who knows, the subject with power over discourse (both his and his patient's), which is the subject position typifying modernism, de Beaugrande claims that although feminism is beginning to have an effect throughout the English profession, as yet "we find no widespread consensus about the detailed consequences that we should expect [from feminism]." He goes on to say that feminism seeks "experimental forms of discourse that attempt to propose and practice a radically different mode of communication" (253). These two statements reveal two of the three standards that work to neutralize *écriture féminine*—namely, communication and consensus. The third occurs in what I believe is de Beaugrande's estimation of the value and promise of (French) feminist discourse. He asks, "Can we deconstruct our entrenched conceptions, and the discourses that presuppose them, to the point where a genuinely non-aligned system of discourse might enable a free and commensurate communication among all humans, be they women or men?" (257). Consensus, commensurability, communication, "non-aligned" discourse—these are the old dreams of the Enlightenment as well as of the philosopher and phallocrat. They are motivated by one desire: the desire for the same mind, the same meaning, the same standard, and the same language. They promise enlightenment, emancipation, and empowerment. Yet in a postmodern culture, *écriture féminine* joins with other forms of postmodern discourse in regarding "consensus [as] an outmoded and suspect value," as an instrument of totalization and totalitarianism (Lyotard, *Postmodern* 66). It breaks with the ideology of communication and seeks instead to explore the limits of language as a communicative system (Kristeva, "Postmodernism"). Although de Beaugrande does not detail what he means by a "genuinely non-aligned system of discourse," my best guess is that "non-aligned" means "neutral"—neutral with respect to position, bias, prejudice, ideology. He might have said "rational" discourse, for this definition precisely reflects the Enlightenment dream of rationality. A "free and commensurate communication among all humans"—male and female—is a communication that transcends or brackets difference. It is communication unmarked by (gender) difference. De Beaugrande quite shrewdly navigates the issue of difference, appropriating *écriture féminine* in a way that makes difference a nonissue when for French feminists it is the only issue. This maneuver strikes me as a rather poignant example of the difference between really thinking differently and thinking the same through the manipulation of difference.

   This kind of appropriation, I suspect, will be the fate of *écriture féminine* in composition studies, especially if the two articles discussed here do in some sense speak the desires of the field. Composition theorists will effectively manipulate *écriture féminine* to shore up the foundations of their field as a modernist discipline committed to the old dreams of the Enlightenment. I say this despite the many overt ways in which the profession has abandoned the rhetoric of totality and opted instead for a rhetoric of multiplicity, suggesting that it wants to locate itself on the side of diversity and heterogeneity and perhaps identify itself with a postmodern sensibility.[13] The notion of distinct discourse communities, for example, which fractures the dominant discourse into many discourses, each with its own conventions for producing and evaluating knowledge, seems to move us toward a sensitivity to difference. In this regard, students' discourse, though few of us would call it particularly spectacular, operates as a subculture openly resisting conventions of academic discourse. Students, by virtue of their marginality to those conventions, seem to occupy a feminine position, regardless of the gender of individual speakers or writers. This, in fact, is Juncker's claim (434).

Yet despite these appearances, the idea of discourse community and the definition of literacy supporting it represent a redeployment, and not a refusal, of the values associated with modernism. The profession is deeply committed to the Englightenment dreams of communication and consensus, emancipation and empowerment, and the idea of discourse community has appeal because it promises to empower students to (re)produce the "proper" kind of discourse by learning, as David Bartholomae says,

> to extend themselves . . . into the commonplaces, set phrases, rituals, and gestures, habits of mind, tricks of persuasion, obligatory conclusions, and necessary connections that determine the "what might be said" and constitute knowledge within the various branches of our academic community.
>
> (146)

Not only does this approach reproduce the ideology of proper meaning criticized by Cixous and Irigaray, it also reproduces the relation of mastery characterizing modernist knowledge. Students must, as Bartholomae says, "appropriate (or be appropriated by) a specialized discourse" (135). It's a big fish–little fish system. Though they may be marginalized with regard to the conventions of academic discourse, students nevertheless are probably conspicuous consumers of the dominant meanings and values of their culture, and these are in no way alien to academic discourse. Students may not move with finesse in the game of academic discourse, but they are well versed, though perhaps unconsciously, in the forms of incorporation and neutralization by which the social order wins their consent and enlists their conformity to a carefully controlled range of values and meanings. If students occupy a feminine position—and I am not at all convinced that they do—it is not because of their marginality in the academy but because they are so thoroughly constructed by the culture in which they live that they are, in effect, exiled from anything remotely resembling "individual expression." The idea of discourse community simply reinforces this relation. It does not individuate; it assimilates. As Bartholomae says, students "have . . . to know what I know and how I know what I know . . . they have to learn to write what I would write, or to offer up some approximation of that discourse" (140). They have to learn to think and write, in other words, like a big fish. This imperative produces a discipleship model of knowledge and education, which, according to Gregory Ulmer, is the least thoughtful relation to knowledge because it only reproduces authorities and the authority of tradition (*Applied Grammatology* 164–69). It is also the antithesis of what French feminists attempt to approach through *écriture féminine*. Our students know only too well the way of life that, despite all the rhetoric of individual choice, demands they take their place in line. The question is whether composition teachers can position themselves so that they do not further prevent individual expression.

In a big fish–little fish system, writing can ultimately evidence possession of or by a dominant framework of meaning or work as a form of resistance. Though the fate of every practice of resistance may be incorporation and neutralization, it is still possible to set resistance in motion again as such. This is the work of *écriture féminine*. If all of us have the responsibility to invent our own styles of resistance, as teachers we are faced with an impossible desire: to teach an unteachable relation to language. While we worry over this problem, and since we have much work yet to do, we can take whatever we glean from the excesses of *écriture féminine* and expand our notions of literacy to their widest possible circumference, to a point where literacy must involve us, and our students, in more than an epistemic relation to the world and to the earth. We can also recognize that *écriture féminine* arises from an ability to read culture, to read the ways hegemony works to win and shape consent so that the power of dominant meanings and dominant groups appears natural and beyond question. This ability can be taught. It involves students in the ongoing criticism of everyday life, of prominent forms of political discourse that shape their lives—such as advertising, film, photography, television, fashion, music, the news media, religious ritual, common sense, and academic discourse. We have numerous "models" to guide us and, within these broad divisions of discourse, numerous cultural texts on which to work, for the desire to give meaning is endless and endlessly fascinating. I find Hebdige's analysis of subcultures particularly suggestive as a reading of attempts by postwar youths to think and live differently. More generally, Hebdige offers an insightful application of Barthes's semiological and rhetorical approach to cultural analysis, which examines not only the literature and images of high art but also the texts of everyday life (eating, drinking, cleaning, vacationing).

The purpose of refashioning composition as cultural criticism, however, is not to stay within an epistemological justification but to liberate a different way of feeling, another sensibility.[14] Our emphasis should shift from the notion of writing as a mode of learning to that of writing as a strategy, without tactics or techniques, whose progress yields "unlearning." This result does not mean that writing produces ignorance; rather, it produces a sense of defamiliarization vis-à-vis unquestioned forms of knowledge. Writing would no longer function primarily as an agency in the articulation of knowledge and redistribution of power; instead, it would become an indispensable agency for making the world strange and infinitely various. Barthes calls this experience *sapientia*: "no power, a little knowledge, a little wisdom, and as much flavor as possible" (478). Students may discover ways to make something of what has been made of them; they may begin to discover and to invent the "flavor" of life in a society whose general tendency is toward conformity. Scholarship in composition, in the meantime, should examine ways in which culture is reproduced in its theory and in its practice—with a view toward becoming a site for the production of difference.

NOTES

[1] In this essay I leave *écriture féminine* untranslated whenever possible, to emphasize its difference from any of our appropriations of it, including my own. Among the translations of this term: "feminine writing," "writing said to be feminine," "writing the body."

[2] Kristeva develops this distinction across several essays; see especially "Psychoanalysis and the Polis," "The System and the Speaking Subject," "Women's Time," "Freud and Love." Her distinction between political and postmodern interpretation closely parallels Jean-François Lyotard's distinction between "metanarratives" of explanation, typical of modernism, and "petite narratives," typical of postmodern knowledge (*Postmodern* 3–23). Also, her definition of political interpretation seems synonymous with Barthes's sense of *myth*, which itself is synonymous with *ideology* (see *Mythologies* 109–59).

[3] For more on the discussion about modernism, the Enlightenment, and postmodernism, see Lyotard's *Postmodern Condition* and Habermas's *Philosophical Discourse of Modernity*. For a discussion of postmodernism and feminism, see Flax; Moi, "Feminism, Postmodernism, and Style."

[4] The analogy proposed here does not attempt to make a perfect match. Significant differences may be observed between *écriture féminine* and spectacular youth subcultures, which Hebdige argues arise out of a working-class ethic and the influence of race and race relations. French feminism, in contrast, has been criticized (e.g., by Spivak) as a phenomenon of and for elite, "First World" women. Most critics, however, see *écriture féminine* as being part of and contributing to a growing consciousness of racial difference (not tension), leading to a politics of diversity (not oppression). In spite of differences between *écriture féminine* and youth subcultures, the similarities seem numerous enough to make speculation productive. This approach, in particular, helps us resist the tendency to see *écriture féminine* simply as an alternative discourse or counterdiscourse constituting a counterculture. Counterculture has been distinguished from subculture by its overtly political and ideological forms of opposition to the dominant culture (e.g., through coherent philosophies giving rise to organized po-

litical action) and by its development of alternative institutions (e.g., alternative newspapers and presses, communes as alternative models of family organization) (Hebdige 148n6). The distinction between counterculture and subculture seems to turn on the degree of organization, formalization, and commitment to the elaboration of a system of meanings. To read French feminism as counterdiscourse therefore would be to freeze it within the demands of political interpretation. *Ecriture féminine* ultimately hopes to create a different culture, a different articulation of meaning and heterogeneity, but it will do so indirectly by first opening a space in dominant culture in which we can begin to think differently. It does not, in or of itself, lead directly to a counterculture.

[5]*Ecriture féminine* is conceived by and for women, who form a subordinate group, in the context of this discussion, in the sense that "they have been driven away [from writing] as violently as from their bodies" (Cixous, "Laugh" 279). Men are not excluded from *écriture féminine*, though women come to it more readily by virtue of their position within phallocentrism. For more on men and *écriture féminine*, see Cixous, "The Laugh of the Medusa"; Kristeva, "Women's Time"; Conley.

[6]Several critics investigate the style of *écriture féminine*. See Duren; Gallop, *Daughter's Seduction*; Jardine, *Gynesis*; Rabine; Richman; Stanton; Suleiman.

[7]Irigaray uses analogy extensively but with no guarantee that her reader will catch the mimic at work. Indeed, her critics often entirely overlook the importance of mimicry and argue that she commits the same errors of thought that brand the philosopher a phallocrat. In defense of her use of analogy, she says:

> And didn't Aristotle, a "giant thinker" according to Marx, determine the relationship between form and matter through an analogy with the relationship between male and female? To return to the question of sexual difference is therefore rather a new passage through analogism.
>
> (*This Sex* 170)

Irigaray, the subcultural bricoleur, steals into the dominant language and uses it against itself. This new passage makes visible what has been rendered invisible by the phallocentric use of analogy—not sameness but difference or, more precisely, differences.

[8]See Eric A. Havelock, who argues that pre-Socratic philosophers began to develop conceptual language once they discovered the power of abstraction and the ideas of system and totality. His discussion, in general, coincides with and supports many of the statements French feminists make about conceptual language, though he is not attempting to expose a sexual ideology at work in the process leading from a narrative logic to a logic of the written text.

[9]Hebdige actually employs Kristeva's notion of language as a signifying practice to discuss the construction of subcultures. He does not, however, extend this discussion to the feminine or to *écriture féminine*.

[10]Heidegger also examines the instrumentalist logic at work in this strategy. He associates it with "the technical interpretation of thought" typical of "research" in the university. See Worsham, "The Question concerning Invention."

[11]For more on humanism, modernism, and postmodernism, see Jardine, *Gynesis*; Moi, *Sexual/Textual Politics*.

[12]I have developed the argument that composition is part of the Enlightenment project at greater length in "The Question of Writing Otherwise."

[13]See Louise Wetherbee Phelps, for example, who situates composition in terms of a postmodern "consciousness."

[14]Gilles Deleuze writes, "The point of critique is not justification but a different way of feeling, another sensibility" (*Foucault* vii).

Feminism and Composition: The Case for Conflict

Susan C. Jarratt

- Heterosexual male students read aloud personal narratives about sexual conquest; women and other male students remain silent.
- White male students write fictional narratives in which a white male protagonist commits violence against a female teacher; the female teachers are unsure how to comment on the papers.
- The blatant sexism in a white male student's reading of a novel is overlooked as his essay is included in a book of model essays for new students because of its honest voice.
- A female student reports two years later that she now feels resentment at having been "manipulated into a position of vulnerability" in a student-centered composition class whose instructor was male.

THESE incidents and others like them—having floated about uneasily in my memory over the last few years—coalesce finally as a question about the relation between feminism and composition. The question especially concerns the kind of composition class that places a high priority on establishing a supportive and accepting climate in which students write primarily about personal experiences. The relation between feminism and composition studies has recently received some careful and productive attention.[1] While I see the powerful potential of the connections between the two realms, my question arises from a less promising tendency that they share: a strong resistance to conflict. Certain advocates of feminism and some composition teachers decline to contend with words. Some feminists vigorously reject argument on the grounds that it is a kind of violence, an instrument specific to patriarchal discourse and unsuitable for women trying to reshape thought and experience by changing forms of language use. For some composition teachers, creating a supportive climate in the classroom and validating student experience leads them to avoid conflict. This stance toward conflict, while it diminishes the power difference between teacher and student, leaves those who adopt it insufficiently prepared to negotiate the oppressive discourses of racism, sexism, and classism surfacing in the composition classroom. Such discourses arise in classes aimed specifically at exposing attitudes toward class, race, and gender (see Ellsworth) but also in classes not necessarily concerned with those issues: for example, in "student-centered" courses, where the instructor allows students a wide range of choice in writing topics. Further, those who avoid conflict minimize unforeseen possibilities for using argument to reconstruct knowledge available to both teacher and student.

First, I review feminist opposition to conflict, especially Sally Miller Gearhart's passionate distillation of the position. Next, I point out similarities in this feminist stance to a particular style of composition teaching. Finally, I argue for a rhetoric historically grounded in the practice of the first Sophists and revived today in overtly confrontational feminist pedagogies as a progressive mode of discourse in the composition classroom.

The Feminist Case against Argument

Feminists have been exploring the political significance of forms of discourse from the beginning of the "second wave" in the seventies. Some theorists condemn conventional academic discourse as the product of a hierarchical, male-dominated system of logic and learning that is oppressive to women (Cixous and Clément; Spender; Lewis and Simon; and many others).[2] In "The Womanization of Rhetoric" Gearhart insists on the material consequences of discourse practices. She speaks with the same tone of urgency and conviction I've heard in conversations and meetings with women who share her view. Gearhart vigorously rejects argument on the grounds that "any intent to persuade is an act of violence" (195). Writing from within a department of speech communication, Gearhart extends her attack on speech and writing even to education as "itself an insidious form of violence" (195). Any attempt to change another person is the expression of a "conquest/conversion mindset," a species feature that Gearhart claims evolved sometime after an earlier golden age when human beings lived in harmony with the earth (196–97). She speculates that this mindset may have developed simultaneously with the birth of language itself.

Despite Gearhart's sometimes extreme claims—"the difference between a persuasive metaphor and a violent artillery attack is obscure and certainly one of degree rather than kind" (197)—the problems troubling her are real and global. Gearhart despairs of the thoughtless destruction of humans, animals, and the earth itself—the product of centuries of male domination —leading us "pell-mell down the path to annihilation" (196). Her socio-biologic reading of a sex-specific tendency to violence resembles Walter J. Ong's in *Fighting for Life: Contest, Sexuality, and Consciousness,* as does her recommendation for change: the "womanization" of rhetoric. Gearhart suggests a shift from a speaker-oriented delivery of truth to a more peaceful context for communication. In her model, no participant seeks to inform or persuade another, but somehow differences are expressed. These communication situations may involve "learning" and "conflict encounter," but each participant must be willing "on the deepest level to yield her/his position entirely to the other(s)" (199).

It's too easy a game to point out the inconsistencies and contradictions in Gearhart's argument (for it is clearly that): decrying the intention to change while calling for change; arguing that arguments are violent. A more generous reading would focus on the distinction she draws between a "male chauvinist" model of speech and a dialogic context for exchange of ideas—a field of communication Gearhart describes as a womblike matrix (199). Like the compositionists of the sixties and seventies who sought to shift the center of the class from teacher to student, to let students write about their experiences, to realign power in the classroom, Gearhart wants to replace an authoritarian model of education with a nurturing atmosphere for human interaction (200). The teacher becomes "co-creator and co-sustainer" of the communication possibilities. These admirable goals aim at real problems still with us.

But problems with Gearhart's proposal arise in the details of the communication context she envisions. She demands that "persons involved feel equal in power to each other" but doesn't explain how, for example, a black student in an all-white class can attain that feeling of equality. Apparently, communication for all is impossible without it. Gearhart acknowledges that communication is difficult and must be worked at, but she provides only the most general suggestions for handling cases when "genuine disagreements" arise (198). And these suggestions come right out of the rhetoric she so violently rejects:

Some unity will have to occur there of personality differences with the principled advocacy of positions; some techniques of interpersonal clarification and openness will have to blend with the use of good reason in the controversy.

(199)

In calling for "principled advocacy of positions," Gearhart redefines rhetoric in a way that differs from her earlier narrow view but that remains quite consistent with a number of classical formulations (e.g., those of Cicero, Quintilian, Augustine). The use of "good reason" relies on a standard of judgment at least as gendered as the rhetoric Gearhart rejects.[3] Those who have enjoyed positions of power in the field of discourse within which Gearhart dwells—namely, white men—have for centuries been responsible for normalizing "reason," with very little interference from other groups. And she provides no method to adjudicate differences about what constitutes "good reason," should they arise. Finally, perhaps the most revealing element in her formula for handling conflict is the implication that difference occurs on the personal level: differences in "personality" can be resolved through "interpersonal" techniques. Despite her identification with feminism, Gearhart fails to anticipate the emergence of differences among groups. She applauds rhetoric's recent turn to an awareness of audience (a singularly ahistorical reading), but she's clearly working on the model of one individual speaking to another.

Gearhart recommends the rediscovery of rhetoric's historical connection with ethics (200), particularly as a corrective to the current social-science orientation of communication theory. But for her that ethical imperative is enacted through a simple inversion, in which persons using the conquest model of speaking and teaching become vessels "out of whose variety messages will emerge" (201). Even if we grant some scope for change through human agency, Gearhart's model pays no attention to the power of institutions to reproduce ideology (see Althusser, *Lenin*) or of discourses in Foucault's sense that speak through members of a culture. While she contributes to a discourse of difference, an important moment in feminism's challenge to a male-dominated status quo,[4] Gearhart does not account for the way other struggling voices can be drowned out, despite the good intentions of the instructor, in specific communication contexts where the dominant discourse is well represented.

Composition without Conflict

Gearhart's rejection of rhetoric reminds me of the attitude toward conflict I see in composition teachers trained in or converted to student-centered writing pedagogies. Though I haven't done a systematic study comparing approaches, I have spent many hours working with graduate-student teachers schooled in a program based on works like Peter Elbow's *Writing without Teachers* and Donald M. Murray's *Write to Learn*. James A. Berlin's analyses of these composition theorists, whom he calls "subjective" or "expressionist," emphasize their interest in self-discovery and the assumption of common human experiences and values underlying their practices (*Rhetoric and Reality* 145; "Rhetoric and Ideology" 484–87).

At their inception, these pedagogies created productive conflict at the institutional level by encouraging students to write about what mattered to them and by challenging an institution of literary studies unresponsive to students' lives. The pedagogies encouraged teachers, through example and practical advice, to loosen their grip on a stiff, academic language taught largely through error-identification and to experiment with alternative styles. In classes and in books guided by these theories I find an intense and genuine desire to break down the barriers between teacher and student, between distant, academic discourse and personally meaningful writing. Teachers who follow these theories nurture rather than act as authority figures. Indeed, the two books cited above have no teachers—only readers, who are most often sympathetic and committed.

Removing the teacher from the center of the classroom—away from the authoritative position as the source of knowledge—is a postmodern move, in the sense that the teacher was taken as the locus of a Truth. But the transformative potential of expressive pedagogy has to be evaluated in the light of the broader political implications of the theory. Berlin has effectively identified the cooptive potential of the emphasis on the individual in expressive pedagogy ("Rhetoric and Ideology" 487). In my experience at a midwestern state university, affirming the voice of a white, middle- or upper-middle-class student often involves teachers in rationalizing a future in corporate anonymity, in endorsing the clichés of competitive self-interest that perpetuate a system of racism, sexism, and classism still very much a part of American culture. The complexities of social differentiation and inequity in late-twentieth-century capitalist society are thrown into the shadows by the bright spotlight focused on the individual. Consider the epigraphs opening Murray's *Write to Learn*: from Jane Austen, "I must keep to my own style, and go on in my own way"; from E. E. Cummings, "To be nobody-but-yourself—in a world which is doing its best, night and day, to make you everybody else" (1).

Paradoxically, when groups do work together in these pedagogies, the ideal is homogeneity, another way of avoiding confrontations over social differences. In *Writing without Teachers*, Elbow describes a group of seven to twelve committed writers, best if they're "people who have a lot in common" (79).

Murray brings the reader into his text *Write to Learn* only on page 195, and then his advice about reading and readers assumes a commonality of experience. Reading as a writer means "reading unwritten texts," like an archaeologist unearthing potential meanings. The reader intuitively fills in the spaces because of an unspoken empathy with writers and their texts. Although conflict is anticipated, it usually occurs because of a lack of clarity in the message—fog or static, in Elbow's terms (127–32). Conflict is a matter of each reader's experience, personal quirks that can't be second-guessed by the writer; the writer's control over the text is paramount (104–05). This vision of communication fails to acknowledge fundamental clashes in values that underlie issues of style, effect, and meaning. How would those differences be negotiated in Elbow's writing group? They wouldn't, because the group is essentially value-free. His advice to readers includes "Never quarrel with someone else's reaction" and "No kind of reaction is wrong" (95). Both writers and readers are "always right and always wrong" (100, 106). Elbow encourages, even demands, uncensored accounts of the experience of reading and self-evaluations of writing. But this view assumes that the writer will be able to do whatever he or she wishes with the responses because of the equality of all group members (126). In our society, men and women, blacks and whites, rich and poor are positioned in "antagonistic and asymmetrical relation," as the feminist theorist Teresa de Lauretis has observed (*Technologies* 38). Because those structural differences pervade the writing classes most of us teach, our students can't merely accept or reject such responses on an equal basis, because of the material realities in our society in which such responses are grounded. Such inequities often make the attempt to create a harmonious and nurturing community of readers an illusory fiction—a superficial suturing of real social divisions.

Although the expressionists are displacing authority and thus enacting a feminist goal, expressive pedagogy presents problems for women and for feminism. Consider, for example, the heavily gendered language with which Peter Elbow instructs the reader of student writing in *Writing without Teachers*. Working against the standard teaching and writing practices of the literary criticism he inherited, Elbow encourages participants in the "believing game" to give up the aggressive, combative, argumentative rigidity required for the "doubting game" (178–79).[5] In so doing, they leave themselves open—but not to "force-feeding" or "rape," Elbow assures us (185); nor will they go "intellectually soft and limp" (181). Rather, Elbow advises, following Conrad, "In the destructive element immerse"; give yourself over to the alien— what threatens to poison or infect (186–87). *Writing without Teachers* is truly a revolutionary text in its feminization of the male writing teacher. But female readers—teachers or students of composition—are positioned differently in relation to these instructions.[6] Demanding that our female students listen openly and acceptingly to every response from a mixed class can lead to a discursive reenactment of the violence carried on daily in the maintenance of an inequitable society (de Lauretis, *Technologies* 34). Advising a female student to "swallow" without reply a conventional male reaction to a woman's experience has serious consequences. Similar problems occur when a female teacher takes a nurturing role in a class of men and women—replicating the traditional female role in our culture. A female teacher who takes a position of uncritical openness toward the male student, especially if social-class differences also apply, invites the exercise of patriarchal domination to which every man in our society is acculturated. Because most high school teachers are women and may be seen as maternal figures, the role of the supportive, nurturing composition teacher repeats that childish pattern and puts the teacher at a disadvantage in any attempt to assert a counterhegemonic authority as a woman.[7] A third problem is that of the female student whose male composition teacher encourages her to make a deep and serious self-examination of personal experience. How is the female student to resist an exposure she feels unwilling but obligated to make under the rules of the institution and the culture? These are the problems surfacing in the incidents I cited in the opening of this essay.

I can hear those who use expressivist methods objecting that none of these scenarios would occur in the classroom of a sensible and sensitive teacher: one who would intervene in an objectionable discourse from a male student, who would simply take on a stronger role as a woman with male students testing the limits of the supportive setting, who would never demand a self-revelation from a resisting student. I am confident that many teachers, male and female, intuitively negotiate such situations with sensitivity to the complexities of gender, race, and class differences. But we can't always control the ways discursive power works in our classes. We can't force female students to speak out against men, or students of color to speak out against whites. We can't always undo the institutional authority of our roles through our instructions and assurances. Despite the efficacy of intuitive responses, I contend that we need more, especially in the area of teacher training. We need a theory and practice more adequately attuned than expressivism is to the social complexities of our classrooms and the political exigencies of our country in this historical moment.

Feminist Adaptations of Expressivist Composition

Some feminists find the work of the expressionists much less troublesome than I do. They agree with Elbow and Murray that the writing teacher should be, above all, nurturing and the writing class, above all, nonconflictual. Elisabeth Däumer and Sandra Runzo elaborate the parallel between the mother and the teacher of writing. Citing the "distinctly female perspective in the works of Janet Emig and Ann E. Berthoff," they create a genealogy for feminist composition theory, emphasizing the supportive context within which students can best learn to write and endorsing the idea of "drawing on maternal practice and the values it cultivates" (48, 50). While they acknowledge the downside of that model—the exploitation of women through the devaluation of women's work and the socializing burden placed on mothers—they keep it as their ideal for the composition teacher. Rather than turn that ambivalence about mothers into a complication of the teacher's role, they direct it toward the pedagogical choices of the teacher-mother. Instead of asking if the teacher should be like a mother or, as Margo Culley et al. do, how we can understand and make the best of the psychological dynamics at work when a woman teaches, the question Däumer and Runzo ask becomes, What does the mother teach? The answer is women's texts. Rejecting an approach to writing embodying a masculine ethic of "aggression and adversarial relationships," they advocate a class in which women write about personal experiences after reading women's autobiography, history, and fiction. Despite the emphasis on women's experience, Däumer and Runzo claim that reading and writing assignments "can easily be modified to include men" (47). What appeals to me about this pedagogy is the opportunity it provides for women's growth in such a composition class. What disturbs me is the easy assumption that male students would have no problem fitting into such a class and the absence of any reference to the psychological complexities around the conjunction of mothering and teaching.[8] Under such circumstances—which the authors acknowledge as the norm—I think we need a more rhetorical composition theory, one providing a model of political conflict and negotiation.

Carol A. Stanger addresses the possibility of gender-related conflicts in the composition classroom more directly. She argues for sex-linked language difference, traces a history of the suppression of women's writing, and seeks the most efficacious mode of composition teaching for encouraging female students to write (32–34). Using a hypothetical student as an example, Stanger contrasts an authoritarian form of one-on-one tutoring with Kenneth Bruffee's collaborative method of reader response. She finds collaboration preferable for drawing out women writers in the group through a dialogue between male and female language:

> Although we would expect that male language would dominate, the new social structure of the peer learning group, the lack of a patriarchal presence "teaching," and the presence of strong and vocal women in the group can combine to give women's language the power to surface and replace men's language.
>
> (42)

Stanger does not guarantee that collaboration works for the woman writer, but she has strong confidence in the possibility of a transcendent, "oceanic" group experience mirroring the experience of "perfect oneness with the mother, a primary intimacy" (40). Again the feminist composition class becomes founded in the maternal, though the teacher is not placed directly in the mothering role. If indeed this transcendent experience comes about—although I can't say I've witnessed it in years of what I considered successful collaborative work in my writing classes—students will most likely see the teachers as the source of this maternal intimacy, since teachers initiate the groups, presumably control the larger process, and ultimately give the grades. Anticipating such a positive response to teacher as mother naively ignores the deep ambivalence toward and repression of the mother in our culture. But what of the occasions when conflicts do arise? Stanger relies on Carol Gilligan's reading of the differences between men's and women's socialization on questions of moral value. While male students fight for the "right" answer, female students seek compromise, and thus the group reaches consensus (41). Doesn't that suggest that the women probably give in to the men's positions? Because consensus is necessary for the pedagogy to work, Stanger can only hope that it includes women's as well as men's voices. Like Elbow, she puts a high priority on placing power in the voices of the students, on shifting power from teacher to students who are undifferentiated by gender—not to mention class or race.

Even when teachers announce the desire to create a particular climate, they can't neutralize by fiat the social positions already occupied by their students. I believe we need to supplement the note of hope sounded in Stanger's essay with a more open acknowledgment of gender, race, and class differences among students and with a pedagogy designed to confront and explore the uneven power relations resulting from these differences. It's not a question of throwing out the innovations of teachers like Elbow and Murray or of shutting down the voices and personal experiences of students; rather, it's a question of relocating those practices and interests in a different theoretical context—getting a larger sense of what produces them and of what the writing based in them should do. It is a question of metaphorically breaking down the classroom walls to examine the ways the infrastructures of society have created those experiences. While these early mappings of feminist pedagogy deserve praise, we must work to strengthen the goal of displacing teacher authority with a more carefully theorized understanding of the multiple forms of power reproduced in the classroom. Differences of gender, race, and class among students and teachers provide situations in which conflict does arise, and we need more than the ideal of the harmonious, nurturing composition class in our repertory of teaching practices to deal with these problems.

Conflict in Historical Rhetoric

A leap back to classical rhetoric can give us a perspective on the political implications of suppressing conflict that may be hard to get at close range. Plato and Aristotle condemn the Sophists for eristic argumentation—that is, a competitive contentiousness allegedly engaged in for its own sake. It is this kind of argument feminists and compositionists reject. Both philosophers replace the sophistic *techne* with more respectable alternatives: for Plato, dialectic; for Aristotle, invention. In each case, the objective method masks the political implications of its appropriation by an interested party. In other words, Plato's metaphysical goals underlie Socrates's questioning in many dialogues but are not themselves brought under examination. Pure scientific knowledge and dialectic differ from the informal logic of rhetorical invention in Aristotle's theory, but such divisions themselves are not matters for rhetorical argument. Both Plato and Aristotle assume that, for any audience in possession of full knowledge, rhetoric would not only lack conflict, it would be unnecessary. That is, each idealizes an audience completely in harmony about fundamental assumptions, even though each acknowledges the persistence of conflict in real human affairs. This understanding fits the ideal political arrangement envisioned by both philosophers: rule by a small, homogeneous group of aristocrats.

In contrast, the first Sophists place at the center of their practice *dissoi logoi*—conflicting views about an issue. Their theory assumes that knowledge is always constructed socially and that public action is guided by informed debate among members of a democratic community (Jarratt, *Rereading*). Conflict is central to their theory of rhetoric and democratic politics. Only through recognition of and argument over differences can conflict be resolved into *homonoia*, like-mindedness. If we can make the same kinds of assessments about contemporary composition pedagogy, then conflict—the place it holds in theory and practice and the ends toward which it is employed—can serve as a measure of the political effect of a discourse practice.

Moving toward Rhetoric

Here I wish to examine two pedagogies moving toward a more politically efficacious use of argument: one offered by the feminist philosopher Joyce Trebilcot in "Dyke Methods or Principles for the Discovery/Creation of the Withstanding" and the other by a more rhetorical Elbow than we saw earlier. Trebilcot, at first glance, appears to be laying out a discourse scenario similar to Gearhart's radical rejection of conflict. But a closer look shows that Trebilcot refines Gearhart's case for nonconflict because she takes into account different situations—places where the rules of nonconflict hold and places where they are debilitating. The methods her essay title refers to apply only when women are speaking together in "safe spaces":

> The principles are not intended to be used in situations that are predominantly patriarchal, that is, when getting something from men is at stake, as when one is working in the patriarchy for money, doing business with men and male-identified women, etc. In these contexts I find that it is usually most effective to operate according to patriarchal ideas of knowledge and truth.
>
> (3)

Trebilcot, a philosopher, seeks to establish methods of using language to account for reality without participating in the "domination inherent in the patriarchal idea of truth." Like Gearhart, she refuses, when talking with other women, to engage in persuasion: "I speak only for myself. I do not try to get other wimmin to accept my beliefs in place of their own" (1).

While Gearhart approaches the issue from a global and historical perspective, Trebilcot arrives at her principles out of personal anger against control. In male-dominated discourse, she often sees herself and other women either excluded or misrepresented. Like the expressionists, Trebilcot wants to unweave the fabric of discourse, separating out the single thread that is hers. Or, in terms of another figure, she wants her voice to sound alone rather than be submerged in the flood of male voices either drowning her out or pretending to sing her part for her. But she is not unaware of a Bakhtinian heteroglossia always present in any discourse: "pure wimmin's spaces can't exist—we are interlarded everywhere with patriarchy" (10). The purpose of Trebilcot's "principle of nonpersuasion" is to avoid, in communication with like-minded women, the exercise of male power and control she experiences in the "truth industry—heteropatriarchal science, religion, scholarship, education media"—and to promote serious respect for the differences among women (7).

Through the dialogic construction of her article, a result of arguing both with herself and with commentators on her work, Trebilcot anticipates and answers a number of objections critics might raise about her principles. She agrees that discourse can persuade even when it isn't intended to, that power relations influence how discourse works, and that her claim to a single voice denies the working of a community. I find the last of these issues the most intriguing because of the way she defines nonpersuasive communication and describes her experience of discourse. When "wimmin" meet to talk in nonhierarchical and noncompetitive communication situations, they tell stories —past, present, and future—and plan action. In a telegraphic way, Trebilcot proposes a version of sophistic rhetoric, the art of representing the past and present so as to suggest a course of action for the future. Trebilcot's definition elides the process of coming to agreement about the particular course of action to be taken, but she does explain that if anyone in a group of compatible women disagrees with a plan, it is dropped (9).

But persuasion of some kind must be going on in the space between telling stories—necessarily different stories—and planning action, even in a group of like-minded people. Further, I think that for pedagogical purposes—that is, as a model for the language of the classroom—it is more productive to bring out and examine the contradictions and conflicts being resolved in that space than to overlook them or minimize their significance. The same kind of sharp dichotomy between argument and agreement appears in Elbow's essay "Methodological Doubting and Believing: Contraries in Inquiry." Seeking to shift the balance in intellectual inquiry away from the critical process of attacking propositions with rigid logical instruments, Elbow argues for the "believing game"—the process of granting provisional assent in order to expand mental abilities and arrive at valid judgments. In this essay (a later version of the appendix to *Writing without Teachers*), Elbow openly acknowledges the gender associations of the two poles: "Believing invites behaviors associated with femininity: accepting, saying Yes, being compliant, listening, absorbing, and swallowing . . . being mute or silent" (266). Indeed, he links his project with feminist theory, because both attempt to emphasize experience and assent, "processes that have been undervalued in a culture deriving its tradition from methodological doubt and male dominance" (266). With Trebilcot, Elbow shares a conviction that storytelling can help listeners envision new worlds (277–78). Like the Sophists, he questions the rules of noncontradiction (279). His plea for believing sounds, at times, like the Sophists' way of making the worse case better. In positive terms, this practice means imagining the unimaginable; he advises storytelling as an aid to this kind of imagining (277–78). In short, Elbow's essay makes a major contribution toward providing a rhetorical foundation for the expressive composition class.

I find his theoretical formulation of the believing game troubling, however, in its reliance on authority for validity and in its silence on the issue of social differences in the practice of believing. While Elbow defends the believing game as a way to ensure that minority opinions are given power against those of the majority, how can that guarantee work when the "proof" of a belief is its acceptance by "a respected group of authorities" who endorse it through participation (266, 267)? Elbow's criterion is open to the same criticisms as Stanley Fish's "interpretive community," which Elbow offers as a parallel to his own model (see Fish, *Is There a Text*). Those educated readers who make up an interpretive community reflect the dominant group and crowd out marginal voices. Aristotle also evaluates the legitimacy of a deduction in terms of its "reputability": it is judged by whether the majority, all, or the most notable of men accept it (*Topics* 100a–b). If it isn't "reputable," it's "contentious." Elbow seems more concerned with the possible corruption of the reputable, the commonsensical, than with the silencing of marginal voices. He counters a charge of mental promiscuity or laxness, the seduction of the thinker into some sort of fringe belief such as "Moonie-ism," but never brings up the much more common problem of what happens to a woman's voice in a group of men or a black voice in a group of whites (283). A gender-sensitive reading of Elbow's rhetoric of belief shows it to be the feminization of a masculinist discourse of logic. That is, if taken to heart by a man, it would really help a male listener experience a female discourse. But for a female listener, the effect is much different. In Lacanian terms, Elbow is taking the position of castration, but because woman is already castrated in patriarchal discourse, placing a female reader in the position of castration (like Jane Gallop does, in *Reading Lacan*) is doubly disempowering (Moi, "Feminism" 15). Elbow advises us to overcome our "archetypal fears" of becoming "the large opening into which anything can be poured—force-fed, raped" (283–84). Though he wishes to offer all readers a way of gaining more control over their minds, because "compulsive doubters [are] more dominated by unaware beliefs than other people are" (284), this loaded language positions its gendered readers differently. Only read Elbow's rhetoric of surrender as a female subject, which I must do, and that positioning becomes frighteningly clear (285). An attitude of complete receptivity, of openness to "any view or hypothesis that a participant seriously wants to advance" (260), still puts a woman, I believe, in a dangerous stance.

Like Trebilcot, Elbow repudiates argument. But he goes much further in describing the process by which the listener participates in a belief. In citing the sophomore who petulantly asserts that argument is pointless, Elbow accepts a definition of argument like Aristotle's use of the eristic for the Sophists. Sometimes translated as "wrangling," eristic discourse is competitive, the point being, as Elbow says of argument, to defeat the opponent. But the Sophist Prodicus in Plato's *Protagoras* provides a synonym and thus an alternative for wrangling: "I . . . would beg you Protagoras and Socrates, . . . that you will dispute (*amphisbetein*) with one another and not wrangle (*erizein*), for friends dispute with friends out of good will, but only adversaries and enemies wrangle" (337b).[9] In place of "eris-ize"—to behave like the Eris, the goddess of discord—Prodicus offers a word meaning loosely to "go both ways." The noun form in fact refers to a serpent that can go forward or backward (Liddell and Scott 45). This ability to move into different positions, paradoxically, seems more consistent with the positive pole of both Trebilcot's and Elbow's oppositions. The kind of argument they reject is a one-sided, combative form of discourse: one that completely shuts out any opposing view. In both these formulations, then, conflict has a place—can be strategically deployed—though it is de-emphasized in favor of "believing" (Elbow) and of the "principle of nonpersuasion" (Trebilcot 5).

Productive Conflict in Feminist Composition Pedagogy

For pedagogies most fully engaged in issues of gender, race, and class— pedagogies in which conflict is central—I turn to the research of Kathleen Weiler and the radical black feminism of Bell Hooks. Weiler's work gives a feminist turn to the critical pedagogy of Paulo Freire, Henry Giroux, and others. Where the male theorists have focused largely on the issue of class, Weiler broadens the venue of critical pedagogy with special attention to gender. Her book *Women Teaching for Change* is particularly interesting for writing teachers because it uses personal narratives as a research methodology (see the chapter "The Dialectics of Gender in the Lives of Women Teachers" 73–100) but also because it moves beyond the supportive context of personal experience in an examination of classroom discussions in which gender, race, and class create conflicts among students and teachers. Weiler grounds her study in an analysis of schools as places where culture is both reproduced and produced. Though educational institutions enforce the power and control of the existing social order, they also allow students and teachers to challenge, oppose, and resist those forces. Her project, then, given that potential, is to work toward "a more fully developed theory of gender in an examination of the lived experiences of teachers and students in schools" (24).

Weiler observed feminist high school teachers in a range of subjects, including composition, who work with students of different classes, races, and genders (130). Like many composition teachers brought up on Elbow, Murray, and Ken Macrorie, these teachers

> expand the limits of discourse by directly addressing the forces that shape their students' lives . . . attempt[ing] to legitimize their students' voices by ac- knowledging their students' own experiences and by calling for their students' own narratives.
>
> (131)

But these teachers go farther than creating a nurturing, student-centered classroom:

> [R]elated to the expansion of discourse, is their own presentation of themselves as gendered subjects with a personal perspective on issues of gender and race. They are overtly political in their presentation and both will use personal anecdotes and will challenge and engage students on these topics.
>
> (131)

In foregrounding their membership in a class, race, and gender, these teachers either conflict with or affirm their students' identities. They create a classroom in which personal experience is important material but openly acknowledge that differences exist and cause conflicts. The negotiation of those conflicts becomes the subject of the dialogue Weiler quotes and comments on. Not all the discussions Weiler relates show teachers smoothly mediating the conflicting positions of their students. In one example, a working-class girl, questioning the morality of the rape victim who left her children at home to go to a bar, is silenced by middle-class feminist students (138). In another, the contribution of a black boy, who wants to discuss a segment of *The Autobiography of Malcolm X* in terms of racism, is passed over by his white teacher, who is making a point about socialization (140). The point of Weiler's account is not to showcase exemplary teachers but rather to capture and analyze the highly complex collisions of gender, race, and class in the classroom. She expresses no aim to rid the classroom of conflict because it is "always a site of conflict, and will be a site of conflict for the feminist or critical teacher . . . just as much as it will be for a traditional or authoritarian teacher" (137) or, I would add, even for the composition teacher seeking a nurturing environment for a heterogeneous group of students writing about personal experiences. Recognizing the inevitability of conflict is not grounds for despair but the starting point for creating a consciousness in students and teachers through which the inequalities generating those conflicts can be acknowledged and transformed (144–45).

The teacher's role in the writing classroom, in a feminist critical pedagogy, varies greatly depending on the makeup of the class in relation to the teacher's subjectivity. Beyond recognizing the institutional power of teachers—the political intervention staged by expressionists—a teacher would recognize, for example, an unequal positioning if she or he were the product of a working-class background but teaching in an elite school. A black man teaching all white students would face a much different situation. In the polyphony of voices, not all will or should sound equally. Ira Shor, using Freire, explains how the teacher, even while creating a "loving matrix" for dialogue, may sometimes need to take on an adversarial role against an abusive student or to voice an unrepresented view in the dialogue (*Critical* 95, 102). As Moi asks, "What dogmatism says that it is *never* feminist to speak with authority?" ("Feminism" 15).

An eloquent and powerful example of how, even among women, voices differ, Hooks speaks directly to the issue of conflict in the title of her recent collection of essays, *Talking Back*. While the stereotype of women's speech under patriarchy is that it is silenced, Hooks remembers women's voices as strong and angry in her experience as a child in a southern black family and community. She was silenced not by men but by the adult women in her family who tried to socialize her as a female child into using the right kind of speech (6). Her account runs counter to the assumptions of feminist compositionists cited earlier whose primary aim is to make a space for the voices of women (Däumer and Runzo) or for an essentialized "women's speech" in dialogue with men's (Stanger). For black women, Hooks explains, the "struggle has not been to emerge from silence into speech but to change the nature and direction of our speech, to make a speech that compels listeners, one that is heard" (6). Perhaps the nurturing, nonconflictual composition classroom could aid in this enterprise, but perhaps not. Hooks's revolutionary feminist pedagogy rejects an exclusive focus on personal experience as a simple inversion of the older pedagogy of domination against which compositionists reacted in the sixties and seventies (52). I agree with Hooks that "[t]his model must be viewed critically because a class can still be reinforcing domination, not transforming consciousness about gender, even as the 'personal' is the ongoing topic of conversation" (52). The incidents recounted in the opening of this essay are examples of domination in the context of classroom conversations about the "personal."

Using her favorite teacher as a model, Hooks endorses a pedagogy grounded in "an oppositional world view"—essential for blacks in a white, racist society (49). Her teachers, almost all black women, "offered . . . a legacy of liberatory pedagogy that demanded active resistance and rebellion against sexism and racism" (50). Hooks's analysis of the current educational climate, oddly similar to a picture of the sixties, calls up a different pedagogy in response. Students today, she writes, "suffer from a crisis of meaning, unsure about what has value in life," and they "long for a context where their subjective needs can be integrated with study" (51). But rather than the safe and nurturing classroom, Hooks recommends a class wherein "the primary focus is a broader spectrum of ideas and modes of inquiry, in short a dialectical context where there is serious and rigorous critical exchange" (51). In this frank description, she marks very pointedly the difference between her pedagogy and the one under critical examination here:

> Unlike the stereotypical feminist model that suggests women best come to voice in an atmosphere of safety (one in which we are all going to be kind and nurturing), I encourage students to work at coming to voice in an atmosphere where they may be afraid or see themselves at risk. The goal is to enable all students, not just an assertive few, to feel empowered in a rigorous, critical discussion. Many students find this pedagogy difficult, frightening, and very demanding. They do not usually come away from my class talking about how much they enjoyed the experience.
>
> (53)

While this account may make advocates of the expressive school uneasy, I suggest that we need now to reassess the criteria by which we evaluate success in the writing class. We must again take a political pulse to determine the effects of our practices and to reconsider strategies. The expressivist focus on student experiences and concerns is an important starting point for feminist pedagogy. But my double concern about those feminist compositionists who advocate such pedagogies is not only that they are positioned unequally in the expressivist discourse but also that they spend too little time helping their students learn how to argue about public issues—making the turn from the personal back out to the public. As Gayatri Chakravorty Spivak points out, a mere inversion of the public-private hierarchy succeeds only in a more rigid division of the two realms. Just as "the so-called public sector is woven of the so-called private, the definition of the private is marked by a public potential, since it *is* the weave, or texture, of public activity" (103). My hopes are pinned on composition courses whose instructors help their students to locate personal experience in historical and social contexts—courses that lead students to see how differences emerging from their texts and discussions have more to do with those contexts than they do with an essential and unarguable individuality. I envision a composition course in which students argue about the ethical implications of discourse on a wide range of subjects and, in so doing, come to identify their personal interests with others, understand those interests as implicated in a larger communal setting, and advance them in a public voice. Such a content for composition would replicate closely the Sophist Protagoras's identification of the subject of rhetoric: "prudence in affairs private as well as public." Through this course, the student will "learn to order his own house in the best manner, and he will be able to speak and act most powerfully in the affairs of the state" (Plato, *Protagoras* 318e–319a).[10]

Feminists are arguing the argument issue, and some of the most prominent voices are advocating a specific alignment of rhetoric and feminism. Examining the ways some feminist theorists discover a productive tension in the differences among feminists' positions, I have argued elsewhere for the parallel positioning of women and sophistic rhetoric against philosophy in the Western intellectual tradition ("First Sophists"), a view Patricia Bizzell extends in a reevaluation of the goals of cultural literacy. The discursive method driving both feminist and sophistic ways of negotiating change through discourse is argument. In both the prephilosophical fifth century, BC, and in the current postmodern antifoundational context, rhetorical positions stand temporarily as grounds for action in the absence of universally verifiable truth (Jarratt, *Rereading*; Bizzell, "Beyond Anti-Foundationalism"). When we recognize the need to confront the different truths our students bring to our classes—not only through self-discovery but in the heat of argument—feminism and rhetoric become allies in contention with the forces of oppression troubling us all.[11]

NOTES

[1]Elizabeth Flynn astutely identifies composition as the "feminization" of the field of literary studies. Using Carol Gilligan's *In a Different Voice*, Flynn demonstrates a gendered reading of student narratives in a first-year writing class. In Cynthia L. Caywood and Gillian R. Overing's collection, *Teaching Writing: Pedagogy, Gender, and Equity*, a number of the essays build on the inherently similar goals of a student-centered writing class and a particular style of feminist pedagogy (e.g., Stanger; Däumer and Runzo).

[2]See Catherine Clément, however, for a defense of women's use of a hegemonic, logical discourse (Cixous and Clément). Jane Tompkins creates a mixed discourse in "Me and My Shadow," encasing a conventional critique of another woman's work within a sympathetic, personal narrative about a woman's experience of academic life.

[3]Elizabeth Ellsworth criticizes the "rationalist assumptions" she finds underlying critical pedagogy (4–5).

[4]The feminist theorist Toril Moi defines *difference* as one of three positions emerging historically since the late sixties in the international women's movement ("Feminism" 5).

[5]Peter Elbow's most rhetorical statement on writing occurs in his "Appendix Essay: The Doubting Game and the Believing Game—An Analysis of the Intellectual Enterprise," an elaborated version of which appears in *Embracing Contraries*.

[6]Barbara Johnson makes a similar observation about Paul de Man's pedagogical posture of "self-resistance":

> [T]he question *can* be asked why de Man's discourse of self-resistance and uncertainty has achieved such authority and visibility, while the self-resistance and uncertainty of *women* has been part of what has insured their lack of authority and their invisibility. It would seem that one has to be positioned in the place of power in order for one's self-resistance to be valued. Self-resistance, indeed, may be one of the few postures remaining for the white male establishment.
>
> (45)

[7]Margo Culley et al. explain the double bind for the women in the academy in terms of the psychological dynamics of the family. On the one hand, the child, needing the mother for nurturance, ultimately comes to resent her power and the child's own dependence. On the other hand, in the role of "father" as an intellectual in the academy, a woman "betrays [her] body's traditional significance." As women academics, "our maternal power is feared, our paternal authority is mistrusted" (14).

[8]A collaborative inquiry in feminist pedagogy at Miami University, based on students' responses on teacher evaluations, indicates that a focus on women's issues in composition classes can create problems for both male and female students (Bauer et al.). In "Pedagogy of the Oppressors?" John Schilb describes the feminist pedagogy he arrived at through his experiences teaching women's studies to "mixed" classes, most of whose members "routinely oppose [his] values" (253). See also Margo Culley et al. on nurturance.

[9]The Sophist Protagoras himself demonstrates goodwill and flexibility in the dia-

logue, using both *mythos* (storytelling) and *logos* (laying out a case) to make a successful argument against Socrates that virtue can be taught.

[10]I maintain the gendered language of the original because of its historical accuracy but assume that its contemporary application will be understood as gender inclusive.

[11]I'd like to thank Dale Marie Bauer, Sara Farris, Peter W. Rose, and John Schilb for helpful comments on an earlier draft of this essay.

The Postdisciplinary Politics

of Lore

❖

Patricia Harkin

ECENTLY, from disparate theoretical perspectives, thinkers such as
Paulo Freire, Louise Wetherbee Phelps, and Richard Ohmann have
asserted that the acts of teaching do not merely disseminate knowledge but actually produce it. This political and conceptual move is
particularly important for teachers of composition, who often find the burdens
of time-consuming paper grading, low salaries, inadequate supplies, and
cramped office space painfully increased by the perception that their work is
"only" a service.

That unfortunate perception is exacerbated by the institutional structures
of most English departments in the United States. As Laurence R. Vesey
shows, American universities have historically served the society that supports
them, preserved its culture, and promoted research into questions it deems
valuable. This history unfolds within a context of "scientism," which Jürgen
Habermas calls "science's belief in itself: that is, the conviction that we can
no longer understand science as *one* form of possible knowledge, but rather
must identify knowledge with science" (*Knowledge* 4). In the American academy, research is understood to produce knowledge on a more or less scientistic

model, while service courses provide practical instruction in the application of that knowledge. In this context, however, departments of English are somewhat anomalous. The "knowledge" most often produced by traditional departments of English (however that knowledge may be defined) has to do with literary studies. But the service course of English departments, composition, does not usually tell its students how to use that literary knowledge. Unlike the research in, say, chemistry departments, where a graduate-level biochemistry course may produce knowledge that is later disseminated in an undergraduate course called Chemistry for Pharmacists, the research activities of English departments frequently have little or no immediate applicability to composition studies. Lately, of course, an increasingly large number of universities describe themselves as supporting research in composition, but that support is, I suspect, more often construed as an investment in improving a service than in advancing knowledge.

The recent attention to teaching, by contrast, seeks to demonstrate that teaching itself makes knowledge in ways that are different from, but not less valuable than, the methods of science. In these discussions, it is not sufficient merely to assert that teaching produces knowledge; we need to have models of knowledge production—concrete accounts of proposed changes in institutional procedures that tell us what kind of knowledge teachers make, how they make it, and why it should count. In that endeavor, one of the most refreshing voices belongs to Stephen M. North.

In *The Making of Knowledge in Composition: Portrait of an Emerging Field*, North delineates a notion he calls "lore": "the accumulated body of traditions, practices, and beliefs in terms of which Practitioners [of composition study and teaching] understand how writing is done, learned and taught" (22). Lore comprises the rituals of our profession, like teaching the modes, sitting in a circle, assigning double-entry notebooks, using a red pen, forming peer-group workshops, commenting on students' papers according to the codes in the *Harbrace Handbook*, establishing a list of "fatal errors," valuing "voice," encouraging revision, and so on. "Literally anything," North writes, "can become a part of lore," and "nothing can ever be dropped from it either" (24).

As a consequence, we cannot speak of a unified "body" of lore as we might speak of the procedures of inquiry that constitute an academic discipline. Lore is nondisciplinary: it is actually defined by its inattention to disciplinary procedures. Lore cannot provide abstract accounts of the writing act; it tells us what practitioners do. And practitioners rarely attend to the theoretical implications of their practice, even if they do adopt, adapt, and apply theoretical articulations. Lore often takes the form of teachers' guides to textbooks, "Staffroom Interchange" in the journal *College Composition and Communication*, lesson plans, syllabi, handouts, and even the narratives about "what I did last Thursday" that we share as friends and professionals. Lore is passed around from person to person and passed on from generation to generation.

This dissemination, North writes, is "driven . . . by a pragmatic logic: It is concerned with what has worked, is working, or might work in teaching, doing, or learning writing. Hence, its structure is primarily experiential" (23). The experiences of lore are not like the experiments of the recognized sciences. Practitioners rarely have the time, resources, or inclination to conduct experiments that meet standards of reliability and validity.

Because its procedures derive from disparate and unarticulated assumptions about writing, lore is frequently contradictory. For example, a practitioner might use sentence-combining exercises that invoke a linguistically based notion of writing as the record of speech. But that same teacher might also assign journal entries that imply a phenomenologically based notion of writing as the making of meaning. That these notions of writing may be incompatible with each other is not a problem for most practitioners. The inconsistency goes unrecognized because the "law" of noncontradiction is simply not invoked and because the teaching practice is successful at achieving its often disparate practical goals.

Although North's colleagues C. H. Knoblauch and Lil Brannon find these contradictions troubling (see ch. 5), North takes pains to make sure that his readers value lore in spite of its difference from more traditional means of knowledge production. He points out that lore has a social function. Its accretive rituals "form an important part of a Practitioner's identity, are the outward signs of community membership," provide "much of the foundation for the Practitioner's authority," and "serve a logistical, practical function" of passing information (30).

More important and more surprising, though, is North's assertion that lore should (sometimes) count as "inquiry" in the fully valorized sense of that term. He writes that when a practitioner identifies a problem, searches for causes, searches for possible solutions, tests solutions in practice, and validates and disseminates that information (36), that practitioner may be said to have conducted an inquiry, even if his or her procedures vary from disciplinary and professional criteria. North's example, par excellence, of the inquiring practitioner is Mina Shaughnessy and her *Errors and Expectations*.

I use Shaughnessy's work as an example to explain (1) my sense that North's account of lore permits us to see some teaching practices as postdisciplinary; (2) my belief that lore therefore has important implications for engaging the problem that Stanley Fish calls "theory hope"; and (3) my proposal to develop lore as an instance of what Fredric Jameson calls "cognitive mapping" and to use it to foreground differences in theories of writing so as to produce an "environmental-impact statement" for writing pedagogy.

Mina Shaughnessy's book begins with that wrenching paragraph that so impressed us in 1977:

> I remember sitting alone in the worn urban classroom where my students had just written their first essays and where I now began to read them, hoping to be able to assess quickly the sort of task that lay ahead of us that semester. But the writing was so stunningly unskilled that I could not begin to define the task or even sort out the difficulties. I could only sit there, reading and rereading the alien papers, wondering what had gone wrong and trying to understand what I at this eleventh hour of my students' academic lives could do about it.
>
> (vi)

North counts the steps in Shaughnessy's inquiry. She identified the problem as a function of her students' expectations about error. She developed exercises to help her students avoid these errors and, hence, change their expectations. The exercises worked, and *Errors and Expectations* was published.

It is important to note how lore differs from "normal" disciplinary inquiries, which usually *end* by establishing the validity of a hypothesis about causal or explanatory relations. A traditional experiment would aim to demonstrate, reliably and validly, why Shaughnessy's open-admissions students wrote nonstandard English sentences. By eliminating other variables, the researcher would perhaps determine, as Shaughnessy did, that these errors were the result of students' expectations that they would fail. But, unlike Shaughnessy, a traditional disciplinary researcher would need to end the inquiry with that knowledge. Another experiment, perhaps, someday, would attempt to establish the efficacy of a particular effort at changing these expectations. Again, however, that inquiry would necessarily limit itself to establishing one cause-and-effect relation. The need to replicate, with its attendant constraints on the kinds of research questions that can be asked, constitutes the main difference between lore and normal science.

Shaughnessy didn't have time to worry about reliable and valid research; she was too constrained by class size; limited funding, time, and energy; and all the other quotidian concerns that make up our lives as academics. In *Errors and Expectations*, she is careful to stipulate that her definitions of terms are not disciplinary ones: for example, she distinguishes her definition of competence from Chomsky's and points out that "syntax is generally, and loosely, used by teachers to mean the 'big' problems in sentences—problems that keep a sentence from 'working' or being understood as opposed to those that keep it from being appropriate to a specific situation" (47). Having made that demurrer, Shaughnessy goes on to discriminate among "skipped words," "blurred patterns," and "consolidation errors," symptoms for which she finds a variety of explanations:

[W]hen academically ill-prepared young adults write, which they rarely do
except in an academic situation, they often mismanage complexity. This mis-
management gets explained in different ways. One explanation focuses on what
the student has not internalized in the way of language patterns characteristic
of written English, another on his unfamiliarity with the composing process
and another on his attitude toward himself within an academic setting.

(72–73)

The first of Shaughnessy's explanations is governed loosely by the discipline
of linguistics, but the second requires sociological warrants and the third,
psychological ones. Each explanation, Shaughnessy continues, implies a pedagogy, but "a teacher should not have to choose from among these pedagogies,
for each addresses but one part of the problem" (73). Shaughnessy's remedies,
exercises generally warranted in linguistics, make no claim to disciplinary
rigor. Indeed their claim is precisely the opposite: a complex problem requires
a complex solution. In a process of informed intuition, Shaughnessy tested
these solutions in practice, not under laboratory conditions, and succeeded
spectacularly—not at "doing science" but at doing what she wanted to do.
More than a decade later, Shaughnessy is revered, but her work is not routinely
offered as paradigmatic of "inquiry." Because lore cannot be validated in
traditional ways, it tends to be undervalued.

Errors and Expectations (and lore in general) is subject to two kinds of
objections: a "slippery slope" ethical one and a rigid disciplinary one. First,
critics charge that because Shaughnessy's exercises are so easy to use, they
can be (mis)used in the service of racist, sexist, or classist agendas. Second,
because lore is nondisciplinary, and therefore not replicable, critics charge
that it is not really knowledge at all.

John Rouse's article "The Politics of Composition" exemplifies both kinds
of objections. Rouse uses Basil B. Bernstein's work in sociolinguistics to
warrant his disciplinary critique of Shaughnessy: specifically, he assumes that
basic writers are persons who possess restricted (as against elaborated) codes.
Rouse summarizes Bernstein in this way:

A restricted code relies on context to give its statements meaning. . . . It is
for all of us a language of intimacy . . . in which little need be made explicit
because so much is understood. . . . But a child who has only that code is at
a disadvantage in school, where the whole educational enterprise is for more
explicitness and for the mind that takes nothing for granted. . . . [By contrast]
children who have been led by their family experience to strive towards their
own role . . . have a sense . . . of separation from others: . . . what "I think"
as against what "you think." . . . And these habits of mind are expressed in
the structure of their sentences, in an elaborated speech code.

(4–5)

Let me fill in some of the disciplinary context that Rouse apparently invokes. Writing, in these frameworks, is understood as a record of speech; speech is the product of a habit of mind; habits of mind are products of social conditions. Once produced, these habits belong to the individual speaker and help to constitute the speaker's "self." But then Rouse begins to make ethical judgments about how teachers should treat that self and concludes that Shaughnessy treats her students badly. One of her writing assignments, Rouse explains, asks students to take a position on the ways children and adults see the physical world. He objects to the topic as one "likely to leave any of us stammering for words," but, more important for my purposes, he asserts that it "disregards the known facts of language learning" (2). A few sentences later, Rouse specifies what I take to be some of these "facts":

> Any writing task involves anxiety, of course—we always wonder if the words will come, if the ideas will make good sense. But our interest in the project keeps us going until finally we have created from out of ourselves and our material an essay, perhaps, that might interest others.
>
> (2)

When "young people are not asked to write about matters that engage them deeply . . . they seem inarticulate or unthinking" (2). Is Bernstein's sociolinguistics the source of this second set of "facts"? I think not.

Rouse neither argues nor asserts a connection between linguistic warrants and ethical "facts." I therefore infer that Rouse thinks that if we encourage students to write about what is important to them, their restricted speech codes can grow into elaborated ones as they desire to communicate with a wider audience. As a consequence, their writing will become a record of elaborated codes more fully contextualized. If, however, a teacher intervenes with exercises designed to regularize the syntax of students' written work, then they develop what Rouse calls "that amorality so useful to authority everywhere" (2), the tendency to write anything at all so long as it adds up to the requisite number of words. In disciplinary terms, Rouse's strategies are to define writing as a record of speech, to discriminate restricted from elaborated codes in speech, to apply those distinctions to writing, to see error as the consequence of restricted codes, and to connect good writing with the truth that arises from engagement with emotions and concerns about which the speaker is capable of elaborating. These strategies solve for Rouse not only a disciplinary problem (what is *the* origin of basic writers' syntactic errors?) but also an ethical one (how should the university treat basic writers?). Rouse claims that Shaughnessy's practice is unsound in two ways. She is scientistically wrong because she ignores or rejects the empirically derived conclusion that "teaching grammar as a method of teaching writing has no support whatever in research evidence" (3). And she is ethically wrong because she exercises control over her students' right to pursue their own interests.

For Rouse, Shaughnessy oppresses the very students she worked so hard to help because she makes a disciplinary mistake that in turn produces the ethical one. When she tries to deal with writing as "a thing apart" from speech, she not only fails to give an accurate account of the problem but also tramples on students' rights. The specific danger Rouse sees is that teachers like Shaughnessy are willfully ignorant of disciplinary knowledge. Shaughnessy, Rouse argues, and practitioners like her, think that they should be "free . . . to ignore modern linguistic scholarship, free to invent their own programs as they go along . . . free to ignore evidence or theory, free to rely on their own insight," free, that is, to ignore "facts" (4).

On the contrary, I think Rouse's disciplinary mistake produces his ethical one. Stephen Toulmin's discussion of the use and evolution of concepts offers a helpful explanation of how this error occurs. A discipline, for Toulmin, is a traditional procedure for raising and answering questions in a regulated way (142). It is precisely the regularity of the procedures of inquiry that produces the facts. A discipline, therefore, is a function of its lexicon (the way it defines its terms), its representation techniques (or traditional ways of sharing that knowledge through lab reports, articles, books, conferences, presentations, maps, charts, diagrams, etc.), and its application procedures (161)—the ways a science demonstrates that it works, that it has a demonstrable effect on the world. Sociolinguistics as a discipline is visible in its definition of writing as the record of speech and in its use of the International Phonetic Alphabet to record speech sounds and patterns. Application procedures, though, create a problem. Would the discipline of sociolinguistics demonstrate that it works by producing accounts of language behavior that are replicable? Could it (should it) involve itself in attempts to change, rather than merely record, that behavior? And if the behavior is to be changed, then how? Here, it seems to me, is the most important locus of divergence between Rouse and Shaughnessy. Both teachers have grafted other considerations over linguistic ones. Both teachers have ethical agendas. The difference is that Shaughnessy straightforwardly acknowledges her importation of sociology and psychology. Rouse, however, seems to think that linguistics is all he needs.

For Rouse, Bernstein's distinctions offer an account of basic writers' difficulties and possible solutions that is both disciplinarily sound and socially correct. I think Rouse's argument provides an example of the institutional blindness that prevents us from seeing how lore produces knowledge. Disciplines look at what they recognize or, more precisely, see only what they recognize no matter where they look. The irregular, ad hoc procedures of lore are nondisciplinary, to be sure. But it seems possible to construe them also as postdisciplinary in their willingness to use, but refusal to be constrained by, existing institutional rules of knowledge production.

When Rouse charges Shaughnessy with ignoring facts, he evidently does not see that these facts are only facts because—and when—they appear in linguistic syntax as part of a disciplinary representation technique. He therefore conflates the disciplinary questions of sociolinguistics with Shaughnessy's questions about error in student writing. Shaughnessy doesn't ask how language works in society; rather, she asks where these errors come from and what we can do about them. Her question is decidedly, consciously, not a disciplinary one. Her answers are "situated" knowledge.

When Rouse accuses Shaughnessy of failing to see Bernstein's formulations, he seems to assume that they are visible to everyone regardless of situation and agenda and that they are valid in all circumstances. Thus, his argument is an example of "foundationalism," Fish's term for an attempt to "ground inquiry and communication in something more firm and stable than mere belief or unexamined practice" (*Doing* 65). From his foundation in sociolinguistics, Rouse argues not only about the facts of language learning but also about the politics of the situations in which Shaughnessy's students find themselves. Fish explains that the

> foundationalist strategy is first to identify [a] ground and then so to order our activities that they become anchored to it and so are rendered objective and principled. The ground so identified must have certain (related) characteristics: it must be invariant across contexts and even cultures; it must stand apart from political, partisan and "subjective" concerns in relation to which it must act as a constraint; and it must provide a reference point or checkpoint against which claims to knowledge and success must be adjudicated.
>
> (*Doing* 342–43)

Thus, in attacking Shaughnessy, Rouse seems to assume that, once established, foundations provide procedures that are replicable and applicable in many disparate situations. If an account of writing or speech or language is adequate, that account can help teachers develop curricula, compose examinations, foster literacy, and so forth. Here, surely, is an instance of what Edward Said calls "travelling theory" and of what more traditional logicians consider a category error (*World* 226–27). But, on the contrary, the very strictness of procedures for replicability makes it likely that foundational knowledge (like delicate wine) does not travel. Facts are only facts in the discipline that constitutes them. Finally, Rouse faults Shaughnessy for not doing something that she never intended to do and, in the process, manages to avoid arguing the ethic of intervention by situating his disagreement with Shaughnessy in the disciplinary field of linguistic facts.

Although this example suggests that something is wrong in our decisions about pedagogy, the problem, it seems to me, is not with lore. The current academic situation offers two kinds of defense of lore. The first works within lore's pragmatic logic and evades or blurs disciplinary questions. In his essay "Writing away from Fear: Mina Shaughnessy and the Uses of Authority," Michael Allen describes his experiences teaching black students at Rust College in Mississippi; there, too, Shaughnessy's procedures work. Allen neither needs nor desires any further foundation. That lore's strategies do travel to other situations is an important aspect of its difference from disciplinary inquiry. Whereas disciplinary knowledge can only be replicated under conditions that duplicate the ones that produced it, lore adapts.

In "The Politics of Composition: A Reply to John Rouse," Gerald Graff defends Shaughnessy with the proverbial good offense: he finds a different set of disciplinary warrants to discredit Rouse's claims. Although Graff accepts Bernstein's foundational distinction between restricted and elaborated codes, he rejects Rouse's application of them and argues forcefully for an opposite ethical conclusion. Repudiating Rouse's claim that Shaughnessy's strategies are oppressive, Graff uses the disciplinary definition of elaborated code to warrant an instructional ethic that empowers students. He frames the issues in terms of his ethicopolitical belief that "to shield students from . . . socialization on the grounds that you are liberating them helps nobody" (852).

In the context of my project, this disagreement clearly shows that the interlocutors' beliefs, not transhistorical truth, govern what they can see in each situation. The ethical question cannot be solved by appeal to linguistic foundations, nor can the disciplinary question be answered by appeal to ethical ones. Although foundations are useful to maintain consistencies and to avoid lapses in logic, they cannot provide universal justifications for practice.

No discipline can deal theoretically with the paradox that "improving" basic writers' syntax may violate their right to their own language. There can be no generalized theory of writing capable of serving as foundation for an ideologically neutral way of teaching that improves both students' practice and their political position. The problems arise from different belief systems. The belief that we could produce a metatheory to resolve this contradiction is a logical error that Fish calls "theory hope."

Thus, Fish rescues Shaughnessy from the charge that her work is not a "contribution to knowledge" by showing that there can be no such thing as "knowledge" (at least, as foundationalists understand it) to contribute to. I suspect that many readers will find this (non)solution ethically unsatisfactory. It's cold comfort to be told that

> practice has nothing to do with theory, at least in the sense of being enabled
> and justified by theory. That leaves me and you only a few worn and familiar
> bromides: practice makes perfect, you learn to write by writing, you must

build on what you already know; but anti-foundationalism tells us that these bromides are enough, tells us that as situated beings our practice can make perfect, and that we already know what we think. . . . . [A]ntifoundationalism offers you nothing but the assurance that what it is unable to give you— knowledge, goals, purposes, strategies—is what you already have. And come to think of it, that may be an offer you can't refuse.

(Fish, *Doing* 355)

We may not be able to refuse, but we can be embarrassed: it is disturbing to be told that theory cannot help us figure out what to do. Perhaps the greatest reason for theory hope is ethical. If we had a generalized theory of writing, surely its first job would be to adjudicate disagreements like the one between Shaughnessy and Rouse, to figure out how to help people.

We can't refuse Fish's argument if we believe, as he does, in the efficacy of logic. But we need to remember that logic is just one of the systems that lore often chooses to ignore. In this context even Fish's position is liable to the very objections he raises. The belief that informal logic may help delineate problems seems to be the one belief that Fish does not get out of. And it's a particularly unfortunate belief if it reduces us to paralysis. I describe my hopes for lore in terms of this problem.

To explain, I borrow some distinctions from Stephen A. Resnick and Richard D. Wolff's *Knowledge and Class: A Marxian Critique of Political Economy*. The foundationalism that for Fish is merely naive becomes for Resnick and Wolff an "essentialism" that is reductive in a particularly dangerous way. They argue that essentialists "organize their fields of inquiry into contrasting poles of cause and effect, phenomenon and essence, and determinant versus determined" (3). These poles, and their contents, are for Resnick and Wolff symptomatic of the ways in which ideology makes us blind to other explanations for phenomena we see. In the concrete terms we have been using, Rouse is an essentialist required by the rules of his inquiry to posit only one cause for the writing behaviors of basic writers: that they suffer from "restricted codes." Practitioners, by contrast, could cite preconditions for a problem named "basic writing": that the students have restricted rather than elaborated codes, that they are poor, that they are disenfranchised, that they "suffer from" secondary orality, that they are not readers, that they expect to fail, that they have no models for writing correct English prose, that they are not white male Anglo-Saxons, that they do not have English as a native language, and so forth, through all the political agendas that characterize discourse about the literacy crisis. The practitioner's activity coincides with Resnick and Wolff's description of antiessentialism, which, they write, rejects the

presumption that complexities are reducible to simplicities of the cause/effect type. Instead the presumption is that every element in the context of any event

plays its distinctive role in determining that event. Every cause is itself also
an effect and vice-versa.

(3)

As lore procedurally and pragmatically blurs relations of cause and effect, it
is able to deal more effectively than traditional science with "overdetermined"
situations. Unlike the linear, cause-and-effect relations that are represented
by disciplinary techniques, lore arranges its data serially, spatially, paratactically, like a rhizome, however they work. A practitioner can say that basic
writers have restricted codes, that restricted codes cause secondary orality,
that secondary orality causes situations in which people do not (need to) read,
that class and race cause a writer to expect to err, that the expectation of
error causes restricted codes, that poverty causes secondary orality, and so
forth. When a practitioner like Shaughnessy "solves" for all these variables
at once by taking into account a multitude of structural determinants of a
given problematic situation, she may—and I think must—be said to have
produced knowledge.

Thus, lore seems (at least potentially) postdisciplinary. In their eclectic
foraging among theories, practitioners are antiessentialist as they deal with
situations in which single causes cannot be stipulated, in which causes cannot
be discriminated from effects. Because it admits contradiction, lore, perhaps
unintentionally but nonetheless effectively, can cope with overdetermination.

Lore, then, is theory in Resnick and Wolff's sense: a "site of a particular
interaction of all the processes stemming from all the other processes com-
prising any society" (2). Through interaction, competing accounts of writing
and ethics determine or cause one another, instead of being determined by
some disciplinary object (writing or the "good"). When I assert that lore is
theory in Resnick and Wolff's sense, I need to address the question of whether
a discourse can unintentionally be theory. I think that it can, in a particularly
postmodern way. Lore is a site and a moment at which differing praxes meet
as praxes. When, through a process of informed intuition, practitioners do
what works, they bring a number of disciplinary projects into a concrete
problem. They certainly do not deny the disciplines, nor do they ignore them.
Rather, they evoke disciplinary language, not to produce knowledge, but to
solve a problem. Lore, in this context, elides without denying the opposition
between theory and practice. And the informed intuition that produces that
elision may, I would assert, be called theory—not in the sense of a metadiscourse, a generalized account of a practice to which all instances of that
practice can be referred, but rather as a way of coping, contending with the
overdetermined words of knowledge production.

But to recuperate lore is not simply to stop being disciplinary and start
acting like a rhizome. Merely embracing lore would mean connecting events
and explanations haphazardly. Such connections may mirror real life, but

they don't help us understand or change it. Thoughtless, accidental seriation or association or both (as Ohmann observes in another context) "subdues temporal relatedness, . . . denies the borders between material and non-material, living and inanimate [and] . . . in the process . . . mystifies social connections, and virtually eliminates causation as a way of understanding things" (*Politics* 100). I certainly do not advocate that mindless, antitheoretical pluralism. Nor do I recommend practitioners' tendency to operate uncritically in terms of dualisms like correct versus incorrect, or process versus product. We should not accept lore uncritically, but we can ask what kinds of problems lore has solved and reexamine those problems with the understanding that they are overdetermined. What I'm suggesting is a way to avoid the unfortunate aspects of disciplinarity, particularly its tendency to simplify to the point of occulting its ideological implications and making us think that its narrowness is normal.

If we learn to use lore well, it can help us see ways of construing relations of relatedness to which our ideology has made us blind. Lore can help us see that disciplinary inquiries can be strategies of containment; these strategies achieve coherence by shutting out or repressing the contradictions that have their source in history. Lore can help us see ways in which solving for one problem causes another.

But these happy effects are not automatic: we need to develop strategies that use the power of lore, that have a reasonable chance of earning the academy's institutionalized respect. We need more than pious platitudes and theoretical arguments about teaching as knowledge production. We need to do more than say we're going to revise our syllabi next term, establish a "teacher of the year" award, or take a part-timer to lunch.

Our problem is nothing less than getting the academy to change its understanding of knowledge production. We need to denaturalize lore to the point at which the institution, having been made aware of it, can learn to value it. Because institutions change slowly, I look first to ways we might adapt existing frameworks to help institutions learn to see lore produce knowledge. In *Professing Literature*, Graff suggests that we adjust our teaching and curricula so as to "foreground conflict" in (literary) English studies. He further implies that the conflict model constitutes a kind of theory for the postmodern era. Under Graff's proposal, theory is no longer understood foundationally, as a generalized account of practice to which individual cases could be referred. Rather, theory is the conflict itself, the contending with words. Graff believes that understanding the conflicts that inform literary and cultural studies empowers students. One locus of conflict that Graff particularly likes is the conference, a postmodern conversation in which different theories interact dialogically.

But Graff's project does not specifically address ways in which these conferences have the production of knowledge as an agenda. Looking at Graff's suggestion in the context of Jameson's (far more overtly political) account of cognitive mapping helps envision and achieve that agenda. Jameson develops the conception of mapping in specific response to a postmodern problem. Whereas narrative has traditionally served us well as a metaphor for the ways in which we know ourselves historically, psychically, and socially, Jameson thinks that the particular complexities of commodity capitalism require a new figure. A narrative is too static, too linear for the situations in which we find ourselves. A narrative functions like an AAA trip-tik, a customized touring book in which maps of highway segments, drawn to a very large scale, are bound together to fit individual itineraries. A trip-tik shows only the shortest, most direct route to a destination, but a map can show us intersections and relative configurations between our itinerary and the itineraries of others. A map can also show empty spaces. An itinerary is "subject-centered," but "cognitive mapping," Jameson writes, "in the broader sense comes to require the coordination of existential data (the empirical position of the subject) with unlived, abstract conceptions of the geographic totality" ("Postmodernism" 90).

A cognitive map, as I understand it, functions like the textbook transparencies in which the viewer sees relations among several anatomical systems. In our context, the notion of a cognitive map allows us to imagine the possibility of representing relations among the various definitions of writing. We might map Linda Flower and John R. Hayes's cognitive strategies for achieving one's rhetorical purpose over Peter Elbow's notion of voice, over E. D. Hirsch's account of cultural literacy. The objective is not to achieve a totalizing metatheory but rather to see where theories intersect, where they contradict, where they form constellations, and, perhaps what is most important, where they form lacunae, where they actually prevent us from doing something that we deem necessary. For example, a map of Shaughnessy's practice shows convergences between the syntactic, sociological, and psychological accounts of her students' writing difficulties. It also shows us that her exercises have no itinerary for preserving her students' right to their own language.

But who are the cartographers? Who gets to wield the power of mapping relations? I suggest that it be vested in the multiple interests of the audience of a conference. My proposal therefore emends Graff's rather significantly: I envision a series of conferences that ask us to work up from the practice of lore, not down from a theory of writing, conferences in which experienced, gifted teachers address a problem delineated for the occasion, a problem like students' writing in open-admissions colleges, cultural literacy, or exit exams. The conference would focus on the teaching practices of these featured guests, much as we now focus on a keynote speaker. I imagine that examples of teachers' praxes would be collected, unobtrusively, by videotape, before the conference. Later, an audience would gather to view the videotape of an interview between a teacher and a client in a writing lab or of a teacher teaching an actual class, discussing revision, commenting on papers, conferencing.

Featured also would be a panel of theorists, representatives of disciplinary ways of knowing, experienced in thinking through the implications of a practice. This conference would reverse the usual practice by which practitioners take from theorists ideas that they think will work. I imagine a format like that of the PBS series *Ethics in America*, with elements of Ted Koppel and Phil Donahue, in which the panel would comment on the implications of a practice that already does work. These theorists (whose function would closely resemble that of the "respondent" at CCCC or NCTE meetings) would be asked to do only what they do best, to provide a kind of environmental-impact statement for the teacher's practice.

Such a panel of theorists might say of Shaughnessy, for example, that her process of regularizing students' syntax is likely to produce results that also inhibit their use of their own language. A panel might suggest to Hirsch that, yes, ignorance of certain information does diminish our workers' competitiveness but that an attempt to codify that information and require students to know it can be, de facto, racist. A panel might point out that, although exit exams are repressive and teachers often teach to them rather than to other student needs, the process of designing and administering a writing test can be one of the most effective faculty-development activities available.

What would characterize this conference is not the either-or logic that, elsewhere in this volume, Susan C. Jarratt and Lynn Worsham describe as masculinist and logocentric. Rather this dialogic conference would embrace a both-and approach to situations. It would say, If you do this, these effects are likely to follow. Do you want them all? Is there any way to redescribe the proposal to eliminate or diminish the results that seem to you, now, in this situation, less desirable than others?

Some administrators may object that this conference does not seem like knowledge production. I suggest making the conference public through an electronic network, to tap into the academy's institutionalized respect for technology. Our teleconference, using a format already familiar to the sciences, would permit "callers" to ask questions about specific problems at specific sites of conflict. Let's assume that a tutor and a client in a basic-writing lab at a large urban university permit the unobtrusive videotaping of a number of their interviews. That series becomes the topic of an interactive conference in which the interviews are "read" by a Carnegie Mellon empiricist, a Marxian, an Elbow-oriented "romanticist," a linguist, a classical rhetorician, a phenomenologist. Each of these theorists interacts with the teacher and student, who are present on the panel. During the presentation, telecast live by closed circuit, the panel members receive a phone call from a teacher in

North Dakota, who points out that a given procedure won't work for students with secondary orality marked by rural rather than urban traits and who makes a suggestion for emending the procedure. At this point, one panelist draws a large diagram explaining that strategies for achieving one's expressive goals "travel," even to North Dakota. But another asserts that the behaviorists act as though "human nature" never changes and that there are no problems that better planning won't solve. On the contrary, the panelist asserts, rhetorical strategies must change to meet each new problem. The rhetorician speaks of the Sophists, who certainly did change strategies to meet new situations, while the romanticist observes that voice is likely to be lost in all this adjusting. In the course of these conflicts, knowledge is produced in ways that count: through the conference the profession demarcates persons and problems that it thinks important. A conference about practitioners working on a problem would create a situation in which that work could be valued. And technology, because it is expensive, is a way of marking that value.

Some critics might object that such a procedure would inevitably change the "nature" of the knowledge produced: that is, that our very gaze would alter the situation. But I suggest that it's precisely the gaze that's important. This proposal denaturalizes teaching to make visible its heretofore secret acts of knowledge production. For the most part, we professional academics (whether or not we think of ourselves as practitioners in North's sense) are silent about our teaching. We tend to discount, hide, and even repudiate our classroom activity. We are proud of low teaching loads. We covet grants and leaves that get us out of the classroom. Perhaps we actually believe what we learn from our annual faculty-evaluation reports, that teaching doesn't count. But perhaps, too, we think of teaching as a site or moment when we are free, behind closed classroom doors, to be eclectic, to ignore recognized procedures, to do what needs to be done without worrying about being watched, evaluated, tested.

Precisely because of its relative obscurity, teaching allows us to escape the panoptic gaze of the disciplines for a silent, secret moment of postdisciplinary knowledge. We should do all we can to bring lore to light.[1]

NOTE

[1] An earlier version of this essay appeared in *Forum*, the journal of the Southeastern Ohio Teachers of English. I'm grateful to Tom Flynn, David Laurence, and John Schilb for their perceptive comments, and I particularly thank the members of the Composition Study Group at the University of Akron—Mary King, Robert Holland, John Stoker, Carol Lipps, Arlene Toth, and Linda Weiner—for helping me think it through.

Three Countertheses: Or, A Critical In(ter)vention into Composition Theories and Pedagogies

❖

Victor J. Vitanza

For Lenny Bruce,
the most perverse of all comics

But I would turn things around.
    —Kenneth Burke, "Rhetoric, Poetics, and Philosophy"

[W]hatever the minority view happens to be at any given time,
one must consider it as "counter."
    —Kenneth Burke, *Counter-statement*

Beginning(s)

THE subject is "perverse comedy," which is an attempt to think—
that is, to let be thought—the opposite. Perverse comedy is not,
however, a mere attack on a status quo but a meditative questioning
of it through an act of ironic "critical in(ter)vention." (Perverse comedy is, when deployed, a critical in[ter]vention.) It is both critical and an
in(ter)vention here in that uncanny criticisms will be deployed heuristically

with the sole purpose of establishing the (postmodern) conditions for the possibilities of discourse in and about writing theory and pedagogy that, heretofore, the field of composition has had to disallow. Perverse comedy is an attempt at a discourse, therefore, that requires itself to bear witness to what has been disallowed by searching for comedic counteridioms that will allow, that will enable. At times, however, this discourse is not easy to follow, for it attempts a discourse that does not follow. Perhaps best described, this discourse searches for new ways of linkage, while it leaves behind traditional ways, which fix a point, plot an order. It, instead, connects paratactically (and . . . and . . . and), at any point, to any and every point. It is a discourse, then, without (a) discipline, nor is it especially in search of (a) discipline.

Why has the field of composition disallowed such a discourse and such a critical in(ter)vention? As we proceed, the possible answers become explicit and plentiful. For now, however, it is enough to say that some composition theorists/pedagogues are well aware (on occasion) that such a discourse would place in post-Cartesian doubt the very (supposed) foundations of the field of composition; would, in other words, place the field in the midst of the "legitimation crisis." This crisis places in doubt humanistic and conventional ways of thinking about authorship, the self, and gender; places in doubt representation; places in doubt the distinction between fiction and truth; places in doubt the modes/aims of exposition (valued as perspicuity) and argumentation (valued as consensus); places in doubt especially the revealed wisdom of even teaching students to write. In general, such a discourse can (if allowed) place in aporia the very value, or even possibility, of community itself, which traditionally has been the end of rhetoric.

But let us reformulate the subject and attempt, nonetheless, this irrepressible, necessary critical and ironic in(ter)vention: in more (tragic) academic terms, the subject of this paper (de)centers on three countertheses that will be stated, elaborated, and celebrated as perverse comedy. The countertheses are counterresponses to the strong *will* of the field of composition; they are counterresponses to (1) the will to systematize (the) language (of composing), (2) the will to be its author(ity), and (3) the will to teach it to students. In short, they are counterresponses to the field's will *to control* (this) language (specifically, its modes of representation) for the general ends of both traditional and modern rhetoric(s) and, hence, for a (homogeneous) community. These ends, as commonly accepted, are noble. And yet, I irrepressibly ask, are they? I would think other(wise): These rhetorics—their modes of representation—are insidious and invidious. While they appear to be informed by a set of assumptions that (democratically-capitalistically) value heterogeneity (in the name of the "individual"), they are, instead, only a reactionary devaluing of heterogeneity through the homogenization of heterogeneity (as mass society). While they allow, they simultaneously disallow and disenable.

Let us begin again, and consider how language can be tamed/socialized so that knowledge might be "mercantilized." (By "controlling language," I mean controlling the perversity of language, the noncongruent, nonisomorphic nature of language that contributes to the possibilities of *ap/op*positional countertheses.) Three sources, whose efforts are occasionally combined, attempt such control: the preacher, the teacher, and the (psycho)therapist. With control in mind, let's contrast two competing psychologies.

One branch of psychology is known as cognitive psychology (it covers everything from psycholinguistics to protocol analyses of problem solvers); the field of composition has appropriated this branch to help students use language with a high degree of formulaic control so that they can solve rhetorical problems. Parallel to this psychology is a social psychology such as Carl Rogers's view of communication (which has given us "Rogerian rhetoric") and Martin Buber's view of dialogue in communication and community (which has given us "Buberian rhetoric"). These humanistic-rationalistic psychologies have as their primary purpose the establishment and maintenance of social bonds.

I label the contrary, competing branch of psychology "French Freudian-Lacanian psychoanalysis–cum–Deleuzian-Guattarian postpsychoanalysis," which the field of composition has *not* used but kept in silence, perhaps for the simple reason that this branch of psychology is ethically and micropolitically against any humanist-rationalist notion of control, or mastery, of language and therefore the control of teaching. This school of psychoanalysis—contrary to American ego psychology—occasionally calls on language for revolutionary ends in a struggle against what it sees as the hegemonic discourses of capitalism and socialism. These French (nonhumanist) psychoanalysts find within language the means of resistance and disruption. While studying "hysterics" or "schizos," Gilles Deleuze and Félix Guattari have come to understand how some patients can be both in and out of the social bond(age). (Lest there be some commonsensical misunderstanding, note that Deleuze and Guattari do not advocate a "breakdown" as a means of liberation. They are interested, instead, in using the processes of hysterical/schizo discourses for a political and ethical "breakthrough" [see *Anti-Oedipus* 341]). Deleuze and Guattari do not advocate "total" politics (for society) but a "micropolitics" (a "minoritarian" politics cum ethics, for the social in the individual).[1] I return to their ideas as I proceed.

No Arguments from Me

In what follows, I leave unargued the dangers of the capitalistic-consumer "game of knowledge," which has as its similar ends—similar to clerical-priestly psychologists' ends—the homogenization and totalization of both modes of production and the codes of consumption. (The arguments can be found from early Marx through post-Marxists.) The reader perhaps has only to spend some time reading Jean-François Lyotard, who speaks of the "mer-cantilization of knowledge." He writes, "Knowledge is and will be produced in order to be sold, it is and will be consumed in order to be valorized in a new production: in both cases, the goal is exchange" (*Postmodern* 4–5). After Lyotard and others—Michel Foucault, Jean Baudrillard, Fredric Jameson, Henry Giroux, and Stanley Aronowitz—perhaps the reader can turn (anew) to composition textbooks to see how the authors answer the question Why write? (The answer, given openly, though unsuspiciously, is in economic-capitalistic terms: Learn to write this way and you, too, can be successful as a white, male, and middle-class *producer* of clear, coherent, easily consumed prose.) Indeed, what James Berlin has to say is cogent: Teaching students how to write is also teaching them a view of (economic) reality and an "identity" for themselves that is to be attempted, though never realized, in "sameness."

But then, Berlin is never suspicious enough; for he simply never "drifts" far enough, nor does Giroux. Berlin (with his predisposition to social-epis-temic rhetoric) and Giroux (with his notion of the "hidden curriculum") both have an exclusive penchant for socialist rationalism or for very early Frankfurt-school Marxist-critical theory or for the British Left and cultural studies and hence for narratives of emancipation.[2] Both speak of the contradictions in society and the curriculum, which must be laid bare so that students might "resist." But this laying bare is to be attempted by way of the game of knowledge. And ah, there's the rub! I reject this approach of "rational" thinking and acting, especially about language. It only further remystifies and disempowers students and us all (see Foucault, "Subject"). Why? Because, as Lyotard says, "Reason and power are one and the same thing. You may disguise the one with dialectics . . . , but you will still have the other in all its crudeness: jails, taboos, public weal, selection, genocide" ("Adrift" 11). Because while reason espouses a cerebral view of history, it blindly neglects, so to speak, a history below the belt or a history of *desire*. And therefore it impoverishes each of us. Let us continue to drift paratactically.

My Notice

Though these are "unfriendly" words toward Berlin and Company, I do, nonetheless, (dis)incorporate their thinking in a broader, though fragmented, spectrum of both reason and desire. Specifically, the countertheses of my title are counterresponses to the politics (really, the *terrorism*) of theory (totality) made into (a) pedagogy founded on capitalism and consumerism as well as on socialism and consensus. In this way, then, I am alongside Berlin and Company—in that I, too, am against founding a pedagogy on capitalism— while I am still unequivocally contra to these social-consensual theory-hopeful rationalists, who through social reengineering and instrumental reason (here, I begin my Nietzschean turn) want to cure society and make the world into a great, good place. (I do not work from the principles of *medicina mentis*.) But, more generally, the countertheses are to be seen as conceptual (re)starting places for modes of resistance that are to be deployed against the game of rationality/knowledge and against the dominant (political) modes of representation, which are expressed throughout the field of composition; in fact, they *are* the field, as it now commonly locates itself in two not very different groupings: the first, foundational; the second, antifoundational.

The first group is composed variously of current traditional rhetoric, of expressionistic rhetoric, and of scientistic, cognitive rhetoric. Scientistic rhetoric, as practiced by Linda Flower and John R. Hayes, has recently been criticized for its exclusive attempt to search for an inner-directed theory of the nature (*physis*) of how the mind solves problems (see Bizzell, "Cognition"; Berlin, "Rhetoric and Ideology"). The second group is called social-epistemic and is interested in outer-directed theories, which look to social situation, context, paradigms, communities, or local *nomoi* as loci of deliberation or judgment. Though a definite improvement over the first, this second group, nonetheless, has numerous problems: besides potentially being both dangerously utopian and blindly ideological, it is, as Stanley Fish says, "nothing more or less than a reinvention of foundationalism" ("Anti-Foundationalism" 72; cf. Cooper). The followers of this group, as I discuss later (in the second and third countertheses), suffer from "theory hope" (Fish, "Consequences" 112) and from what I call pedagogy hope (in the third counterthesis) and have simply not been suspicious enough of their rationalistic motives, which are best described as the will to knowledge and power. This second group, however flawed, is strong and steadily growing—it will be the wave of the nineties—and, therefore, must be resisted strongly and, if necessary, comedically-perversely (cf. Trimbur, "Cultural Studies"; Freedman).

Contrary Coordinates within Critical Theories

How is this resistance to be accomplished? One possible way of answering this question is through subversive modes of resistance. These modes, however, are not engaged in by, nor do they belong to, any group. (There is no third group of composition theorists—at least, not as I have represented the field of composition—though there may be a "molecular agglomerate" of paratheorists, who may form a fifth column. Furthermore, though this antigroup of paratheorists has no faith in the traditional/realist perspectives and terribly little faith in Marxist or modernist-revisionary perspectives, it is at times comedically and perversely informed, as in a poststructuralist bricolage, with Marxist ideas.) The subversive modes of resistance, which I give the (im)proper name of three countertheses, are abstracted from postmodern views of antilanguage and a counterculture and a nonhumanistic psychology, as I referred to it earlier, and finally they are abstracted from what I see as contrary, contested issues located at the contrary coordinates where contemporary, "uncanny" critical theories variously interact. (This act of location is the commencement of my critical and ironic in[ter]vention.) The three countertheses, once again, are counterresponses to the strong *will* of the field of composition; they are counterresponses to (1) the will to systematize (the) language (of composing), (2) the will to be its author(ity), and (3) the will to teach it to students. The three countertheses are not always distinct, for they inevitably and progressively imbricate as we proceed "across" them. And yet, the countertheses are conceptually located according to Gorgias's trilemma of negative propositions: "Nothing exists"; "If it does exist, it cannot be known"; and "If it can be known, it cannot be communicated" (Sprague 42–46).[3]

In the attempt to pinpoint one actual manifestation of these contrary, contested issues that inform the countertheses, I call on the contemporary debate between Jürgen Habermas and Lyotard.[4] (In addition, however, I must call on Deleuze and Guattari and on Michel Serres to further extend Lyotard's less-than-radical thinking.) The two views of the debate might be summarized as follows: Habermas favors a critical rationalism, a legitimation of knowledge, the "universal conditions of possible understanding" in discursive practices (*Communication* 1), whereas Lyotard questions any possible universal conditions or legitimation of knowledge. He sees legitimation eroding and consensus (philosophical rhetoric) as an outmoded and suspect value. Habermas looks back to the Enlightenment in his attempt to construct a totalizing, universal pragmatics for a hermeneutical understanding. He attempts to avoid the Nietzschean turn to irrationalism that Habermas says befell Max Horkheimer and Theodor W. Adorno in *Dialectic of Enlightenment* (*Philosophical* 106–30). Habermas is not attempting, however, to establish philosophical knowledge claims (for him, truth is "warranted assertability"). But, at the same time, his position differs greatly from Hans-Georg Gadamer's philosophical hermeneutics (see *Philosophical; Truth*); it is at best a strong form of philosophical rhetoric; that is, his rhetoric suffers from a nostalgia for universals (Kantian—at least, as in the first two critiques), which he wants to establish in the form of ideal speech acts. Attempting to avoid "instrumental reason," which Horkheimer and Adorno had critiqued, Habermas establishes his ideal speech acts on what he calls the "Life World" (based on a phenomenological sociology) and on systems theory (see *Legitimation*, pt. 1). His game is the game of knowledge. In contrast, Lyotard is a child of the post-Enlightenment, a postmodernist who confronts the crisis of rationality, the (fortunate) fall from a loss of overriding (grand) narratives or accounts of knowledge, science, literature, morality, or the arts. His objective is not to lament this loss but to discover a different set of language games, or experimental discourses, that will allow us not merely to survive the (legitimation) crisis but to flourish within it and to fend off attempts, like Habermas's, to bring us out of the crisis and return us to the nightmare of the Enlightenment, to return us to the *idea* of political totality. (For Lyotard, learning to flourish is a matter of "just gaming" or drifting, which is an idea he takes from Kant's third critique and from Montaigne's genre of the essay and which is Lyotard's primary counterstrategy of resistance, disruption, and (dis)continuation. Lyotard's game, then, is the "game of avant-garde [paralogical] art.")

Three Countertheses

Counterthesis 1

The first counterthesis (de)centers on the age-old issue of whether knowledge can be legitimized or grounded either on some universal, ontogenetic theory (that is, on some universal law, or *physis*) or rhetorically on consensus theory (that is, on homology, or local *nomoi*). This first counterthesis, which is contrary to such knowledge, is informed by the Gorgian proposition "Nothing [of essence] exists." The thesis is counter, more specifically, to foundationalism (universal laws) or structure (as found in, say, the Porphyrian tree of genus-species, of subdivision and pyramidal hierarchization [see Eco 46–86]) or consensus (discourse/interpretive communities, for the most part by way of "pragmatics"). This last view—that of consensus—sometimes mistakenly goes by the name of antifoundationalism. (For an expression of such a mistake, see Bizzell, "On the Possibility.")

For Habermas, knowledge can be based on rational consensus, but he offers his strong view of consensus as a general theory of communication and labels it a *"universal pragmatics"* (*Communication* 5). Unlike Aristotle and his view of a prudential judge situated in a Greek world, Habermas presents us with a set of universal criteria—he says a priori that they are universal—for communication, responsibility, and judgment. If other cultures do not share these criteria—and many, of course, don't—they simply have not yet evolved to our superior state of potential knowing, doing, and making.

Lyotard, however, speaks against criteria and therefore against a universal theory of pragmatics for two primary reasons (*Just Gaming* 26). First, he says that such a universal theory is currently not possible because of the loss of grand narratives, which originally founded knowledge claims (*Postmodern* 27–31; cf. *Differend* 151–81). In other words, each grand narrative (at least, so it was believed) had "warranted," or had legitimized, the discourses of disciplines, whether in the natural or the human sciences. The grand narratives informed and unified the pragmatics (or speculative discourses) of science, which Habermas adheres to (see Lyotard, *Postmodern* 23–37). This pragmatics is based on "homologous structures of consciousness in the histories of the individual and the species" (*Communication* 99).

Lyotard's second reason for opposing a universal theory is quite simply that it does not emancipate but only enslaves and impoverishes us. Such a universal theory—in the form of a pragmatics of science based on rational consensus (*homologia*)—is finally ineffective. Lyotard says that with the inevitable collapse of such a theory a "delegitimation" of knowledge claims occurred, which eventually manifested itself in nihilism. Lyotard succinctly states, agreeing with Nietzsche, that "'European nihilism' resulted from the truth requirement of science being turned back against itself" (*Postmodern* 39). With nihilism comes a yearning (again), however, for a totality of meaning. Thereby, science was resurrected and, hence, lives on. And in living on, and ever so successfully in its "death," science and its quest for consensus—at least, as it stubbornly holds on to its speculative language game—does "violence to the heterogeneity of language games" (*Postmodern* xxv). Lyotard says that we, therefore, must *resist* the pragmatics or "narratives of science" (*Postmodern* 23–37). We must also resist through "paralogy" (*heterologia*). As Lyotard says, "[I]t is now dissension [not consensus] that must be emphasized." Why not consensus? Lyotard answers, "[C]onsensus is only a particular state of discussion, not its end. Its end, on the contrary, is paralogy" (*Postmodern* 61, 65–66).

Paralogy can be seen as a means of discovering "what is at stake in a literature, in a philosophy, in a politics." It is "to bear witness to differends"; that is, it is to bear witness to the unintelligible or to disputes or differences of opinion that are systematically disallowed by the dominant language game of homological science and are therefore "silenced"; it is to bear witness "by finding idioms" for these differends (*Differend* 13; cf. Feyerabend 256–57). This notion of paralogy is comparable to what I have called *dissoi paralogoi* (see "Critical Sub/Versions"); however, paralogy is an attempt not only to make the weaker argument the stronger but also to favor a radical heterogeneity of discourses over either the favored protocol of One or the homogeneity of the Many.

From time to time I return to a discussion of paralogy. This complicated issue is best dealt with through a series of returns. Paralogy means, for Lyotard, several things: it is both a means of resistance to *homologia* and a means of legitimation (*Postmodern* 60). In this second sense, I distinguish paralogy from traditional or modern "invention" (*Postmodern* 61–62), which is smooth, continuous, and controlled and accounted for by a system or a paradigm of knowledge and which is used to promote the capitalistic, socialistic, scientific "efficiency" of that system or paradigm (or is used, in Thomas Kuhn's phrase, to promote "normal science"). Paralogy, however, is "discontinuous, catastrophic, nonrectifiable, and paradoxical." It (re)turns— that is, radically tropes—against the system, or paradigm of knowledge, "changing the meaning of the word *knowledge*" (*Postmodern* 60); in Kuhn's phrase, it promotes "revolutionary science"; in Richard Rorty's phrase, it promotes "abnormal"/"revolutionary" discourse ("Habermas" 320). Whereas invention is used for traditional or modern science, paralogy is used by postmodern science.

In sum, Lyotard's view, in contrast to Habermas's systemic-synecdochic view, is metaphoric, paratactic, paralogical, pararhetorical, and, as I discuss later, proleptic. His view is one of just gaming, moving from one language game to the next, or drifting or just linking (paratactically, paralogically). Specifically, then, with (dis)respect to Habermas's universal theory of pragmatics/speech-act theory and to the rules of consensus, Lyotard writes:

> For there to be no phrase is impossible, for there to be *And a phrase* [parataxis instead of traditional syntax or hypotaxis] is necessary. It is necessary to make linkage [for example, for justice]. This is not an obligation, . . . but a necessity. . . . To link is necessary, but how to link is not.
>
> (*Differend* 66; cf. Deleuze and Guattari, *Thousand* 7–8)

For Deleuze and Guattari, there are no (either real or acceptable fictive) foundational principles, though, to be sure, there is the will to these principles. Even two of the "hermeneuts of suspicion" fall prey to this will: for the Freudians-Lacanians, the foundational principle is Oedipus; for the orthodox Marxists, it's rationalism and economics (see Deleuze, "Nomad" 142). More generally, however, theorists have made attempts at totalization by way of the dictum "Think like a tree," that is, a Porphyrian tree (Eco 58).

Specifically, they are referring to thinking (of state philosophy) in the form of species, genera, divisions, differentiae, whether that thinking is done in the form of Aristotle's homologous categories, Ramus's dialectical tree, Bacon's divisions of human learning, Chomsky's linguistic trees, or Flower and Hayes's flowchart (branching) computer models of the composing process. Deleuze and Guattari, like Lyotard, insist that all attempts to universalize (or to make "molar" by the logic of "arborescence") must be resisted and disrupted through "radical multiplicities," through what they call thinking (by the "molecular" unconsciousness) like a rhizome (see *Anti-Oedipus* 283–96; *Thousand* 3–25). Instead of consensus, they focus on "outsider thought," "nomad thought," and schizo-"dissensus."

Relevance to Composition. This first counterthesis suggests two possible conclusions—namely, either that there can no longer be or that ethically, micropolitically, there should not be any foundational principle or covering law or ontogenetic model for composition theory and pedagogy. It does not matter whether that principle is based on a conceptual theory or a tropology of composition (D'Angelo), on a cognitive/computer model (Flower and Hayes), on a universal pragmatics (speech acts) of rational communication (Habermas; Kinneavy, *Theory*), or on social consensus, social construction of reality, or interpretive communities (Bizzell; Bartholomae).

Language, of which we have many foundational models, turns against the models that are constructed in its name, ever delegitimizing the models of language processing itself. Such models are not isomorphic with the very (perverse) processes that they are designed to represent (see Deleuze and Guattari, *Thousand* 75–110). Flower and Hayes speak of their model of *the* composing process as a metaphor of that process ("Cognitive" 368); it is a metaphor and, to boot cum heel, a dogmatic one that is appropriate only for a computer (machine) simulation doing an unintended parody of captured—not captivated—human beings composing. Lyotard says it best:

[I]t is common knowledge that the miniaturization and commercialization of machines is already changing the way in which learning is acquired, classified, made available, and exploited. . . .

The nature of knowledge cannot survive unchanged within this context of general transformation. It can fit into the new channels, and become operational, only if learning is translated into quantities of information. We can predict that anything in the constituted body of knowledge that is not translatable in this way will be abandoned and that the direction of new research will be dictated by the possibility of its eventual results being translatable into computer language.

(*Postmodern* 4)

In this light, the model of the composing process that Flower and Hayes build is a metaphor of knowledge determined by the ending of their step-by-step method of research—namely, the final testing (validation and reproduction) by computer simulation, which is necessary to satisfy the game of knowledge. It is the end (the preassigned *telos*) that determines the beginning and middle of the research project. This is a bad-faith use of *prolepsis* (cf. Baudrillard 166–84). Flower and Hayes's metaphor—as Deleuze and Guattari would claim—is oppressive, mechanically and politically so. It is an unintended political metaphor of human beings as capitalistically controlled "desiring machines" (see *Anti-Oedipus* 36–50), which must be resisted by a baroque (unstable) allegory or countered by an antiperformative of rhizome-thinking or by nomad thought. The issue here, then, for Deleuze and Guattari, is the modes of production, which are (again, given Flower and Hayes's metaphor) also the modes of enslavement. Though Flower and Hayes's intention seems good—to invent, so to speak, the grand narrative of writing so as to emancipate student writers—their work, in appropriate words from Deleuze and Guattari, only promises to "reterritorialize" (or reenslave) these students. We should, instead, deterritorialize students and turn them into drifters.[5]

How is this to be understood? Flower and Hayes practice a "Royal, or State [legalistic, technological] science" as opposed to a "Nomad [postmodern] science." State science is "hard" (privileged) science; nomad science, a parascience. Whereas the former values "civil, static, and ordinal rules," the latter favors "becoming, heterogeneity, infinitesimal, passage to the limit, continuous variation" (*Thousand* 363, 365, 367–68). A (baroque) metaphor offers further explanation. Deleuze and Guattari point out that the state for political reasons must have a "hydraulic science" (a hydraulic engineer) when confronted with a "hydraulic force"—specifically, a science that can

> subordinate hydraulic force to conduits, pipes, embankments, which prevent turbulence, which constrain movement to go from one point to another, and space itself to be striated and measured, which makes the fluid depend on the solid, and flows proceed by parallel, laminar layers.
>
> (*Thousand* 363)

Such a science controls the hydraulic model of "nomad thought," which

> consists in being distributed by turbulence across a smooth space, in producing a movement that holds space and simultaneously affects all of its points, instead of being held by space in a local movement from one specified point to another.
>
> (*Thousand* 363; see Prigogine and Stengers)

Is there another way of saying all this? On the one hand, Flower and Hayes are working out of a capitalistic model that promises, "Do it this way: Submit yourself to the branchings of the tree diagram (the conduits) and submit yourself to the audience. Then you, too, through the investment of your desire (that is, cerebral and somatic energy) will be fulfilled. (This is the way of state philosophy and education, the way to economic power.) Therefore, embrace this approach so that you, too, might tap into this power that we (the state, department of engineering) have contained for your use. Your investment of desire will perhaps have really made something of consumable value not only for you but for us all." This state-engineering-hydraulic model slouches toward uniformity with (dis)respect to molecular, nomadic styles of thinking; it also reduces *all* (totally) to *the* style of problem solving, which again is a style of thinking devised to serve the state apparatus (a "notion of style as [micro-]politics" resists and disrupts such a model [Deleuze, "Nomad" 143]). Moreover, what appears to be writing as discovery is only—unbeknown to its unself-conscious mystified self—writing that uncovers what has already been predetermined by the modes, or the social codes, of production and representation. (The so-called successful writers make nothing, for they have already been made.)

On the other hand, Deleuze (a postphilosopher) and Guattari (a postpsychoanalyst) are working with an antimodel based simultaneously on desire and on schizoexcess, on capitalism and schizophrenia cum schizoanalysis. This antimodel, moreover, is based on what I referred to earlier as deterritorialization, which also goes by the name of schizoanalysis and which has the antipurpose to critique the modes of representation and, more important, to *decode* them so as to free libidinal energy or, rather, desire.

In this respect, Deleuze and Guattari speak, first, of a "Body without Organs" (*Anti-Oedipus* 9–15). And *why* a (student) body "without"? For the simple reason that organs have (economic) codes stored in them that stop and start the free flow of desire and attempt to curb excess. *Organ*izations, after all, are *the* modes of scarcity, placed strategically by the state hydraulic engineers to contain the flow of information and meaning and thus to give capitalistic/consumer value to them; organs are identical to Flower and Hayes's boxes in their flowcharts, their conduits. (The *flow*charts control the other[wise] free *flow*[er] of desire, or schizoexcess. Insidiously, they frequently say, Return to Go and *do* collect $200!) However, a body without organs (that has been thoroughly decoded, deterritorialized) is a body of free-flowing desire, a body of excess (which finally threatens hegemonic-capitalist thought patterns through a surplus value of the code); it is a body (antistrategically) without and beyond the will to capitalism and to totalization.

Deleuze and Guattari speak, second, of rhizomes as opposed to trees or arborescence and its model. Why are they against trees? As already suggested, trees signify the modes of production and representation of the state philosophy and education, that is, the paideia and its idea of arborescent culture (Massumi xi–xii). The rhizome, however, is an antitree. It has no beginning, middle, and end; it's all middle, unlike Flower and Hayes's research method, which is based on David E. Wojick's "issue analysis." Some characteristics of a rhizome are *connection* and *heterogeneity* ("any point of a rhizome can be connected to anything other, and must be"); *multiplicity* (it is neither one nor many but "radicals" that refuse homogeneity or arborescence); and *asignifying rupture* ("a rhizome may be broken, shattered at a given spot, but it will start up again on one of its old lines, or on new lines" or it "is an anti-genealogy") (Deleuze and Guattari, *Thousand* 7–11).

With these two concepts (a body without organs and rhizomes), let us ask, what *is* wanted as writing (as a mode of resistance) by Deleuze and Guattari? They work with the notion of

> writing inscribed on the very surface of the Real: a strangely polyvocal kind of writing, never a biunivocalized, linearalized one; a transcursive system of writing, never a discursive one; a writing that constitutes the entire domain of the "real inorganization" of the passive syntheses, where we would search in vain for something that might be labeled the Signifier—writing that ceaselessly composes and decomposes the chains into signs that have nothing that impels them to become signifying. The one vocation of the sign is to produce desire, engineering it in every direction.
>
> (*Anti-Oedipus* 39; also see 132–33; cf. 130–37, for "The Process")

Or again, they say:

> Write to the *n*th power, the $n - 1$ power, write with slogans: Make rhizomes, not roots, never plant! Don't sow, grow offshoots! Don't be one or multiple, be multiplicities! Run lines, never plot a point! Speed turns the point into a line! Be quick, even when standing still! Line of chance, line of hips, line of flight. Don't bring out the General in you! Don't have just ideas, just have an idea. . . . Have short-term ideas.
>
> (*Thousand* 24–25)

Just drift! Just be pagan!

A corollary to this counterthesis is that argumentation, which is based on a variety of (apparent) legitimation principles that we call warrants (according to Toulmin), grand narratives (according to Lyotard), and representative anecdotes (according to Burke) and which has as its primary goal rational consensus (or hermeneutic understanding), is questionable and, therefore, problematic; so-called rational consensus, in the light of the discussion, is seen by Lyotard and Deleuze and Guattari suspiciously as political oppression. Commonplaces have an insidious way of only fostering the dominant discourse;

commonplaces are in no way revolutionary. What we desire instead of po-
litical-argumentative discourse (either dialectics/didactics or argumentation),
what we desire instead of politics, then, is rhizomatic-"polylectics," or radical
multiplicities, as means of resistance.[6]

Counterthesis 2

The second counterthesis centers on the Nietzschean-Freudian question Who
speaks when something is spoken? (It's a question of author[ship].) For
Habermas and the rest of the humanist tradition, human beings speak. For
Lyotard, however, this statement by Habermas is a grammatical, though
nonetheless dangerous, fiction. (Not too unlike Nietzsche, Lyotard would say
that people believe in their egos insofar as they have faith in the first-person
pronoun of their grammar or have blind faith in a reified, universalized
language game.) One possible conclusion for Lyotard might be that if human
beings do not speak, they are spoken. Or as Jacques Lacan has it, "La langue
[et lalangue] se parle" (*Ecrits* 123).

This global, unrefined notion of being spoken, however, is a complicated
one in its particularity in Lyotard's thinking and needs to be both attenuated
and elaborated on here. (It becomes somewhat clear that this second counterthesis is locally informed by the second Gorgian proposition that if anything
exists, it cannot [should not/ought not to] be known.) The best way to
understand this notion of being spoken is to place it, at least initially, in a
larger framework of Lyotard's view of language games or pragmatics, which
he locates within the exclusive categories of either addressor or addressee
(*Just Gaming* 38). Lyotard's pragmatics, which are *not* universal, might be
seen as direct counterstatements to Habermas's universal pragmatics and as
indirect counterstatements to the Kinneavy model of the communications
triangle (*Theory*). Lyotard describes three different pragmatics (*Just Gaming*
38–39):

1. The *addressor* as in control of language, as its author(ity). (This pragmatic
   is grounded in the presuppositions of philosophical discourse; it is the
   "Parmenides game.")
2. The *addressee* as in obligation to listen and, therefore, not in control of
   language. (This pragmatic is grounded in the "theological" Judaic tradition and is the "Moses game.")
3. The *addressee* as in the addressee without an addressor or a receiver without
   a sender. (This last pragmatic is situated in a postmodern countertradition,
   which Lyotard calls the "Pagan game.")

Since this third pragmatic stands in direct contradistinction to the first two
and since it is Lyotard's main contribution to pragmatics, it needs further

elaboration. The conditions for the possibilities of an addressee (receiver) without an addressor (sender) have been suppressed/oppressed by homological-totalitarian, philosophical-political thinking. Such thinking favors a rhetoric of the speaking subject or an authoritarian, but only apparently humanistic, ideology that favors language as the function of the speaking subject. For Lyotard, there must be and, in fact, there is a counterrhetoric (or pragmatics) to both the traditional (pragmatic 1, above) speaker authority (autonomy) and (pragmatic 2) speaking language (obligation). Such a rhetoric/pragmatics—which he finds in the narrative pragmatics of the native American Cashinahua (*Just Gaming* 32–35; *Postmodern* 20–21; *Differend* 154–55)—can be described as a subject that is the function of the listener, or the addressee. (But this is not a speaking language as it is with pragmatic 2, above.)

Let me clarify this idea further. Lyotard writes of the distinction between language as a spoken game and language as a listening game, favoring the latter. (The spoken game corresponds with pragmatic 1, above, and, in part, with pragmatic 2, while the listening game corresponds specifically with pragmatic 3.) He says,

> For us, a language is first and foremost someone talking. But there are language games in which the important thing is to listen, in which the rule deals with audition. Such a game is the game of the just. And in this game, one speaks only inasmuch as one listens, that is, one speaks as a listener, and not as an author. It is a game without an author. In the same way as the speculative game of the West is a game without a listener, because the only listener tolerated by the speculative philosopher is the disciple. Well, what is a disciple? Someone who can become an author, who will be able to take the master's place. . . . One of the basic rules is indeed that the position of sender must remain empty. No one may put herself or himself there; no one may be the authority.
>
> (*Just Gaming* 71–72)

I explore the specific implications of this position for a pedagogy in the third counterthesis.

To recapitulate, the notion of a language as speaking game is a turn against philosophy and the paideia discourse of traditional-modern composition theories, whose goals have been to control/master language and knowledge or, in other words, to "totalize" (such is pragmatic 1).[7] As Nietzsche says, the will to knowledge is the will to power or the will to critical mastery, which leads to political disaster and violence. The loss of autonomy is, furthermore, a complete Nietzschean turn against the Judaic-Christian tradition of a singular God speaking (such is pragmatic 2). What remains then, in reference to pragmatic 3, is still the (il)legitimate question Who, if anyone or more, is speaking to us as listeners, so that we might speak as listeners? For Lyotard (if "who" or "it" exists), perhaps it is the gods.

He develops his major concept of (sophistic, postmodern) paganism in *Just Gaming*. But this concept can be misleading, for the "gods do not speak," Lyotard tells us, "even when I consult them. As they say, they signify, they do not speak. It cannot be said that the gods speak to me, certainly not in the Jewish sense," that is, in the sense of pragmatic 2, above (*Just Gaming* 42). Moreover, the gods do not speak because they are not masters (authors/addressors) of the word or of us. The gods have no "metalinguistic position," have no outside-of-speaking position from and by which to judge. They signify "with the same degree of uncertainty, of deception, of ruse, and of chance" that occurs in human communication. They and what they have to say are "very dangerous" because, like the oracles, their statements "lend themselves to misunderstanding" (*Just Gaming* 42, 43). Lyotard writes:

> [T]hey are not gods in [the sense that they are] all-knowing [and so goes our troubling model of the *omniscient* God]. They just have their stories, that humans do not know. And humans have their own stories. And these two sets of stories are, if you will, not two blocks but two centers that send out their elements to negotiate . . . on the boundaries. This is paganism. One does not know whom one is speaking to; one must be very prudent; one must negotiate; one must ruse; and one must be on the lookout when one has won.
>
> (*Just Gaming* 43)

Or when *One* (as in homogeneity/consensus) has *Won!* The gods are metaphors for linguistic paganism or agnosticism and for political heteronomy. (Hence, if "who" or "it" exists, "it" cannot be known.) What Lyotard has done, then, is to exclude the dominant, humanistic position of the speaker: Specifically, he has placed the speaker-writer (encoder) in a situation of nonauthority; for the speaker (of the traditional communications triangle) can only be a speaker now by virtue of having been, more so, a listener (decoder, reader). But this explanation via the communications triangle is misleading, for in Lyotard's conception, the speaker is only a listener but not a listener as in pragmatic 2 above (cf. White's "middle voice" and Spivak's "rumor" [213]). Lyotard's speaker as listener is even more complicated than I have intimated; hence, I return to it later with (dis)respect to David Bartholomae's concept of "inventing the university."

If Lyotard limits his pragmatics to addressor-addressee and then to only an addressee, Deleuze and Guattari and Serres find other, more radical ways of resisting and disrupting the speaker as authority. Serres, in his antischeme, retains the addressor-addressee, but he includes a third concept or antispeaker, who is, in communications theory, sometimes called "noise" (babel) or is generally conceived of as an outcast, victim, or the vanquished. It is this third concept, or antispeaker, that the addressor and addressee work hard at excluding. Serres tells us:

> *To hold a dialogue is to suppose a third man and to seek to exclude him*; a successful
> communication is the exclusion of the third man. . . . We might call this
> third man the *demon*, the prosopopoeia of noise. . . . Dialectic [in the Socratic-
> Platonic dialogues] makes the two interlocutors play on the same side; they
> do battle together to produce a truth on which they can agree, that is, to
> produce a successful communication. In a certain sense, they struggle together
> against interference, against the demon, against the third man. Obviously,
> this battle is not always successful. In the aporetic dialogues, victory rests with
> the powers of noise; in the other dialogues, the battle is fierce—attesting to
> the power of the third man. Serenity returns little by little when the exorcism
> is definitely (?) obtained.
>
> (67; cf. 126; see Deleuze and Guattari, *Thousand* 146–48; Guattari)

A careful reading of the Platonic dialogues, however, discloses that not only
the third but even the second (wo)man is excluded. What appears to be the
philosopher's give-and-take dialogue/dialectic is really none other than a
didactic. The best example of this occurs in the *Sophist*, when the Stranger
says that he would prefer to speak alone but will agree to speak with another
if he is obedient and lets himself be guided (217d). (See Lyotard, "Theory
as Art," esp. 73–74.)[8]

Let's now recapitulate in (dis)order to re(dis)orient: What have we done
in examining models of communication (or pragmatics)? And where do we
intend to go? First of all, I have only implied here—since it is already well
known—the model that is universal, philosophical, and *ideal* (it is identical
to Habermas's notion of universal pragmatics and Lyotard's first category of
the addressor as in control of language). What I have also implied is a second
model, one that is local, rhetorical-(but still)-philosophical, and *actual* (the
model is manifested by a variety of local interpretive communities, and it
informs, but only in part, the thinking of Lyotard, Serres, and Deleuze and
Guattari). I say "in part" because these "paratheorists," especially Deleuze
and Guattari, aspire not only to local knowledge (*nomoi*) but also to radical,
noncodifiable (nonrational, minoritarian) ways of knowing or, in other words,
to greater levels of noise (Deleuze and Guattari would say deterritorializations)
than the model based on "actuality" alone could account or would even allow
for. Specifically, their antimodel, then, includes a third, (dis)integrating
element beyond the binary (of the two general models), an element that I
have called "Third Sophistic possibilisms"[9] and that can be seen as "the *demon*,
the prosopopoeia of noise" that all four paratheorists, in innumerous ways,
are after. As Deleuze and Guattari say, for example, "Stammer language, be
a foreigner [a Sophist, not a Socratic] in one's own tongue" (*Thousand* 134).
Let's now take a stammering, stumbling step toward (de)composition.

Relevance to Composition. The second counterthesis (Who speaks when someone speaks?) can have and has had in composition theory two very general

answers. The question Who speaks? is a question of origins, groundings, sources, capacities. If we conceive of it in this manner, we end up (or begin again) with some groupings that are not true to what is commonly thought. (To simplify and to root the distinction, if only temporarily, I use Berlin's labels from "Rhetoric and Ideology," along with others from traditional pragmatics, as Lyotard already does.)

The first answer to the question Who speaks? then, is to be found(ed) in the addressor, who shapes the world when he or she speaks (this answer can be associated with expressionist or cognitive rhetorics and could even be called humanist; it is identical to Lyotard's view of the addressor as in control of language). The second answer, however, is found(ed) "relationally" between an addressor and addressee or an addressor and the code/signal, who speak only by virtue of conventions of discourse, situations, contexts, interpretive communities (this answer can be associated with social-epistemic rhetoric but can only be dangerously confused with Lyotard's other two views of pragmatics, those based on the addressee).

Moreover, the first answer *founds* a humanist philosophy and educational system. It assumes that the (rhetorical) self is free and, therefore, an appropriate conceptual starting place for pedagogy of emancipation. (When humanists become scientists, as Flower has, they "found" the self/subject "cognitively.") The self or subject or ethos, however, is not "free," as humanists are so found of touting. The self cannot be the liberating grounds/foundations for a society/education (any more than consensus can be) because to be a subject in our society is inevitably to be subjected, individually and collectively. Foucault, in his discussions of power-knowledge relations, has already disclosed to us how subjects are constituted (see Rabinow 7–11; Foucault, "Subject").[10] Furthermore, a reading of a Platonic dialogue (such as the *Meno*) can disclose that the slave boy is, indeed, a slave to and subjected to the questions being asked. (I continue this discussion of the dialogues in the third counterthesis.) Then, of course, there are Lacan's and Derrida's notions of the subject as an effect, as "divided" and "fading" (see Lacan, *Fundamental* 199 and "Function" 65–71; Derrida, "Differance" 11–12, 15, and *Positions* 28; cf. my "Concerning"). We can conclude, then, as I have suggested throughout, that subjects are constituted—or "hailed" as Louis Althusser would say ("Ideology" 170–77)—by the prevailing modes of representation, by the prevailing ideologies of the production of knowledge, by the prevailing dominant discourse, all of which are fostered by the humanistic curriculum, which is (put) in place to "invent the university." The self/subject apparently is forever in a master/slave dialectic, with the master being the dominant discourse and the slave being the so-called (invented-liberated) self. What, then, is (far) left to us? For now, I can only answer that we must continue to search for ways to problematize the subject, especially as it is conceived of in pragmatics. It is no longer, in our profession, *just* a question (or a *just* question) of "the students' rights to their own language" or of "teaching the other self" or of "empowering students," which I think is the biggest hoax ever perpetrated on "the student body." It is a question of students' resistance to and disruptions of these so-called rights and other self.

The second answer to the question Who speaks? is, as I have said, founded on the notion of social bond. Recent work by Patricia Bizzell ("Foundationalism"), Bartholomae ("Inventing"), John Trimbur ("Consensus"), and Karen Burke LeFevre (*Invention as a Social Act*) shifts the conceptual starting place for a theory of composition from the self as inventor (or *ethos* or the cognitive perspective) to the community as inventor (or *pathos* or the social perspective). Though these three theorists, along with others, have contributed some invaluable insights, they have neglected to continue to counterquestion their conclusions, that is, to be suspicious, to drift enough. (And here, in part, lies an understanding that they are not antifoundationalist but only incipient foundationalists.) Though they point out that the self (the inventor) is constructed socially, they neglect to point out similarly that the social (or *pathos* or consensus) is itself previously (and insidiously and invidiously) constructed (see Lyotard, *Differend* 110–15). If they in passing do suggest, however, that the social is saturated with ideological constructs that "speak us," they finally, in these instances, continue to advocate a certain, uncertain view of emancipation. How? Again, by returning to the social. I agree with them that the romantic individual is not the means of solving the problem, but neither is romantic socialism. Simply put, they have not fully confronted and embraced the problem of the ethical subject or the gross limitations of the rationalist-leftist approach to this problem. They, like their predecessors, neglect to be suspicious of their "narrative of emancipation." If we, therefore, cannot/ought not to accept the first answer to the question Who speaks? (which only places the self in bondage to the dominant-hegemonic discourse), why should we accept the second answer? (It only places a bunch of already enslaved selves in an equally unacceptable—that is, nonemancipating—locus.)[11]

But—instead of ending this point with a rhetorical question—let us (ever) return to the narrative of emancipation founded on local *nomoi-techne* (on social bond or social convention methodized), and, in doing so, let's now get suspicious. As an example, let's look at one social theorist in composition theory who wishes to place value in fields of discourse, specifically in academic discourses. Instead of inventing the self/subject in relation to another self, it is, for this theorist, a strategy of inventing the university (that is, founding one's self on the modes of university discourse). Student writers now would be "invented" by engaging in the conventions of academic discourse. This position (aptly presented by Bartholomae) answers the question Who is speaking, when someone speaks? by saying, Language speaks, but specifically, Academic language speaks. To be sure, this is a poststructuralist position (which Bartholomae takes from Barthes), but it is a position that greatly differs from one advocated by Lyotard in his notion of "language as a listening genre" (*Just Gaming* 71).

Let me explain exactly how this position differs from Lyotard's, but first I locate some troubling words that make a difference. Bartholomae writes:

> The writer who can successfully manipulate an audience . . . is a writer who can both imagine and write from a position of privilege. She must, that is, see herself within a privileged [academic] discourse, one that already includes and excludes groups of readers. She must be either equal to or more powerful than those she would address.
>
> (139–40)

And again Bartholomae says, "I think that all writers, in order to write, must imagine for themselves the privilege of being 'insiders'—that is, the privilege both of being inside an established and powerful discourse and of being granted a special right to speak" (143). Unfortunately, I find much to agree with here at a descriptive level but not at a prescriptive level. First, Bartholomae is talking about "the language game of knowledge," which has as its primary function the maintenance of the integrity of the paideia and the university and the state (see Lyotard, *Postmodern* 31–37; cf. Althusser, "Ideology"). Lyotard, however, thinks of his discourse as "the language game of art," which has the primary motive and function of resistance and disruption (*Just Gaming* 50). It might, indeed, be a game of art that Lyotard is privileged to play within philosophical circles, but it is, nonetheless, a primary form of resistance against state-philosophical (pedagogical, terrorist) politics. Lyotard's game of art is against what he calls the "research game" and the "teaching game" (*Postmodern* 23–27); it is against inventing (students by political virtue—*arete*—of) the university. His language game of art does not issue "truth claims" (sentences), nor does it issue exclusively from authority/performatives (speech acts); it issues from what I call "postmodern theatricks" (pagan *theos*-tricks), whose sole purpose is not faithfulness to the story of knowledge (i.e., to the dictum "ye shall seek knowledge and it shall set you free!") but to "just gaming" or to hamming it up or cutting up (i.e., to Foucault's idea "ye shall free yourself from knowledge by cutting up") (see *Just Gaming* 33; Foucault, *Language* 154).

Second, whereas Bartholomae speaks of a position of privilege (of being an insider), Lyotard is against privilege and all that it entails; he is diametrically opposed to writing from such a position, within academic discourse, because it does, indeed, finally exclude others (that is, both people and ideas) from being "expressed" within that discourse. Lyotard attempts to extend the boundaries—if not tear them down—of what stands as academic discourse. He tries to write from inside but as an outsider. This does not mean, however, that he writes so that any and every reader can follow; if he were to write in this transparent, plain style, what he says would not get said at all. Such fetishist clarity would only perpetuate the exclusion of his ideas, would only maintain the so-called privileged over the silenced. The choice here, then, is between including the greatest number of audiences or including ideas—or what Lyotard calls "differends" (*Differend* 13)—that, heretofore, have been disallowed and excluded. But this logic is tricky, for the choice is not really disjunctive. If we choose wider audience appeal over the differend, we do, indeed, exclude the differend. But if we choose the differend over wider audience appeal, we create the (postmodern) conditions for the possibilities of eventually including wider audience appeal. The notion is that the ideas make the audience, not the opposite; Bartholomae himself gives credence to this notion. But then, Lyotard calls this notion "romantic" (*Just Gaming* 11). As a postmodernist, he does not have a traditional-classical view of audience (as a priori) or as romantic (as made or invoked); he believes not in a "pathos of conviction" (as Habermas and other social-epistemic theorists do) but in a "pathos of distance" (as Nietzsche does) (*Just Gaming* 3–18; Nietzsche, *Twilight* 91).

Akademia and (the exchange of) its discourse, its symbolic kapital, no doubt, foster a private club: it excludes not only nonacademics (those not at all familiar with the discourse) but also nonacademic academics and their ideas (those who know the discourse but who have views that are only silenced by the so-called privileged academic-discourse strategies). My position with respect to Bartholomae's, therefore, is not that of inventing the university but that of *paralogizing* (the opposite of paralyzing) the university so that it might become a (polymorphous) perversity.

Counterthesis 3

The third counterthesis is more of an indirect meditation on the consequences of the Habermas-Lyotard debate (which we are steadily leaving behind, so as to drift on). Specifically, it states (from a postmodern, "third sophistic" perspective) that theory as the game of knowledge cannot help as a resource, because theory of this sort resists finally being theorized, totalized. (The set of all sets in the universe does not constitute a set.) This third counterthesis is in reference to the third, but modified, proposition of Gorgias (if "it" could be known, it cannot and should not be communicated [that is, taught]). The counterthesis can be restated (with greater precision) in two other ways, which have an overall immediate, direct relevance to rhetoric and composition and, most important, a direct relevance to pedagogy.

The first way to restate counterthesis 3 is to declare a moratorium on attempting to turn theory into praxis/pedagogy. The field of composition demonstrates a resistance *to* theory by rushing to apply theory to praxis without ever realizing the resistance *of* theory itself to be theorized and applied. To paraphrase Paul de Man, the field's collective resistance to theory (the field's attempt to turn its back on theory altogether and to embrace applied theory exclusively) is matched only by a still greater force of theory itself, which perversely resists being known, being totalized. Therefore, we have "theory and not theory at the same time, the universal theory of the impossibility of theory." (This is what I have said spawns paratheorists.) To the extent that pedagogical applications (i.e., rhetorical reading and writings based on a cognitive model) are, in turn, based on theory, "that is to say teachable, generalizable and highly responsive to systemization," de Man continues, "rhetorical readings [and writings] still avoid and resist the reading [and writing] they advocate" ("Resistance" 20).

The second restatement is that during the moratorium, we will gain time (yes, I'm optimistic!) for enough of us to realize that (critical) theory para-doxically can, but cannot, be employed to critique and to found theoretical praxis. Theory has become, for the field of composition, the will to unified theory (see a nostalgic expression of this will in Bizzell, "On the Possibility"); it has become "theory hope" (Fish, "Consequences" 112; also see "Anti-Foundationlism"). Theory, then, as I suggest in the second counterthesis, is currently based on either a cognitive (psychology) model, as foundational, or on a social (hegemonic discourse) model, as supposedly antifoundational. As de Man says, "The equation of rhetoric with psychology [or sociology] rather than with epistemology opens up dreary prospects of pragmatic banality" ("Resistance" 19), which is just one way that theory manifests its resistance. But de Man speaks against linking rhetoric not just with cognitive psychology but also with the social-construction-of-reality model itself, which attempts to "grammatize" rhetoric (i.e., to subject rhetoric to codification, in the name of situation and interpretive community) and to blind its user to ideological underpinnings. De Man is, instead, an advocate of an unstable—postmodern, third-sophistic—paraepistemology and pararhetoric, both founded, but un-founded, on the perversity of a rhetoric of tropes: those specifically that resist unified theories and consequently resist totality and totalitarian knowing-doing-making. Like Lyotard and myself, de Man is against a stable topology—that is, a rhetoric of persuasion—and for an unstable "tropology"; he is against the game of knowledge as a means of totality and for the "game of avant-garde theory-art" as a means of resistance.

If, during the moratorium, there will have been time gained—I am relying on the Lacanian "future anterior" here—for enough of us to realize that critical theory paradoxically can, but cannot, be employed to critique and to found praxis, this realization may, in turn, allow us to realize that our will to pedagogy is, like theory hope, only a form of pedagogy hope. Pedagogy hope has, as its supposed beneficient ends, the improvement of our teaching of composition. (Pedagogy hope is the dream of the paideia.) We hope for improved modes of production (a set of *techne*) to create an improved product; we hope for *arete* (political virtue) that will sustain the capitalist/socialist polis at the expense of the social in the individual. (I am not speaking here of the bourgeois individual.) Such revisionary modes of production, however, contribute to a pedagogy (not unlike a pederasty) that we can/should no longer see as acceptable; it must/ought to come to light as a thing of the "philosophical" past that also must (and will) wither away in the (un)place of what is coming to be called a postpedagogy.[12] What we want, then, is a *pedagogy other(wise)*, what we want is a pedagogy without criteria (*Just Gaming* 14–16, 26), what we desire is a counterpedagogy, which expresses the "desire to escape the pedagogical imperative: a desire . . . to do away with pedagogy altogether" (Felman 23; cf. Crowley; Berthoff, "Teaching").

I state the language of the last counterthesis in strong words and suggest catastrophic self-acknowledgments and changes, which a practical-minded and recently proud profession must reject as ridiculous. I do not, of course, expect that the complementary suggestions will be acted on. (After all, the field of composition is self-congratulatory in that it touts its alleged "empowerment" of students.) Can any one of my (even more open-minded) readers, therefore, imagine the National Council of Teachers of English or the College Composition and Communication Conference having as its conference theme the question Should writing be taught? (This is no mere question of whether writing can be taught; obviously it can be as either craft or *techne*. This is no mere position based on "vitalism.") As far as I'm concerned, this political-cum-ethical question can/should no longer be begged. And yet, it must be begged; for if it were, indeed, asked and then acted on, it might very well put an end to the NCTE or the CCCC or at least change their ends radically. (The asking might bring with it insight and then disempower the field.) Blindness here may be necessary. As both Burke and de Man tell us, a way of seeing is a way of not seeing: The dominant (therefore, blinding) language game of the profession of composition (i.e., the language game of knowledge) must disregard, or actually can make little immediate sense of, the two aspects of this third counterthesis. My suggestions (perhaps made by a jester), therefore, automatically have to be ruled out of court. (That's often the fate of the differend.) One could say quite reasonably that the two aspects (concerning both theory and pedagogy) leave no room for us to teach writing, and, after all, we are a teaching profession, not purely a contemplative profession. And then, the very idea that we might be *pederasts!*[13]

A postpedagogy, however, appears irrepressible (in the light of counter, uncanny criticisms) and contributes to a counterposition against Ciceronian and Quintilian pedagogical rhetorics and all that is their heritage up through the eighties (see Kinneavy, "Restoring"; Murphy, "Rhetorical History"). It also contributes to a counterposition against Marxist and social-epistemic, exclusively rational rhetorics and all that is their heritage up through the nineties (see Berlin, "Rhetoric and Ideology"; Bizzell, "Cognition"; Trimbur, "Cultural Studies").

Such pedagogical-social rhetorics are composed of old, myopic, utopian grand narratives that stubbornly hang on and that are fundamental to the language game of knowledge. What is the status of this language game? The basic assumption in many of the Socratic dialogues is that to know something, to call it knowledge, one has to be able to teach it, to reproduce the means by which it is transferred to and acquired by another human being. Socrates is always asking his interlocutors, Can *rhetoric . . . piety . . .* whatever . . . be taught? This question is not innocent; it is a step in the major language game called Socratic dialectic. If any of these concepts or activities is unique, then it cannot be taught and is discarded as being "irrational." (This is the kind of violence that Lyotard sees perpetrated on the differend and hence on the heterogeneity of language games.) If, however, any of the concepts or activities is generic (or if it can fit into the scheme of a computer model, which, as Lyotard says, determines what "knowledge is" [*Postmodern* 4]), then it can be codified, and if codified, taught. (Plato—is it not clear by now? —with his dialectical procedure, was a protoprogrammer.) Again, that which does not fit into this scheme of reasoning simply falls by the wayside; worst of all, it is deflected. It is negatively associated, in the "scholarship" of the field of composition, with Romanticism, with Croce or Bergson, or with vitalism.[14] (Aristotle, though often seen in a favorable light, further builds on this grand narrative. Specifically, art, or *techne*, is founded on scientific understanding and is divided into theoretical, practical, and productive sciences [which eventually become disciplines or metadisciplines]; into respectively knowing, doing, and making; into mathematics, ethics, and poetics.)[15]

To be sure, it is no longer necessary to run Socrates's gamut of questions to achieve quasi accreditation for those concepts and activities that do not appear to be generic. It has been amply demonstrated by Michael Polanyi's concept of tacit (personal) knowledge that we can know a great deal more than we can ever articulate and that tacit knowledge is present in all disciplines and is transferable, even though we know not how it is "taught" (see Sam Watson). But I am not exclusively interested in this kind of knowledge and nonteaching; I prefer the kind associated with Lyotard's notion of postmodernism and with his interest in the game of (avant-garde) art. (In this respect, Lyotard is influenced by Nietzsche: We have art lest we perish of the truth.) Whereas Habermas needs to unify (like Bizzell and others) the various language games; whereas he specifically wants "to bridge the gap between cognitive, ethical, and political discourses" for "a unity of experience" (see *Postmodern* 72); and whereas he, therefore, wants to turn these language games into metanarratives, into unified knowledge, into truth—Lyotard, on the contrary, wants to disunify them all. Lyotard, as a postmodernist, expresses an "incredulity toward metanarratives" and such unified language games (*Postmodern* xxiv). Hence, he turns away from metanarratives (or grand narratives) such as consensus or emancipation to what he calls "little narratives," which I discussed in the second counterthesis as narratives without an addressor but with only an addressee. (Such a little-narrative pragmatics he takes from the Cashinahua.) These little narratives (which may be associated with the Sophist's local *nomoi* or Deleuze and Guattari's radical multiplicities such as "schizowriting" or a "a thousand plateaus" or Lyotard's avant-garde art) are discourse strategies as art, which attempt to keep knowledge from being realized as system, as categories, as generic, as *techne*, as political "linking"—and more so, as "teachable." The game of art is played in such a manner, then, so that art cannot (that is, its rules of linking cannot) be known. It is a game of dispersion, diaspora. It is a game of paralinkage. And it is a game played proleptically. Lyotard writes that the artist or writer "work[s] without rules in order to formulate the rules of what *will have been done. . . . Post modern* would have to be understood according to the paradox of the future (*post*) anterior (*modo*)" (*Postmodern* 81). But finally having discovered the rules for linkage does not mean then that they are to be codified; instead, another game (of [dis]linkage) is to be played, another game that "will have been done" (cf. Coles 11). This game is not of the *polis* but of the *pagus*—"a border zone where genres of discourse enter into conflict over the mode of linking" (*Differend* 151).

It might be easier now to understand Lyotard's discourse strategies—specifically, his concepts of paganism and "speaking as hearer" (which removes the dangerous metanarrative of "authorship" [*Just Gaming* 38–43, 71–72]) and parataxis (which resists hypotactic thinking, which is the thinking/linking of the game of knowledge [*Differend* 65–66]) and little narratives (which resist/disperse the grand narratives) and paralogy. All these strategies are designed to resist totality, humanity's rottenness, with perfection. But unlike the modernist, nostalgic Burke in *A Grammar of Motives*, they make no attempt to systematize ambiguity. Though perhaps by now these several discourse strategies are understandable even in this cursory manner, the last two strategies deserve more attention as a means of further establishing this third counterthesis and specifically a postpedagogy.

These little narratives not only are something new, something incommensurable and unintelligible, but also (if after a while they were to become "intelligible") are and remain, at all costs, unacceptable, for they are (and must forever remain) in direct conflict with the always already commonplaces, or the acceptable. For example, they violate the rules of forensic/judicial evidence. (See Lyotard's discussion of the Nazi war-crime trials in *Differend* 56–58.) In general, little narratives are found in the differend (in phrases in dispute): "The differend is the unstable state and instant of language wherein something which must be able to be put into phrases cannot yet be. . . . What is at stake in a literature, in a philosophy, in a politics perhaps, is to bear witness to differends by finding idioms for them" (13). Little narratives are attempts at such idioms (so are my countertheses). Differends and little narratives are found elsewhere in the "excluded third" or in "noise" (Serres), that which is not just outside but unjustly outside the game of knowledge (didactic or dialectic).[16]

Linked to the notion of little narratives is paralogy—that which does not logically follow (cf. Aristotle, who could accept paralogy in his *Poetics* [1460a] but not in his *Sophistical Refutations* [166b20]). The relation between grand narratives and little narratives doesn't make much sense if it is not understood that paralogy is the means by which resistance to, and disruption of, totality are to be brought about. (Paralogy is the paramethod of constructing little narratives.) Paralogy takes on two meanings for Lyotard: That which is against *homologia* but in favor of (para)analogies and that which "means searching for and 'inventing' counterexamples, in other words, the unintelligible" (*Postmodern* 54). Both, once again, are against the game of knowledge, which dreams of *homologia* and intelligibility. And they are "artfully against" this dominant-hegemonic game. What is meant by (para)analogies? As Lyotard says, "To link is necessary, but how to link is not." His favorite example of linkage by way of (para)analogy is found in the way Kant (or Lyotard) (dis)connects the three "faculties" in the critiques of understanding (pure reason), will (practical reason), and judgment (aesthetics) (see *Differend* 130–35). The three are not generically-codifiably connected (they are heterogeneous genres; each is, Lyotard says, an "archipelago" and an "island"). Consequently, none has a metalinguistic position by which to dominate the others; more important, the first two do not have a superior position over judgment (the aesthetic). Thus it should not be difficult to understand why Lyotard has as his conceptual starting place the third critique—that of art—which says, after all, that "how to link is not necessary." *Homologia*, then, becomes politically less threatening and (para)analogies more promising as a means of resistance to the will to *homologia*. Most important of all for Lyotard, however, is that the "Critique of Political Reason was never written" (*Differend* 130).

Now let's return (again) to a pedagogy other(wise)—unlinking it from the game of knowledge and (re)linking it (instead) to the game of art. And let's accomplish such a linkage specifically with paralogy. What we want is a way to proceed without foundations and without criteria (the first counterthesis) and without knowing as a subject (the second) and without conventional theory and pedagogy (the third). What we want, then, is not a discipline or metadiscipline but a "nondiscipline," which—heretofore referred to as a postpedagogy—is more accurately labeled (after Lyotard) a paralogic peda-gogy. Such a postpedagogy would include counterstrategies already alluded to and taken from Lyotard, Deleuze and Guattari, and Serres; they are also taken from Derrida, with his concern for the educational institution versus the state; Barthes, with his concern for the individual professor versus the students; and Paul Feyerabend, with his concern for thinking by counter-example, or counterinduction. (There are precedents aplenty.) These strategies would attempt to lessen the oppressive forces of discursive language; would attempt to be discontinuous, random, and filled with fragmented thoughts and digressions; would attempt to call each previous statement into (rhetorical) question; and would attempt to use sophistic ruse and counterruse. It would be, then, a matter of contrary language games—specifically, those that are anti-Socratic, -Platonic, -Aristotelian, -Habermasian; those that are more (sub)versive than Socratic/Platonic dialectics and didactics could ever be; and those that are prosophistic in the finest (revolutionary) sense of that word and subtradition with its contrary language game of *dissoi logoi*. This latter tech-nique of argument-counterargument, employed to keep the whole (which is always more than the sum) afloat, would have to be modified to reflect the above strategies and to be reconceived as *dissoi paralogi*.[17] Argument in this modification is not a means of achieving or accounting for consensus. It is, instead, a means of continuous "dissensus"; it "counterhopes" to achieve an occasional, if not permanent, place of misology (i.e., a distrust of *logos*), a place that Plato and Socrates saw as anathema (*Phaedo* 89dl–90c7) but that must be seen as the beginning of what Deleuze and Guattari would call a "nomadology" (*Thousand* 351–423) or what Montaigne and Lyotard combined would see as "just drifting/gaming." It is a place outside the philosophical and rhetorical polis; it is places (exploded and) realized through diaspora/ dispersion. It is the *pagus*.

I'm speaking of, and have variously defined indirectly, a postpedagogy that realizes legitimation by paralogy, which is achieved through heterology. Let me explain further, this time in relation to rhetorical invention, which has become the driving force behind composing. As a (para)process, paralogy is contrary to such commonly accepted virtues as control and efficiency. Paralogy (contrary[wise] as it is) echoes L. M. Brillouin's argument—namely, that "the idea (or ideology) of perfect control over a system, which is supposed to improve its performance, is inconsistent with respect to the law of contradiction: it in fact lowers the performance level it claims to raise" (*Postmodern* 55–56). Brillouin refers to "the game of bureaucracies" and how it "stifles" any creativity. The game never allows anyone to go outside that secretly dreamed-of "perfect control over a system" in search of any possible counterlegitimation from another, but "incommensurable," system. The primary, unstated purpose of the system is to maintain itself. Though it can indeed think the opposite, think the contrary/contrast, it does not (it cannot) think its own annihilation or question itself as an organization. It could think only uneasily but never act, for example, on the three countertheses of this essay. But processes of rhetorical invention (which are conceptual starting places for metagames of knowledge), with their built-in control and efficiency, are seemingly different from the game of bureaucracies. They are designed to raise the performance level. If "raising the performance level" means that the performer of the invention process, who is "originating" solutions to problems, can conceptually account for and therefore legitimate her or his solutions across the matrix of possibilities, then for "invention" this performance has succeeded; the mode of production authorizes what it produces. (Kuhn calls this kind of activity "normal science.") For paralogy, however, this performance has failed. For paralogy, the goal is not renovation but innovation; not a stochastic series based on rules that allow us to guess effectively and efficiently but a paradoxical series that invites us to break with the former rules altogether. Thinking paralogically is thinking counterinductively in terms that are counterexamples (that are perverse to the norm; see Feyerabend, ch. 2). Thinking paralogically, Lyotard says, means "searching for . . . the unintelligible; supporting an argument means looking for a 'paradox' and legitimating it with new rules in the games of reasoning" (*Postmodern* 54).

Now with (dis)respect to conventional teaching, teaching paralogically is a turn against the Socratic pedagogy (pederasty) of philosocratizing and of "verbal insemination." Teaching paralogically must force us to recognize and to offer an alternative to such "abnormal" teaching. Its recognition is not easily achieved, but it has been variously attempted. Burke best describes this Socratic pedagogy in his discussion on "principles of merger and division" (*Grammar* 410–18)—specifically, his example of a card trick in which an inquisitor uses a series of questions that force an interlocutor to always give the desired answers, thereby leading the interlocutor to arrive at the predetermined conclusion to the inquiry. It's a philosophical trick and a language game all too damaging to human beings. Moreover, Lyotard—who employs a more revolutionary manner than Burke does—has discussed this kind of trickery as it was played on the Jews who were asked to testify against Nazi war criminals. Such trickery made the witnesses for the prosecution speechless, ineffective, and once again victims. A final solution to the problem had been achieved but this time in an international court of law. What was on trial in those postwar courtrooms were not only Nazi war criminals but the judiciary tradition (the forensic speech act) of a language game called "the rules of evidence." What was wanted were paralogic, counterrules of evidence.

To begin (again), if these are some ways of achieving recognition of "abnormal" teaching, then what are the alternatives to such teaching? Perhaps the reader—if still necessary—should go back to the beginning(s) of this paper. Attempt it again, and learn to drift. With its three "little counter narratives." But to paraphrase the closing of Lyotard's paper, it might/ought to be remembered that we can't make macropedagogical political programs with the little counternarratives, but we can bear witness to them (*Differend* 181).[18]

NOTES

[1]In addition to Deleuze and Guattari's view of psychoanalysis and language, Lacanian psychoanalysis deals with what Jacques Lacan has called *"lalangue,"* which is "general equivocation," "Babel," "Babelonianisms"; it is contrary to de Saussure's two-word concept *"la langue"*; and, therefore, it is contrary to system/totality: synecdoche, control, and "logophilia." Though Lacan does not advocate the widespread use of *lalangue* for revolutionary, micropolitical ends (for resistance and disruption of the hegemonic discourse of the dominant class), he does himself, nonetheless, use *lalangue*, especially in his "scene of teaching and writing," as a "minoritarian discourse" (Lacan, "Television" 10).

This Lacanian question of the control and mastery of language is best discussed by Jane Gallop, *Reading Lacan*; see especially chapter 1, "Reading Lacan's *Ecrits.*"

Needless to say, I have no faith in the "Rogerian strategy," which in the long (insidious) run is really no different from the "Pavlovian strategy" or the "Freudian strategy" (see Young, Becker, and Pike 6–8). All three strategies are after control (see note 7, below) and, therefore, are for (perhaps unintentionally) maintaining the master-slave dialectic. (Rogerian rhetoric is simply more subtle in its ends.) This strategy of listen/talk is insidiously perpetuated by Tullio Maranhao in *Therapeutic Discourse*. Maranhao's strategy, as well as the other strategies, must be checked/resisted/disrupted by antipsychiatry. Some possible help: Sedgwick; Guattari. For both Rogers and especially Buber, see the Levinas Notice in Lyotard (*Differend* 110–15). For another view of psychology and writing theory, which I cannot stand with, see Baumlin and Baumlin. For an excellent book on Buber's view of communication and community, see Arnett.

[2]I say "very early" Frankfurt school because Max Horkheimer and Theodor W.

Adorno in *Dialectic of Enlightenment* enact, in 1947, their "Nietzschean turn" against their previous Marxist rationalism, a "turn" with which I generally agree. Jürgen Habermas, however, later critiques his former "teachers," for example, in "Entwinement of Myth," in *Philosophical Discourse* (see Hohendahl, *"Dialectic"*).

[3]From Sextus's version of Gorgias's "On the Non-Being: Or, On Nature" (cf. Aristotle's version, in *Melissus, Xenophanes, and Gorgias* 979a11–980b21). In *The Differend*, Lyotard does not think favorably about Gorgias. His interpretation of "Non-Being," however, is only one among many competing interpretations. Lyotard does not recognize the possibilities in Gorgias's work and thereby performs a terrible violence to its heterogeneous possibilities. My interpretation is in line with Mario Untersteiner's interpretation, which (curiously enough) is in line with Lyotard's idea of bearing witness to the differend.

[4]Lest there be some misperception, my interests do not lie in a detailed exposition of this complex debate, which has already been examined by others (see Rorty, "Habermas"; Stephen Watson). The debate is included here, instead, only as a set of conceptual starting places, or contrary coordinates, across which I might critically intervene into composition theory and pedagogy. In my in(ter)vention, I move (unsynthesizeably in the form of *dissoi logoi* or comedic perversities) from Habermas to Lyotard but eventually and apparently leave behind direct references to Habermas and, in his place, refer to composition theory and pedagogy, which as far as I am concerned already represents the spirit of Habermas's thinking.

The work of Habermas that I concentrate on is *Communication and the Evolution of Society*. A reader coming to Habermas for the first time should perhaps begin with *Legitimation Crisis*. His most recent work that responds to postmodern thought (specifically to the thought of Nietzsche, Foucault, Heidegger, Derrida, and Bataille) is the collection of twelve lectures in *Philosophical Discourse*. For an introduction to Habermas, see Foss, Foss, and Trapp, which has an excellent bibliography; in addition, see McCarthy. See also Hohendahl, "Critical Theory"; Mendelson, for the Habermas-Gadamer debate; Francesconi, for application of Habermas to rhetorical criticism; and Grady and Wells, for application to rhetoric and composition. For a set of excellent arguments against Habermas's penchant for control of and mastery over language (communication), see Nägele.

The works of Lyotard that I most make reference to are *The Postmodern Condition, Just Gaming*, and *The Differend*. See the special issue of *Diacritics* 14.3 (1984). I am especially indebted to David Carroll for several insights into Lyotard's thinking. To my knowledge, no one in composition theory has given any detailed attention to Lyotard, though he has been used by Harvey Kail.

[5]Another way of discussing Flower and Hayes's metaphor is in relation to Paul de Man's critique of aesthetic ideology. He views metaphor (as I do here) as the trope of unification/totalization and instead views "allegory" in a more favorable light as the trope of dispersion. See, for example, de Man's "Aesthetic Formalization" in *Rhetoric of Romanticism*, in which he critiques, with the help of Heinrich von Kleist, Schiller's *On the Aesthetic Education of Man*. See also Norris.

[6]I have already discussed elsewhere, with the help of Paul Feyerabend, the problem of argumentation; see "Critical Sub/Versions" 44–45. See also Lyotard in *The Differend*, where he strongly questions the genre of argumentation—specifically forensic/judiciary discourse—and even questions epideictic (the good death) and deliberative

(consensus) discourses. In fact, he speaks of the *demise* of these three classical (grand-narrative) speech acts.

⁷Concerning control, see, for example, Young, Becker, and Pike's comments about their book's structure. It is, they write, "a consequence of our belief that the discipline of rhetoric is primarily concerned with the control of a process. Mastering rhetoric means not only mastering a theory of how and why one communicates but mastering the process of communication as well" (9). I am indebted to Lynn Worsham for pointing out this passage to me.

⁸Commenting on the notion of "the excluded third," Serres conceives of it as constructed on the model of mathematical abstraction (68–69). Or it is based, as John Poulakos conceives of it, on "the ideal" (the Platonic) at the expense of the "actual" (the Aristotelian) or, more important, at the expense of the "possible" (the [Gorgian, *kairotic*] sophistic). What gets expelled here, then, is the possibility of "making something new, irrational" (Untersteiner 161) or "unintelligible" (Lyotard, *Postmodern* 54). Serres reminds us, "The order of reasons [ideal and at times local-actual] is repetitive, and the train of thought that comes from it, infinitely iterative, is but a science of death. . . . Stable, unchanging redundant, it recopies the same writing in the same atoms-letters" (100). I have made much of this notion of the excluded third in "Concerning a Post-Classical *Ethos*"—specifically, its value for writing histories of rhetoric and for our attitude adjustments toward language.

⁹I take my lead here not only from John Poulakos—who makes this distinction among ideal, actual, possible—but also from Robert Darnton, who answers the question What was the French Revolution? with the concept of "possibilism," which is defined as being "against the givenness of things" (10).

This discussion of the two models as forming a binary and the addition of the third antimodel is crucial, for it discloses (contrary to what people have previously thought) that I am not working with a binary system. The element of the third explodes/detonates the binary, as I tried to explain in "Critical Sub/Versions," when I worked with the binary of traditional and revisionary histories and then introduced the third antielement of "sub/versive," which explodes the previous two. I have further developed this theme—sophistic possibilisms destructing binaries—in " 'Some More' Notes."

¹⁰For an excellent article on the problem of the subject in relation to the present-day writing curriculum, see Zavarzadeh and Morton. For additional and exceptionally important discussions, see Silverman; Smith, *Discerning*; Dews; Butler; de Man, *Allegories* 160–87. See also my "Concerning a Post-Classical *Ethos*."

¹¹By now, some readers may have begun to wonder if I even believe a liberating rhetoric is humanly possible or even desirable. Lyotard says that the "metanarrative of emancipation" is dead. I personally was disabused of the notion of liberation when I read Vincent Farenga's account of the (mythic, periphrastic) origins of rhetoric. But then again, if a liberating rhetoric is possible, I do not think that it should/ought to be realized, that is, as a traditionalist, realist attempt to realize it. More important, I do not think it should/ought to be longed after (especially nostalgically, as a modernist does). Instead, let us engage in postmodern rhetorics. Let's be pagan. Let's be hysterical. (Let's engage in ruse after ruse.) Instead of a liberating rhetoric, there can/should/ought to be rhetorics of resistance.

¹²Gregory Ulmer speaks of a "post(e)pedagogy" (I take only the phrase from him

and not his particular approach, which I find lacking). For other examples of attempts at postpedagogies, see *Yale French Studies* 36, which has fifteen articles on the subject; moreover, the collections of Nelson and of Atkins and Johnson have several fine articles. See Elbow, *Embracing Contraries*, in which he advocates and describes a nondisciplinary pedagogy. But the pedagogy to which I allude is (politically and radically) different from Elbow's, for it does not wish to "embrace" and to "lie" with its contrary. Instead, it wishes to maintain what Nietzsche calls a "pathos of distance."

After writing this essay, I discovered Mas'ud Zavarzadeh's "Theory as Resistance," which distinguishes among a "humanist pedagogy," a "pedagogy of pleasure," and a "political [Marxist] pedagogy." He and I are in agreement about the first pedagogy—namely, that it is dangerous and therefore unacceptable. About the second and third, however, we disagree radically. He would view what I am advocating as a pedagogy of pleasure; I view his position as advocating totalization. Zavarzadeh bases what he calls the pedagogy of pleasure almost exclusively on Ulmer (in practice) and on de Man (in theory). However, his selecting Ulmer seems a diversionary tactic, and his reading of de Man grossly "mistakes" de Man's view of theory (which is theory as resistance, though not as a Marxist would have it). Further, Zavarzadeh does not even mention de Man's repeated attacks on aesthetic ideology, which are attacks on any effort to totalize; but then, a social totality *is* what Zavarzadeh is all about. Along these same lines, Zavarzadeh, however, presents no view of the social as problematic; I find this omission curious since he, along with Morton, earlier sees the subject/self as problematic and wishes to use "pleasurable" thinkers to "problematize" the subject. Evidently, the common social-(Marxist)-struggle—what Fredric Jameson sees as "the unity of a single great collective story"—is liberating in itself for and from bourgeois individuality (*Political* 19). Finally, I find fault with Zavarzadeh's philosophical view of rhetoric, which is as Platonic as Plato's; Zavarzadeh sees the role of rhetoric as secondary, as managerial, as propagandistic for his own (i.e., a socialist-Marxist) position. A great deal more needs to be said, but since Zavarzadeh's article is part of a forthcoming book, I leave the rest for a review article.

[13]The words *pedagogy* and *pederasty* are not only metaphorically but etymologically associated. Gallop writes:

> Pederasty is undoubtedly a useful paradigm for classic Western pedagogy. A greater man penetrates a lesser man with his knowledge. The student is empty, a receptacle for the phallus; the teacher is the phallic fullness of knowledge. In the classroom the students are many; the teacher unique. Unicity is a primary phallic attribute. The fact that teacher and student are of the same sex but of different ages contributes to the interpretation that the student has no otherness, nothing different than the teacher, simply less.
>
> ("Immoral Teachers" 118)

In *The Daughter's Seduction*, Gallop offers a slightly different version of this passage:

> There is a certain pederasty implicit in pedagogy. A greater man penetrates a lesser man with his knowledge. The *homo*sexuality means that both are measurable by the same standards by which measure one is greater than the other. Irigaray [in *This Sex Which Is Not One*] uncovers a sublimated male homosexuality structuring all our insti-

tutions: pedagogy, marriage, commerce, even Freud's theory of so-called heterosexuality. Those structures necessarily exclude women, but are unquestioned because sublimated —raised from suspect homo*sexuality* to secure homo*logy*, to the sexually indifferent *logos*, science, logic.

(63–64)

Also see Bersani; Marrou.

[14]See Young; Weidner. Although Weidner's dissertation has numerous problems, Young (and the profession through Young) accepts them as being nonproblematic. For one, the chapter on Coleridge is based primarily on secondary material and does not acknowledge that, indeed, Coleridge does have "methods"—for example, his "Essay on Method" and his "noetic pentad." (The methods, to be sure, are very different from the *techne* of the Platonic and Aristotelian traditions.) For another, neither Young nor Weidner takes nontechnological thinking (i.e., nonsystematic heuristics) seriously, and each cavalierly dismisses it as vitalism or mere Romanticism. It is an unfortunate historiographical terministic screen (classicism/neoclassicism versus Romanticism/neo-Romanticism) that we have come to use, for it blinds us from seeing writers such as Coleridge from more profitable vantage points (cf. Kameen, especially his discussion of Coleridge and Heidegger).

[15]Lyotard is predisposed to think favorably about Aristotle (see *Just Gaming* 29; *Differend* 72–75). However, I see Aristotle as a major developer of the game of knowledge (what Foucault calls species/genus analytics), whether that game is based on universal or social norms. The fields of composition and rhetoric are equally predisposed to think good thoughts about Aristotle. He, indeed, looks like a good guy in comparison to Plato. Again, he is not. See Poulakos.

[16]It is difficult to place the ideal of little narratives in Kinneavy's communications triangle, which after all is only one—though currently the dominant—game of the game of knowledge. First, the little-narrative strategies are narratives, not descriptions, arguments, or expositions. Second, the discourse strategy of little narratives should not be placed under "literary," for such a placement would be only a (dis)placement of a radical game of art, whose very moves are contra the triangle itself. But placement involves still other problems: though Walter Fisher sees narrative as having the force of argumentation, it must be kept in mind that consensus (*homologia*) is unacceptable to Lyotard, just as Fisher's view of narrative would be. If the narratives as arguments have persuasive or rational force, it is because they are the commonplaces of the dominant culture or because they are fables with acceptable morals. Indeed, they are protoarguments, the stuff from which informal or formal logic got abstracted into conventional categories of knowledge. For Lyotard, however, such protoarguments must be resisted through counternarratives, little narratives. (Or, as I have been saying, they must be resisted across [mis]representative antidotes.)

[17]For a discussion of *dissoi paralogoi* as an antimethodology of postmodern or subversive (third-sophistic) rhetorics, see my "Critical Sub/Versions." John Poulakos has suggested to me that I might modify the term to read *dissoi polylogoi* to emphasize the multiplicities of competing *logoi* (or ways of knowing and unknowing, which cannot be systemized).

[18]This essay is a much abbreviated version of a chapter in a manuscript in progress, an exploration of the theory and pedagogy of writing and how they establish both a social bond and bondage. It can be read as a complementary paper to "Critical Sub/Versions," which raises in passing the question of a postpedagogy, and can also be read as a counterresponse to George Kennedy's, Robert L. Scott's, and Michael Leff's questions concerning my position on the teaching of writing.

Cultural Studies, Postmodernism, and Composition

❖

John Schilb

Cultural Studies *and* Postmodernism: *Terms for Literary Studies*

IN RECENT years, professors of literature have considered changing the name of their field to *cultural studies*, even though they have not yet pinpointed what this term covers. Hundreds of them attended the 1988 MLA convention forum entitled What Should Cultural Studies Be? Similarly, literary theorists have increasingly supplanted the word *poststructuralism* with *postmodernism*, even though this new term has also proved ambiguous. Note their involvement with edited collections like Jonathan Arac's *Postmodernism and Politics* and *After Foucault: Humanistic Knowledge, Postmodern Challenges*, E. Ann Kaplan's *Postmodernism and Its Discontents*, John Fekete's *Life after Postmodernism,* and Andrew Ross's *Universal Abandon? The Politics of Postmodernism.* Neither *cultural studies* nor *postmodernism* is new to literary analysis. The term *cultural studies* has long been associated with Raymond Williams and the Birmingham Center for Contemporary Cultural Studies. *Postmodernism* has long denoted a style of fiction, was exalted by Ihab Hassan in the early seventies, and has preoccupied the journal *Boundary 2* since then as well. Yet each term now enjoys wider currency within the field.

The change signifies a desire to move literary studies beyond its traditional practices toward larger social concerns. At least four developments have stirred this impulse. First, literary scholars have deployed poststructuralist criticism long enough to see how it can illuminate other discourses besides literature if pushed in their direction and inflected with greater social consciousness. In particular, deconstruction now seems unduly limited by the literary canon and traditions of formalist exegesis. Second, as literary theorists raided other disciplines like philosophy to formulate poststructuralist concepts and as those fields appropriated literary terms to analyze their own texts, traditional boundaries wavered. Third, the sheer demographics of current students—who vary in gender, ethnic background, financial status, and age yet share an immersion in the electronic media—have made literature teachers doubt the relevance of traditional texts and pedagogies. Finally, literary scholars are increasingly identifying with or at least supporting the struggles of feminists, minorities, the poor, gays, Third World peoples, and other marginalized groups. Since these movements look beyond electoral politics to consider how power shapes everyday life, teachers affiliated with them resist bracketing English as an autonomous aesthetic pursuit.

Because we are still delineating cultural studies and postmodernism, their ability to guide more socially conscious inquiry remains unclear. Among other tasks, advocates of cultural studies must ponder how to push beyond Arnoldian aesthetics and view culture as "a constitutive social process, creating specific and different 'ways of life' " (Williams, *Marxism* 19). Williams urges scholars to grasp the materialist dimensions of culture without reducing it to the merely "superstructural status" that Marxists have so often accorded it. This task requires examining ways in which the realm of culture relates to the economy and to the state.

Theorists of postmodernism must keep in mind that the term can designate a critique of traditional epistemology, a set of artistic practices, and an ensemble of larger social conditions—just as modernism referred to intellectual developments, artistic trends, and transformations in the wider social landscape. Indeed, the relation of postmodernism to modernism remains to be elucidated. Furthermore, just as modernism still elicits diverse moral and political judgments, so it remains undecided whether we should celebrate or disdain postmodernism.

Whether we should link or oppose cultural studies and postmodernism also needs exploring. Various analysts of culture hesitate to accept the notion of postmodernism as a conceptual tool. Many worry that the antifoundationalism of much postmodern thought—its "incredulity toward metanarratives," to quote Jean-François Lyotard's notorious phrase (*Postmodern* xxiv)—rules out appeals to truth, objectivity, ethics, and identity that social critics have traditionally made. Jürgen Habermas most prominently raises this objection. Even certain social critics who do wish to discredit the universal, rationalistic, humanist self—believing its image masks power relations and cultural differences—feel that postmodern theorists still neglect oppressed groups. For example, Meaghan Morris and Craig Owens criticize the way various postmodern manifestos have elided women.

Fredric Jameson's 1984 essay "Postmodernism: Or, The Cultural Logic of Late Capitalism" has provoked several questions about the term's diagnostic power. Jameson considers postmodernism a widespread cultural phenomenon spawned by capitalism's latest stage, one in which commodification has supposedly become total. In this new world order, he claims, people have lost critical distance and historical perspective, wallowing in images, simulacra, and pastiche. While no one disputes that Jameson captures at least some aspects of contemporary life, many challenge his basic argument. Dana Polan and Warren Montag question Jameson's and others' reliance on postmodernism as a prime instrument of analysis, believing that it may unjustifiably exclude other diagnostic terms. Lawrence Grossberg and Richard Kearney believe Jameson underestimates human agency; Gayatri Chakravorty Spivak, however, thinks Jameson assumes that the theorist of postmodernism can become "history-transcendent" (171). Montag, Grossberg, and Mike Davis accuse him of departing from traditional Marxism by neglecting social contradictions, yet Stanley Aronowitz and Paul Smith ("Visiting") believe he puts too much faith in Marxism's explanatory value. Meanwhile, Jim Collins insists that Jameson fails to appreciate the virtues of postmodern art. I cite these positions not to provide a minicasebook on Jameson's particular text but to show that attempts at fusing cultural studies and postmodernism can trigger intense debate.

The Role of Composition

Several of us in the emerging field of composition have grown just as interested as literature colleagues in cultural studies and postmodernism and how they may relate. Indeed, I think our field can even more powerfully illuminate these two terms and examine the wisdom of linking them. Yet we should not automatically ingest a particular version of either; instead, through our scholarship and pedagogy we should ponder issues of the sort I mention here. A composition program would therefore examine various theories of cultural studies and postmodernism as well as how they diverge or mesh.

This agenda might appear to threaten the field's current pluralism, its range of scholarly concerns and methodological approaches. But these concerns could be productively juxtaposed even as teachers undertake a collective study. Such study could actually help writing teachers avoid the fragmentation that Gerald Graff says plagues literary scholars who fail to admit and work through their conflicts. And just as Graff proposes that literary studies foreground conflict in a way that is useful and involving for students, so too should we enlist students in the composition project I am suggesting rather than regard them as mere recipients of its fruits.

Composition is well situated for this inquiry. Because the field currently comprises diverse topics and methods and has ties to numerous disciplines, it can analyze broad social questions better than literary studies can. Andrea Lunsford notes this flexibility when she dubs composition a postmodern discipline. Furthermore, because composition deals with a range of texts besides traditional belles lettres, it can better resist the temptation Catherine Gallagher warns of: equating culture once again with Matthew Arnold's version of it. This advantage does not mean that composition ought to claim final authority on cultural questions. For one thing, the field needs to learn more about sociocultural issues—including those raised by the various theorists cited in this volume—if it is to examine them acutely. More important, composition need not aspire to become a supreme court for theories of culture; it can serve as an especially good arena to formulate, test, and exchange them.

Composition can embody the preoccupation with discourse associated with cultural studies and postmodernism. Both have evoked various cultural phenomena as texts; hence, a field identified with broad textual inquiry seems quite relevant to them. Composition's rhetorical bent has, in fact, grown more pertinent as certain theorists of these terms have questioned theory's generalizing bent and stressed that discourse operates in particular conjunctures: in other words, that specific discourses specifically affect specific people at specific times in specific places. Polan contends that "a theory of postmodernity . . . requires historical analysis, investigation of the specific sites in which spectacles, roles and meanings circulate" (54). In criticizing Jameson, Spivak calls for attempts *"to specify the postmodern space-specific subject-production"* (171), especially because the particular situation of Third World peoples might otherwise be neglected. Andreas Huyssen demonstrates that critics should not automatically assume or deny the political efficacy of postmodern art but instead consider the shifting power of the avant-garde in different countries.

Consider, too, that three recent books on the pretensions of theory align themselves explicitly with rhetoric, thereby opening up a leading role for composition in cultural research. Of course, in the last several years deconstructionists have often invoked Nietzsche's sense of rhetoric as tropes. But the books I have in mind revive the classical concern with how particular discursive acts yield particular social effects. Morris's *Pirate's Fiancée: Feminism,*

Reading, Postmodernism begins by emphasizing that "producing a [theoretical] 'position' is a problem of rhetoric, of developing enunciative strategies . . . precisely in relation to the cultural and social conventions that make speaking difficult or impossible for *women*" (7). With this premise, Morris skeptically ponders, for example, how Lyotard promotes dissensus and Jean Baudrillard embraces simulation. Terry Eagleton's *Literary Theory: An Introduction* ultimately discredits literature as an ontologically distinct body of texts, dismisses the study of literature as not just philosophically misguided but also politically blind, and proposes that literary study be replaced by work in rhetoric that studies mass culture as well as the canon. Stanley Fish's *Doing What Comes Naturally* repeatedly attacks contemporary theorists' efforts to rise above the constraints of practice; Fish says we must acknowledge "that we live in a rhetorical world" (25). While these books differ significantly—Fish seems more comfortable with academic professionalism and less driven by political agendas than Morris and Eagleton do—their common esteem for rhetoric dovetails with composition's interest in it.

Composition's concern with the production of discourse also prepares it to investigate cultural studies and postmodernism. Williams points out that "a central intellectual movement of the bourgeois period" was the "replacement of the disciplines of grammar and rhetoric (which speak to the multiplicities of intention and performance) by the discipline of criticism (which speaks of effect, and only through effect to intention and performance)." He contends that "[a]ny social theory . . . requires the activation of both poles: not merely their interaction . . . but their profound interlocking in actual composition" (*Marxism* 149). Williams's last word suggests that composition as a field can help build adequate social theories precisely because it resists the lopsided attention to criticism typical of literary studies. Since composition encourages writing and discussion of writing, it can more comprehensively probe the generation of culture.

The Present Limitations of Composition

In describing ways composition might address cultural studies and postmodernism, I am underscoring the potential of the field rather than its present sense of mission. We are far from realizing that potential, because of institutional and ideological factors embedded in composition's past. In identifying these factors, I think it useful to invoke modernism as a historical force that encouraged a certain conception of the field, a force that now discourages it from examining what postmodernism and cultural studies could mean.

Historians agree that composition was invented purely to train students in the mechanics of language, to help them face the newly specialized demands of higher education and the emerging circumstances of corporate life (Berlin, *Rhetoric and Reality*; Crowley; Douglas). The field is thus a product of modernism. We can clarify its historical situation even more by comparing it with another field: if, as Richard Rorty explains in *Philosophy and the Mirror of Nature*, philosophy became modern when Kant deemed it the very foundation of knowledge, then composition's duty to inculcate mechanical skills made it a low parody of this development. It was further debased by another modern legacy of Kant and other thinkers like Arnold: the idea that certain works of culture embody noble aesthetic values that clearly demarcate them from merely utilitarian discourse. While this hierarchy validated the literature component of English departments, it denigrated the writing courses housed within them.

One result was an ethos that envelops composition to this day: a belief that it exists only to serve the "real" disciplines, which are best served when composition focuses on students' "basic skills." Even if composition specialists want to adopt the agenda I propose, they will need to consider whether this belief still reigns at their college. For remedying such a political situation, no advice is universally applicable; which strategies to choose depends on the particular exigencies of each school. Sometimes, the writing program can forthrightly integrate the mission I am suggesting with the rest of the college; other situations may require a demand for more autonomy, with secession from the English department a distinct possibility; in still other settings, more subtle transformations might prove wise. To boost their institutional significance, though, composition faculty members usually have to articulate for themselves a mission that transcends skills-and-drills obeisance to the disciplines and emphasizes the interrelations of discourse, culture, and society—whether or not *cultural studies* and *postmodernism* serve as guiding terms. What most worries me is that many composition teachers retain the service ethos or residues of it.

Admittedly, composition teachers have long included in their syllabi argument papers and model essays dealing with political controversies. But instead of providing for coherent and expansive inquiry, such topics primarily enable atomistic exercises, during which students are expected to follow certain discursive regimens. In this context, as Ann E. Berthoff observes, " 'Who is to get the kidney machine?' is no advance at all over 'Which is greater, fire or water?' " ("Teaching" 754). The kind of assignment she mocks exemplifies, too, a tendency of the field that Richard Ohmann noted back in the seventies: the habit of framing social issues in a problem-solution format that belies their complexity (see *English in America*). Underlying these practices is a difficulty that, as Sharon Crowley explains, has afflicted composition since its beginning: when writing courses concentrate ultimately on mechanical training, then the texts and topics ushered into them as content inevitably seem artificial. Ironically, the incoherence students often experience in composition as a result of its modern origins can be seen as a quintessentially postmodern phenomenon. Because writing instructors often distress their students by commenting mainly on errors, Jasper Neel wryly suggests that "most composition teachers have always read their students' work with the eye of a deconstructor" (134). When Polan writes that postmodern features of mass culture like superficiality, pastiche, and bricolage encourage "a serialized sense of the social totality as something one can never understand and that always eludes one's grasp" (53), he could be describing the random controversies routinely unrolled by English 101.

We should not minimize how much composition has sought to transcend "current-traditional rhetoric," Daniel Fogarty's and Richard E. Young's label for its long devotion to a small set of modes and error-free prose. It has certainly developed wider, more sophisticated notions of rhetoric over the last two decades. While the seventies' preoccupation with process ultimately degenerated into lockstep formulas, it at least opened up a whole universe of considerations besides the surface features of text. The eighties' and nineties' fascination with discourse communities involves serious efforts to view writing in social contexts.

Unfortunately, a squeamishness about worldly matters of power still infuses even leading scholarship in composition, thus handicapping the field's ability to investigate what *cultural studies* and *postmodernism* can denote. This hesitancy even marks composition theorists who have identified themselves with postmodernism or its associated figures. Four theorists in particular have displayed an attenuated sense of history that could unduly channel exploration of the term: Gregory Ulmer, Richard A. Lanham, Louise Wetherbee Phelps, and Kenneth Bruffee.

Ulmer works mostly in literary studies, but he seeks to revise freshman English and has coauthored a composition textbook. He in effect summarizes ways writing classes might operate when he declares, "The postmodernizing of pedagogy is based on the recognition that knowledge in and of the humanities is precisely a knowledge of enframing, of media and *mise en scène* understood not as a representation of something else but as itself a mode of action in the cultural world" (*Applied Grammatology* 183). The composition classroom thus becomes a "textshop" in which students mainly replicate the formally experimental techniques of certain twentieth-century figures: not only other theorists like Jacques Derrida, Roland Barthes, and Jacques Lacan but also artists like Marcel Duchamp, André Breton, Joseph Beuys, and Mary Kelly. In one article, for instance, Ulmer discusses how he has students "produce a fragment of a 'false novel' using the technique of automatic writing" championed by surrealists like Breton, as well as "a modified ready-made sculpture" following the example of Duchamp ("Textshop for Psychoanalysis" 761).

Ulmer deserves credit for suggesting that composition should note developments in the arts, since the field has basically neglected the possibility that the arts might contribute to the study of discourse. He warrants praise, too, for seeking to expand the stylistic repertoire of students at a time when the field is more preoccupied with training them in disciplinary prose. Yet when he insinuates that formal experimentation inevitably aids social revolution, Ulmer avoids probing the actual relation between the two, and thus he misleads students about the effect of "textshop" activities.

When Ulmer continually advocates play as an inherently subversive force—declaring, for example, that the "textshop . . . [is] to the sciences what the carnival once was to the Church" ("Textshop for Post(e)pedagogy" 61)—he ignores that the Church did, after all, keep the carnival in its place.[1] When he proclaims that "textshop teaches surrealism as one of the ideas that changed our view of culture" ("Textshop for Psychoanalysis" 760), he simply dismisses the shifting historical fortunes of the movement. He fails to consider that, as Huyssen points out, the progressive force of surrealism weakened when it was disconnected from large-scale political movements, commercially deployed by mass culture, and merely commemorated in museums. He forgets that even when enlisted in various causes, avant-garde techniques have served different political masters. Benjamin Buchloh traces, for example, the way photomontage was wielded in turn by Russian constructivism, Fascist propaganda, and the American popular-culture industry. Criticizing students for not respecting "the easily recognized influence of surrealist style on the entertainment and advertising industries" ("Textshop for Psychoanalysis" 762), Ulmer himself seems unwilling to recognize that the legacy of Breton has now been appropriated by consumer capitalism. Similarly, his embrace of Duchampian readymades fails to notice that museums now enshrine them as artifacts and that such pieces no longer shock the art world. As Peter Burger observes, "If an artist today signs a stove pipe and exhibits it, that artist certainly does not denounce the art market but adapts to it. . . . Since now the protest of the historical avant-garde against art as institution is accepted as *art*, the gesture of protest of the neo-avant-garde becomes inauthentic" (52–53). Furthermore, even though Ulmer sometimes contextualizes Beuys's work, he slights its ultimate social fate, neglecting its commodification. Kearney notes that "Beuys' so-called 'artless' collages . . . have become, despite the artist's anti-establishment stance, prime cultural assets of the German government and coveted exhibits of major international banks" (375). The *New York Times* reported in 1989 that Christie's auctioned off pieces by Beuys to various collectors for a total of $1.86 million (Reif). None of these trends means that avant-garde art has lost all power to transform society. They simply indicate that any course based on it should consider its troubled history as a "mode of action in the cultural world."

At the end of his key article "The Rhetorical Paideia," Lanham resembles Ulmer in envisioning the humanities curriculum as a work of post-modern art, unstable, unfinished, interactive, not a certified canon of revealed cultural truth but a participatory drama in which the student must take part, a drama which is set on a stage but not set in concrete, with dialogue which is there to revise and a plot which licenses us to collaborate with chance—all these together aiming to teach not only knowledge but the way knowledge is held.

(141)

Lanham's credo here reflects his often-expressed belief that the academy should recognize that human life is "an uneasy balance of three kinds of motive—play, game, and purpose" (133). These motives are affirmed, he thinks, not only in contemporary artistic developments but also in sociobiology, recent social theories, and uses of new technology like the computer. Moreover, as his title indicates, Lanham believes that these motives are embodied by the rhetorical education that persisted in the West for thousands of years.

Lanham's perspective yields significant insights into composition, the chief one being that the field unwisely retains "a common-sense positivism that finds a real world out there, a sincere soul inside all of us, and a prose style that opens a transparent window between the two" (136). In making this diagnosis, he highlights the variety of styles writers use to advance their versions of the world. As with Ulmer, composition teachers following Lanham's views expose their students to a greater range of discursive forms than the field normally honors.

Yet Lanham unfortunately joins Ulmer in depicting history too simplistically. When he affirms postmodern art as a challenge to "revealed cultural truth," he flatly declares a cultural truth of his own and thus, like Ulmer, slights the various functions postmodern art can perform. By emphasizing, along with Ulmer, that we should incorporate play into the curriculum more often, Lanham, too, fails to address its frequently curtailed power to liberate. When he suggests that the computer "is intrinsically a *humanistic* device" because it "draws deeply on all three ranges of human motive, game, play, and purpose, and invites us to capitalize on its almost natural orchestration of them" (140), he brushes aside other, more insidious "capitalizations" on computers that are possible in our competitive information economy.

Lanham's reliance on the history of rhetoric is especially disquieting. Like many other composition scholars today, he reduces thousands of years of rhetorical education to a few simple principles we should now heed. His version of rhetorical history proves susceptible to feminist questioning too. He blithely links his motive of "game" with "the male primate's centripetal gaze" (135). The hegemony of "the male gaze" has, of course, preoccupied feminist film critics like Teresa de Lauretis (*Alice Doesn't*), Laura Mulvey, and Mary Ann Doane, but Lanham simply perpetuates it instead of examining how it can marginalize the perspectives of women. After declaring, "As for the essential primacy of agonistic struggle, of contest, as the central motive, all of rhetorical education is built around it," he observes only parenthetically, "I am of course leaving out half the human race here, all of womankind, but alas so did rhetorical education" (135). These remarks cry out for the sort of critique that Luce Irigaray, for example, gives Freud (see *Speculum*). Like him, Lanham basically takes men as the norm for "human" psychology, as well as for the rhetorical history that supposedly incarnates it. Irigaray's approach would press him to consider the expression of different values in women's lives and the exclusion of women from "agonistic struggles" when they have sought to engage in them. Scholars may come up with various answers, but a curricular model that is frankly androcentric merits serious review.

Phelps's book *Composition as a Human Science: Contributions to the Self-Understanding of a Discipline* announces as its thesis "that composition awakens in the initial moment of its disciplinary project to find itself already situated, prereflectively, within a specific cultural field of meaning—that of postmodern thought, with its characteristic preoccupations and world vision" (3; see also my review of Phelps's book). Phelps then spells out practices that would follow if composition embraced her notion of postmodern thought. She usefully suggests, for example, that composition adopt a view of rationality as dialogic rhetoric; consider human understanding to be "deeply scenic and pragmatic, actively constructive, holistic, structured, and dynamic" (166); try out different perspectives on discourse for different purposes; see rhetorical features like coherence as emerging from the interaction of writer and reader; remember that "[t]eaching teaches writing to developing persons within concrete life situations" (70); and recognize "that Theory and praxis mutually discipline each other" (238).

Despite her many sound observations, though, Phelps lapses even more than Ulmer and Lanham do into a prophetic mode of discourse that slights historical complexity. At one point, she does allude to the "incessant clash of methodologies" (183) that marks composition. Yet in her subtitle linking composition with selfhood, her reference to composition's "awakening," and her further description of the field in other life-cycle metaphors like "adolescent growth" (4), she depicts composition as an organically unified agent of history, thus eliding the differences within it. Indeed, not everyone in composition shares her fondness for hermeneutics, phenomenology, cognitive psychology, and physics. Acknowledging in her preface that she emphasizes certain theorists and omits others, Phelps claims that "[i]n a postmodern culture the writer needs to read what she needs in order to think, to make sense, not in order to know what is fashionable. There can be no canon of theory, any more than of literature" (xii). Yet she ignores the canon she promulgates through her highly selective references, ultimately using it to characterize the whole planet. Her image of the autonomous scholar who can simply overlook rival theories of postmodernism offers no real way to adjudicate them.

More specifically, in narrating the emergence of "postmodern thought," Phelps confines herself to a traditional history of ideas. While she promises "to make the cultural scene manifest" (3), she reduces culture to a monolithic trend in philosophy and science. On this limited basis, she welcomes her version of postmodernism as the outcome of "a fundamental crisis in human consciousness some regard as one of the revolutionary transitions that transform history" (4). In other words, she explains cultural change by focusing on certain academic fields and positing a universal mind that expresses itself similarly within them. Unfortunately, this return to the historicism of Hegel and Lovejoy brackets the material processes at work in the formation of society and thought. Moreover, as with her attribution of selfhood to composition, it minimizes differences within fields. It overlooks, too, the sheer range of social situations and the relations of power that structure them—in Spivak's words, *"the post-modern space-specific subject-production"* (171). Studying these matters would presumably mitigate against outright worship of a postmodern world. To be fair, Phelps does concede in her preface that she has "neglected power and the political dimension of composition and its praxis" (xiii). She then suggests that she could not do otherwise, since "most current frames for discourse" are "uncomfortably masculine" (xiii). Yet she does not go on to explain how "frames for discourse" are intrinsically gendered; she just proceeds with her romanticized, constricted version of the "cultural scene."

While Bruffee does not explicitly focus on postmodernism, he refers to several theorists associated with the term in formulating his enormously influential notion of the social construction of knowledge. Drawing on figures like Rorty, Fish, Thomas Kuhn, and Clifford Geertz, he maintains that a "social constructionist position in any discipline assumes that entities we normally call reality, knowledge, thought, facts, texts, selves, and so on are constructs generated by communities of like-minded peers" ("Social Construction" 774). Admittedly, his view not only encourages collaborative learning in the writing classroom but also spurs composition scholars to investigate the social contexts of discourse. At the same time, however, his concept of social construction unduly narrows the set of questions that ought to mark historical research.

Bruffee ignores the social constructionists' differing visions of the social. In particular, he slights those who probe configurations of power based on gender, race, and class. His 1986 bibliographic essay on social construction omits feminists (out of forty entries, only three are by women), Marxists, African American theorists, Third World theorists, and other analysts of power like Michel Foucault and Pierre Bourdieu. Furthermore, by championing the word *social*, he fails to consider its function in different historical conjunctures. In her recent book *"Am I That Name?"* Denise Riley explains how, in the nineteenth century, the concept of the social enabled middle-class women in England and America to extend the concerns of the domestic sphere into the wider public realm but kept them from actually gaining the franchise, since the political and the social were regarded as separate. Bruffee's constant use of warm, positive words like *communities* and *conversation* also threatens to obscure processes of domination and struggle.[2]

Overall, Bruffee resembles Phelps in focusing on a particular strand within the history of ideas rather than elaborating the complex, mutifaceted history of a broadly defined cultural scene. He warrants the same criticism Cornel West has made of Rorty, whom Bruffee adopts as a mentor: "Rorty's neopragmatism has no place—and rightly so—for ahistoric philosophical justifications, yet his truncated historicism rests content with intellectual and homogeneous historical narratives and distrusts social and heterogeneous genealogical accounts" (208–09). Bruffee exhibits this flaw when he treats Cartesian epistemology as the driving force in world affairs until the twentieth century, holding it responsible for most ills. In his bibliographic essay, he complains that "the way we normally think about our professional work as scholars and teachers derives from the epistemological tradition that every academic field has followed since at least the seventeenth century" (776). Just as Allan Bloom traces all our contemporary vices to Locke and Hobbes, so Bruffee traces the decline of civilization to Descartes—although whereas Bloom's historiography matches his foundationalist claims, Bruffee's positing of a single origin contradicts his professed antifoundationalism. Indeed, a variety of traditions and social forces have affected the constitution of academic fields, including the rise of the research university in the second half of the nineteenth century.

If Bruffee were to modify the supreme causal status he gives to Cartesianism, though, he would undercut another of his moves: deeming Cartesianism inherently repressive and his own liberalism inherently liberatory. Consider his response to critics of his bibliographic essay. Declaring himself one of the "middle-of-the-road or liberal social constructionists," Bruffee decries "the inherent authoritarianism of cognitive thought and its Cartesian faith in the individual"; submits that "for social constructionists, change occurs peacefully through the formation of new communities of knowledgeable peers"; and claims that Marxist references to "struggle" imply "that only violence can make any impact on the way things are" ("Bruffee Responds" 714–15). Whatever the ultimate merits of liberalism, Bruffee needs to recognize the many social theories and the many historical accounts suggesting that change is not always peaceful, no matter how much we would like it to be. At present, he seems to confuse description and prescription. He should realize as well that many theorists who call for struggle are not simply advocating violence; remember Martin Luther King, Jr. Most of all, by insinuating that a proper attention to the social must make one a liberal and that "cognitive thought," along with "Cartesian faith in the individual," is "inherently authoritarian," he simply dodges the hard empirical work needed to substantiate such inferences—work that again requires precise analysis of shifting historical conditions.

When Bruffee ultimately foregrounds disciplinary knowledge in the name of social construction, he begs other questions. In his famous essay "Collaborative Learning and the 'Conversation of Mankind' " he asserts:

> Much of what we teach today—or should be teaching—in composition courses is the normal discourse of most academic, professional, and business communities. The rhetoric taught in our composition textbooks comprises—or should comprise—the conventions of normal discourse of those communities.
>
> (643)

Bruffee derives his notion of normal and abnormal discourse from Rorty, who in turn is inspired by Kuhn's distinction between normal and revolutionary science. Rorty defines normal discourse as "that which is conducted within an agreed-upon set of conventions about what counts as a relevant contribution, what counts as answering a question, what counts as having a good argument for that answer or a good criticism of it." Abnormal discourse, however, "is what happens when someone joins in the discourse who is ignorant of these conventions or who sets them aside" (*Philosophy* 320). Rorty goes on to note that intellectual fields exhibit normal discourse at certain times and abnormal discourse at others. Bruffee's essay also briefly acknowledges that the term *normal discourse* might not always apply to a given field: he writes, "In contrast to normal discourse, abnormal discourse occurs between coherent communities or within communities when consensus no longer operates with regard to rules, assumptions, goals, values, or mores" (648). Yet in his statement of goals for composition and through much of the article, Bruffee suggests that most disciplines and professions always display normal discourse. He does not posit varying degrees of normality among them, nor does he anatomize their current discourses to verify his claim. He seriously misrepresents his own discipline of English, I believe, when he identifies deconstructive criticism as one of "the tools of normal discourse" (648). Many English teachers still resist that approach, deeming it a symptom of corruption. By minimizing the way conflicts like this beset fields, Bruffee seems to advocate "normalizing" discourse for administrative convenience.[3]

Bruffee's emphasis on normal discourse is misleading as well in its suggestion that academic fields have remained distinct from one another, their purity intact. He does not position students to analyze the border crossings that he, for one, undertakes when he borrows concepts from a host of disciplines. He also fails to probe the academy's political relation to the larger world. Indeed, after theorizing the aims of education, he falls back on the crass practicality of giving teachers what they want:

> Teaching normal discourse in its written form is central to a college curriculum
> . . . because one thing college teachers in most fields commonly want students
> to acquire, and what teachers in most fields consistently reward students for,
> is the ability to carry on in speech and writing the normal discourse of the
> field in question.
>
> (643)

Not only does he thus sidestep the issue of how unified in their conventions particular fields are, he also resurrects composition's service ethos with a vengeance, leaving the social effect of disciplinary behavior unchallenged and, indeed, unexamined. Another of West's criticisms of Rorty applies here:

> After the philosophical smoke clears, the crucial task is to pursue social and
> heterogeneous genealogies, that is, detailed accounts for the emergence, de-
> velopment, sustenance, and decline of vocabularies, discourses, and (non-dis-
> cursive) practices in the natural and human sciences against the background
> of dynamic changes in specific (and often coexisting) modes of production,
> potential conflicts, cultural configurations, and personal turmoil.
>
> (208)

If composition teachers and students launched such an inquiry, they clearly would not discount the importance of disciplinary discourse but would place it in a wider context than Bruffee stresses and would evaluate its worth more carefully than he does. Presumably they would consult not only him but also those who have extensively studied intellectuals' demographic backgrounds, class positions, cultural power, and ideological investments. I have in mind scholars like West, Foucault, Williams, Ohmann, Spivak, Pierre Bourdieu, Antonio Gramsci, Louis Althusser, Edward Said, Frank Lentricchia, Jim Merod, Paul Bové, and the thousands who have developed programs in minority and women's studies.

I use multiple references to emphasize the variety of considerations we should face and the many conceptual resources we should draw on when applying notions of cultural studies and postmodernism to composition pro- grams. The four theorists I have discussed raise issues provoked by these terms but choke off the investigation of social dynamics and the review of social theories they should also elicit. They thus reinforce composition's disinclination to stray much beyond its traditional horizons. Yet even though I encourage composition programs to dwell on the points I have made, I want to reiterate the value of delaying firm conclusions about cultural studies and postmodernism, given the varying perspectives at work in current elaborations of the terms. Again, the task is not to develop a program based on premature resolution of the issues they have generated but to make investigation of these issues the program's ongoing project.

The Composition Student as Theorist of Cultural Studies and Postmodernism

As I have said, the project should involve students as coinquirers into the ramifications of cultural studies and postmodernism. I focus on students' roles because composition programs—and, indeed, the academy in general—often regard them as would-be consumers of previously formulated wisdom. Although composition teachers may fear that the issues I have mentioned will discompose their students, traditional composition pedagogy can also strike students as incoherent. Moreover, they may hunger for genuine intellectual substance. True literacy means examining one's society, not simply manipulating surface features of text. Any composition program must, nevertheless, acknowledge its students' current levels of understanding.

Certainly program faculty members must decide what reading and writing their students can handle before they include students in this sort of inquiry. Some students can comprehend an article by Jameson; others navigate it with a teacher's nudging translations; still others depend on a summary of its points. Although theorists of cultural studies and postmodernism often write formidably, students can produce various kinds of discourse in sharing these scholars' concerns. Since the two terms raise questions about the political significance of play and pastiche, students might satirize the languages of various cultural phenomena and then consider what leverage they have gained. Teachers who want their students to engage first in personal, expressive writing may feel inspired by the attention to daily life that theorists of cultural studies and postmodernism have shown. No matter how arcane their vocabularies, these theorists have probed what it means to lead a concrete existence in the contemporary world—what it means to experience the influence of the media, the lure of commodities, the pressures of schooling, the limits of a certain social status, the virtues and illusions of theories themselves. Of course, teachers may have to encourage students to see how their personal narratives tie into larger geopolitical conditions. In particular, students may need help recognizing that autobiographies can differ with shifts in gender, race, class, sexual preference, and nation.

Students' stories can be woven into and contextualized through peer review groups and larger class discussions. Yet students can also benefit from relating their research into cultural studies and postmodernism to the whole composition program. The process involves forging connections among the program's individual classes through such activities as team teaching, joint section meetings, program colloquia, letters between classes, and even program publications. If the literature camp is willing to join in, so much the better. Through such a collective endeavor, students may find composition not a distressing trial of the self but a stimulating exploration of global forces. The series of exchanges may also help counteract an unfortunate habit of contemporary theorists: the tendency to fix on a narrow cluster of precepts and consecrate them as dogma. Most of all, the exchanges can help composition become what it deserves to become: not a plodding servant of other disciplines but a key force in the diagnosis of the contemporary world.

NOTES

[1]For another critique of Ulmer, emphasizing the limits of his "politics of pleasure," see Zavarzadeh.

[2]In his article "The Idea of Community in the Study of Writing," Joseph Harris explains how other terms might serve better than *community* to designate particular social interactions. See also Patricia Bizzell's essay in this volume.

[3]For other critiques of Bruffee's insistence on consensus see Myers; Smit; Trimbur, "Consensus."

Reimagining the Writing Scene: Curmudgeonly Remarks about Contending with Words

Sharon Crowley

HISTORICALLY, composition studies has entertained only two theoretical controversies that substantially altered the teaching of writing. In one early controversy, just after the turn of the century, teachers argued about whether required composition courses should equip students with practical writing skills or introduce them to the finer things in life (see Berlin, *Rhetoric and Reality* 35–51). Never satisfactorily resolved, this debate still affects the design of composition programs, which waver uneasily between courses introducing students to good reading on the one hand and skills-and-drills approaches to grammar, mechanics, and the modes of discourse on the other.

In the late sixties, a second controversy focused on whether writing should be taught as a process or a product (see, e.g., Murray, "Teach Writing"). This argument, also still alive, is reflected in textbooks or course syllabi that feature a few heuristic exercises alongside prescriptions for producing formally correct compositions.

Although informed teachers may have altered their classroom practices or taken sides as a result of reading or hearing about either controversy, they were not required to change the way they conceived the scene of teaching writing. Since its beginning, composition studies has imagined this scene as an isolated, insulated classroom containing a teacher who administered and graded writing assignments and a group of students who carried out the assignments. In this imaginary scenario, teachers and students worked together to achieve a common goal: improving the students' ability to read and write.

But this communal and harmonious picture just doesn't wash in a postmodern age. The scene of teaching described in *Contending with Words* is immeasurably more complex and considerably less naive. Its site is still the composition classroom. But this room is populated by persons who may not be able to work in harmony, since they inevitably bring with them the patriarchal, racist, or classist discourses of the dominant culture—unless, of course, they identify primarily with one or another minority culture. As a result, they may not always speak (if they speak at all) in mutually constructive terms. The composition classroom imagined in these essays is located within and penetrated by the social, institutional, and cultural contexts that surround it and that dictate how we define and carry on the practice of teaching.

Contending with Words also reimagines composition teachers. They are no longer people conscripted into teaching writing, who, as a result, know nothing about it. This view is indisputably portrayed in popular collections of essays on teaching composition, such as those edited by Gary Tate and Edward P. J. Corbett or by Richard L. Graves. The common and obvious object of these collections is to describe and hence to influence teaching practice. They feature sections on style and the sentence or on motivating student writers. They introduce teachers of writing to the traditional vocabulary associated with their craft—commonplaces, paragraphs, revision strategies, rhetorical stance, writing as a process.

The authors in *Contending with Words*, however, do not imagine their readers as teachers who need to catch up on the latest teaching techniques. Instead, these teachers are on top of the practical game, and they are also conversant with a wide range of theoretical discourses. They still enjoy relative authority within the classroom setting, but they assume this authority uneasily, knowing that it has been conferred on them by an institution whose hierarchical structure marginalizes them and their profession, as well as their students and their students' work.

In other words, the essays collected here demand, more or less explicitly, that composition teachers change the ways in which they imagine their role as teachers. Specifically, these authors expect composition teachers to redirect their goals; to examine the political commitments they bring to their teaching; to reject much of what now passes for composition theory; and to learn to tolerate ambiguity, variety, and conflict instead of valuing clarity, identity, and harmony.

These are tall orders.

All the writers in this collection take their starting points from theory. Some ask us to examine this or that theory of discourse on its own merits and hint at some of its classroom applications (as Bizzell or Herzberg do, for example). Others use theory to throw new light on established practices (Jarratt and Covino). Two authors (Harkin and Vitanza) question the relation of theory to practice.

Patricia Harkin rejects the distinction between theory and practice, partly because contemporary theory authorizes her to do so and probably because she is tired (as I am) of being on the underside of the status hierarchy that relegates "practitioners" (i.e., teachers of composition) to the basement of the liberal arts building. Whatever her motivation, Harkin wants to develop a flexible model of practice that incorporates—and celebrates—teacher lore. Thus, she distinguishes lore as theory from disciplinarity, which is a set of "rules of knowledge production." She characterizes the practical experience of composition teachers as a way into theory, arguing that since they regularly forage among the discourses of linguistics, sociology, ethics, rhetoric, politics, and so on, composition teachers are uniquely situated to develop flexible strategies for both knowing and doing. (I add the curmudgeonly observation that their immediately proximate colleagues, who for political reasons are more tightly bound to disciplinarity, are not so situated). Harkin's charming scenario, depicting an "Oprah cum Elbow" television show of the future, testifies to the inventive potential that is resident in the yoking of practice to theory.

Harkin's celebration of theory-lore implicitly recommends enormously eclectic learning for composition teachers, a view John Schilb shares. He argues that composition studies is an appropriate site in which to formulate, test, and evaluate theory, since "the field currently comprises diverse topics and methods, with ties to numerous disciplines." This position assumes, of course, that composition teachers can easily take time and energy away from reading students' papers to read the theoretical conversations going on among university-level compositionists. Indeed, both Schilb and Harkin suggest that composition teachers need to become scholarly *bricoleurs*. While I, too, hope that writing teachers can saturate their practice with theory every time they meet a class, the material conditions surrounding the teaching of composition in most universities and colleges must undergo substantial reform before we can dream such a dream.

Nevertheless, compositionists must hold the image of the writing teacher as foraging scholar firmly in view, for a couple of reasons. First, we'll never get writing teachers out of the basement without using such an image (unless we can somehow undercut the privilege accorded to theory in the academy). Second, for the first time in our history, the eclecticism that composition teachers have always practiced now redounds to our credit. Schilb alludes to a notorious fact of composition's history: because composition cheerfully operates without a founding theory, it has never generated a readily identifiable discipline (see Crowley). It made no founding disciplinary gesture, allowing composition teachers to borrow freely from any body of thought with enough prominence to be plundered for lesson plans. By virtue of our seedy institutional past, then, compositionists have always been comfortable exploring far-flung disciplinary arenas. But today a qualitative difference exists in that now our habitual eclecticism also enhances our professional prospects.

Certainly the writers in this volume don't apologize for being inclusive. They exploit, willy-nilly, French and American feminisms, literary theory, neo-Marxisms, sociology, various new pragmatisms, and a variety of post-structuralisms. Composition teachers who seek a unified theory of literacy (and there are some) are bound to be disappointed by this valorization of our historic tendency to bounce all over the disciplinary map.

But, as Victor Vitanza argues in his first counterthesis, to hope for a single legitimizing ground of knowledge is to risk entangling ourselves and our students in a hegemonic discourse that "only enslaves and impoverishes." Like Harkin, he understands that a given disciplinary way of seeing may both enable and blind. I suspect that Vitanza is especially sensitive to the hegemony of dominant discourses because he is a versatile theorist working within a practice-oriented field. As a consequence, his work displays a certain cynicism about the composition establishment, which rewrites or simply resists theories that threaten its preservation instead of foraging through them in an effort to rethink itself and its potential complicity with traditional academic values. The composition establishment certainly ought to pay attention to Vitanza, since his subversive project amounts to nothing less than rewriting the history of rhetoric and composition.

Composition theory has traditionally borrowed from classical or modern rhetoric to describe writing situations and from cognitive or Rogerian or association psychology to describe the composing process. But the authors in *Contending with Words* are not interested in traditional rhetorics or in psychology. They mention classical rhetoric only to rewrite it (as Covino does with the classical notion of ethos, for example). The subtitle of this collection is *Composition and Rhetoric in a Postmodern Age*, but readers who believe that their teaching practices should be informed by postmodern theories of discourse must face a hard fact: postmodern rhetorical theories question the validity of the very concepts with which traditional rhetorics began—author, intention, purpose, audience, message, common grounds, and so forth.

As I have said, Vitanza looks this necessity squarely in the face. But most of us—and even some of the authors in this collection—have not fully realized the enormity of the project. Don Bialostosky, for example, wants to salvage the notion of voice by tempering it with Mikhail Bakhtin's theory of discursive multivocality. This reconstituted version of voice, however, may not stand up to postmodern critiques that modify or reject altogether the traditional concept of the authoring subject as a sovereign individual working alone, isolated from and superior to culture or history. As Bruce Herzberg notes in his discussion of Foucauldian epistemology, such critiques "must lead us, therefore, to question many of the available ways for representing the source and purpose of writing to students—that the source of writing is the self, one's voice, experience, or observations" (see also Vitanza's second counterthesis).

In other words, postmodern composition theory rejects the model of authoring found in modern psychology, philosophy, and traditional composition theory. Rather, postmodern theories of discourse represent any writer as "the site of contradiction, as being written by social or psychological forces that might diminish the clarity of consciousness or the singularity of individual intentions" (Clifford). In short, composition theory must rewrite its notion of authors as integral, autonomous, individual selves and substitute instead the notion of collective but shifting "subject positions" that contemporary feminist and neo-Marxist discourses adumbrate.

If we are to rewrite composition theory for a postmodern age, we must also stand ready to dismiss the work of composition theorists who confine their thinking to traditional rhetoric or psychology. Their work seems too idealizing, too generalizing, too totalizing to be useful to postmodern teachers. Many of us may find it difficult to accept the necessity of revising our canon, since our embattled professional status has imbued us with a fierce sense of protectiveness toward our own. Even though we admit to one another in private that we think a colleague's recent work is hopelessly old-fashioned, off the mark, self-serving, or worse, we have generally been reluctant to take one another on in print. Nonetheless, some of the authors represented in *Contending with Words* have, however gently, breached the decorous professional walls that ordinarily shelter one compositionist's work from attack by another.

For example, Ann E. Berthoff, Louise Wetherbee Phelps, and David Bartholomae are singled out for commentary in these pages because their work is regarded as insufficiently responsive to cultural contexts. Since Berthoff and Phelps attempt to philosophize composition in their signature works, it is not surprising that their efforts are depicted in these pages as counterproductive to postmodern agendas. That Bartholomae is characterized here as a "bad guy" is a bit more curious, because his theoretical impetus derives precisely from his poststructural suspicion of individual authority.

Indeed, Bialostosky admires Bartholomae's acknowledgment that "the presence of the 'already written' " can "stand in defiance of a writer's desire for originality and determine what might be said." Noting the authority of already written voices, Bialostosky (implicating Bartholomae by proximity) admits that "[o]ur only choice, if we wish to participate in the writing they empower, is to move inside them and assume the position of privilege they grant us." I am not sure, however, that this solution—giving students access to the assumed privilege enjoyed by academic discourse—stands up to the criticisms of privileged discourse that other writers in this collection make.

If we accept John Clifford's argument, Bartholomae's notion of "academic community" has insidious overtones in the context of writing instruction. Clifford writes:

> The teaching of writing is inevitably an ideological act and thereby one part of any culture's attempt to reproduce itself, both intellectually and economically, by creating accommodating students who are eager to fill designated positions of influence within various institutional landscapes.

If we endorse this idea, we must also accept that composition teachers who subscribe to wish-fulfillment notions of community are locally complicit in the reproduction of the dominant ideology. Such teachers cover over the disruptive and alienating forces that daily affect their students' lives, both in and out of class, with an image of democratic harmony.

Patricia Bizzell, however, is discomfited by the element of patronage that resides in the notion of academic discourse, since this genre marks out a position of privilege for the writing teacher, whose "professional expertise smooths the way for students and manages their introduction to academe."

Bartholomae's attractive vision of the composition classroom as a temporary refuge—where students can heal their wounds and learn to cope with an undemocratic and abusive outside world—is open to question, then, not least because the notion of academic community is a comforting distortion. Several authors in *Contending with Words* readily admit that writing classrooms are not sites of harmony and community. Indeed, themes of struggle, strife, and conflict echo throughout the collection, and the title of this volume underscores their appropriateness. Whether we like it or not, the alienating conflicts that exist in our culture surround and infiltrate our writing classrooms.

In short, Bartholomae sins because his vision of community, however well intentioned, just doesn't jibe with our experience as teachers. Nor does it make good theoretical sense from a postmodern point of view. Vitanza resists altogether the assumption that discourses, academic or otherwise, have insuperable boundaries that demarcate and separate insiders from outsiders.

Furthermore, Bartholomae's work is just too damn liberal to suit the more radical authors in this collection. For the first time since the thirties (and a brief moment in the early seventies), influential voices are being raised from the radical left of composition studies. If my readers doubt this, I suggest that they make a list of the theorists whose work energizes these essays (for starters: Althusser, Bakhtin, Burke, Cixous, Freire, Giroux, Irigaray, Spivak). The work of radical compositionists poses major difficulties for mainstream composition theory, since the very project adumbrated within the mainstream is suffused with liberalism.[1] Composition teachers try to improve their students' levels of literacy or to inculcate literacy in students who do not possess it at all. They profess many reasons for trying to accomplish these goals, but most of the reasons reflect the belief that literacy helps students cope with a variety of obstacles in life after composition. Whatever else we may say about this hope, it indubitably smacks of liberal social agendas, which ordinarily try to right the immediate wrong without analyzing the more powerful, hidden relations that produce it.

Composition teachers' habitual liberalism surfaces now and again in this collection. No doubt unfairly, I choose William Covino's wonderful essay on magic and rhetoric to demonstrate the point. Composition teachers, including Covino, treat literacy as though it were truly magic. We believe—hope— that inoculation with literacy will somehow solve this country's social problems.[2] I am not sure that this hope differs substantially from the hopes entertained by readers of the *National Enquirer*. According to Covino, *Enquirer* readers look for authoritative and noncomplex solutions to the daily social difficulties they face, difficulties imposed on them partly or wholly by the sexism and classism embedded in our capitalist economy. I wonder if Covino thinks that *Enquirer* readers who believe in its magic, albeit a false magic, are responding inappropriately to their social and economic circumstances.[3] I want to ask further if their achievement of literacy—Burke's "true magic" that suspends the laws of motion, that creates "everything out of nothing" —enables them to change these circumstances.

We composition teachers can criticize mass culture, sure enough, and we can deplore nonreflective acceptance of the quack nostrums and quick fixes purveyed within it. But I'm not sure that our magic is any more powerful than the *Enquirer*'s—or more comforting, for that matter, to anyone except ourselves. If the history of literacy education has anything to teach us, it is that people learn to read and write only if they have some compelling economic or social reason to do so (see Pattison). Our professional history constitutes a large part of this country's efforts to help relatively privileged members of the culture to achieve higher levels of literacy. The more reflective among us readily admit that we have not always met with unqualified success in this effort. One reason for this difficulty no doubt has to do with our failure to ask ourselves why students resist our efforts to invest them with our version of "true magic."

Since most of us are liberals, we may also fail to ask in whose service we perform our magic. As Lynn Worsham observes, too often the drive to instill literacy in those who are supposedly without it only reinforces "the power of those already in a position to order and give meaning to the social world." Could it be that we invest literacy with more liberatory potency than it actually has? Could it be that we purvey a model of literacy that has a great deal more to do with our wishes and hopes and professional successes than it does with our students' wishes and hopes and needs? And could it be that by insisting on literacy as a means of liberation we are masking our profound complicity with the status quo? *Contending with Words* raises these questions, and I don't think that any of them will go away in the foreseeable future.

Some of the radical compositionists represented here do lay down specific agendas for literacy education. Clifford disappoints only a little when he posits that "writers seem better poised to understand their intellectual and psychological possibilities in institutions." But Bizzell imagines two uses for critical literacy: developing a critique of the dominant ideology and recovering discourses that have been excluded from academic conversation. Both writers would put literacy to work with the specific goal of effecting social change. Clifford urges teachers to study and practice writing with their students "in a rich sociopolitical context." Doing so, he argues, "can open spaces for the kind of informed resistance that can actually affect hegemonic structures." Bizzell is confident that the development of critical consciousness will help us all to understand "broader patterns of domination" and to imagine ways in which to resist that domination—a project that she admits is utopian.

Bizzell and Clifford, then, advocate two goals that writing teachers should adopt. First, we should alert students to the ways in which a dominant discourse affirms its dominance and thus retains hegemony over those discourses it defines as nonprivileged or secondary or unimportant or dismissible. Second, we should equip students with means of resisting this hegemony. Bizzell suggests that we can carry out this second project by awarding privilege, in the writing classroom at least, to nondominant discourses—by foregrounding, for instance, the language used by women and members of cultural minorities.

Because nearly every student who enters an American college or university is required to take a composition course, this project indeed has potential for bringing about social reform.[4] However, because composition students are in some sense our captives, we must give up our traditional subscription to liberal tolerance if we are to bring about social change through them. We must also admit that we enact our own hegemonic desire when we use the required composition course to teach our preferred politics.

Of course, teachers everywhere have always used their courses to do exactly that. Historically, the required composition course has usually been yoked into the service of dominant discourses. But never before has it been so persuasively evoked as a site where minority discourses could be liberated, much less celebrated or even utilized as a means of dislodging discursive structures that are less than just to all peoples.

It remains to be seen whether or not freshman composition can be radicalized in the service of social justice. Some of us seem willing to try.

NOTES

[1]I except from this generalization those composition teachers who define their task as forcing students' writing to conform to ideal standards. Conservative prescriptivism has been as central to the history of composition instruction as has the liberalism I discuss in the text.

[2]I can't resist comparing our liberal hopes for literacy to the false magic reflected in the "Just Say No" campaign. Proponents of this willfully ignorant and arrogant policy seem to think that "just saying no" can protect an eight-year-old ghetto child from the horrors of drug trafficking. "Just Say No" is a means of deflecting attention from the social realities that condemn certain Americans to ignorance, poverty, brutality, and early death. To their credit, some composition teachers' hopes for literacy do not ignore these realities. See, for example, Cooper and Holzman; Rose.

[3]Michael Holzman notes that many Americans

live in a world that is at once magical and violent. The violence is real. . . . The world they see on television and in the movies, is magical in a pernicious way. In that magical world things are not connected. One day you are a typical high-school student, the next you have a contract from a professional football team. There is a link between television magic and street violence, a link that makes the magic in a sense believable. . . . [I]n [the] everyday world the transitions are television-sudden if always negative. One day you are a typical high-school student, the next you are dead.

("Teaching" 226–27)

[4]This project is not entirely new, of course. As Jarratt implies, the older Sophists were up to something similar in fifth-century Athens. Circuitously enough, they called themselves "rhetoricians." In different ways, both postmodern and sophistic rhetorics yield a useful insight: where physical coercion is not in use, social change comes about by means of the manipulation and circulation of discourse.

Postmodern Teachers in Their Postmodern Classrooms: Socrates Begone!

❖

James J. Sosnoski

WHEN I was asked to write a response to *Contending with Words*, I read the essays collected in this volume, taking notes that would have led to a predictable commentary. Because of my investment as a postmodern critic, I intended to contest various interpretations of postmodernism. My work on this project was interrupted, however, and those notes never reached draft form. By the time I returned to *Contending with Words*, I found myself reading it from a very different point of view. A memo requesting a list of my textbooks for the following semester had intervened, and I could not help reading these essays in the light of designing my next semester's composition course.

I reread *Contending with Words* intending to be a postmodern teacher in a postmodern classroom. Thus, I had to ask myself several pointed questions:[1] What would the aim of the course be? Would it have an aim? How would I relate to my students? Should I have a syllabus? What writing assignments should I give? How should I grade them? I began thinking about the introductory material I usually hand out on the first day of class: a statement about the course objectives, a list of writing assignments, a syllabus, and a description of the course requirements and my grading procedures.

Instantly, I found myself in a dilemma. Could I turn anything I had read into a pedagogy? Victor Vitanza's third counterthesis includes the statement that "theory . . . cannot help as a resource." Even more pointedly, he recommends "a moratorium on attempting to turn theory into praxis/pedagogy." Similarly, Lynn Worsham maintains that once postmodern discourse becomes a pedagogy, it is neutralized. Though not all the writers in the volume agree with this view of postmodern theory, I felt that I had to deal with it. That institutions appropriate critiques directed at them is an axiom of postmodern thought.[2] In the light of this axiom, doesn't Bruce Herzberg appropriate Michel Foucault and doesn't Don Bialostosky appropriate Mikhail Bakhtin in the way Worsham says Clara Juncker and Robert de Beaugrande domesticate Hélène Cixous and Luce Irigaray? According to Vitanza, are Herzberg and Bialostosky not implicated in "the politics (really, the *terrorism*) of theory (totality) made into (a) pedagogy founded on capitalism and consumerism as well as on socialism and consensus"? Or, I thought, was I not, in Worsham's terms, "trivializing" postmodern thought in postulating a postmodern pedagogy? Since my own impulse matched Herzberg's and Bialostosky's, I felt compelled to answer Vitanza's and Worsham's challenge before I proceeded in designing my next semester's English 111.

Both Vitanza and Worsham distinguish between theory as a form of metacommentary and parallel postmodern discourses that resist becoming theories. In their writings, the word *theory* refers to a modernist notion of an explanatory metacommentary. At the same time, both draw on generalizations about cultural practices from the works of Cixous, Irigaray, Jean-François Lyotard, Gilles Deleuze and Félix Guattari, and others. Customarily, such generalizations get called "theory." To clarify this ambiguity, I typically distinguish (modern) theory from (postmodern) theorizing.[3] Theories, in the modern sense, are paradigmatic explanations of natural phenomena on which predictions can be based. Thus, the explanation becomes a metadiscourse in its relation to the ways what it explains is talked about. Postmodern theorizing is not "meta" to other discourses. It cannot be turned into a pedagogy that, in explaining how students learn, prescribes how teachers should teach. Like other teachers, I want to base my teaching on an understanding of what my students need to learn about writing. Since postmodern thinkers have much to say about writing, I borrow whatever allows me to anticipate the needs of students. However, I have little interest in a total, unified theory that I can apply to my situation. Nor do I regard the content of a writing course as "information" that I can teach, that is, reproduce (see Vitanza's third counterthesis). My effort is entirely ad hoc, localized, and multivalent because it attempts to reduce the painful situations in which inarticulate students find themselves. My strategy may suggest parallel strategies for parallel situations. If so, that does not make it a unified, totalizing pedagogy that claims explanatory power. What follows is tactical and strategic.

I doubt that either Vitanza or Worsham will be happy with my answer to their challenge. Vitanza will doubtless accuse me of "theory hope," which leads to "pedagogy hope," and Worsham will doubtless warn me against making an assignment based on *écriture féminine*. Finally, as Wittgenstein says, I will run out of answers. My bottom line is that persons are not equivalent to ideas about persons. The "theories" of Julia Kristeva, Louis Althusser, Lyotard, Cixous—if they mean anything at all—are valuable as hypothetical notions about problems that affect persons.[4] I am not concerned with Kristeva's or Lyotard's or any postmodern thinker's authorship of a discourse, their "author(ity)" over it. I readily distort their ideas in my own discourse.[5] The students to whom I must speak next semester author my pedagogical discourse, or, in more accurate terms, they make me beg, borrow, and steal specific articulations in a manner that matches Patricia Harkin's delineation of the postdisciplinary politics of lore. In other words, rather than take *écriture féminine* as a discourse founded by Cixous and developed by other French feminists, I take it as French "lore." It is of interest to me only if it can be transported into my situation. In short, I am not concerned with protecting the "integrity" of a theory. Protecting theory from the classroom seems to me a very unpostmodern attitude. Why protect theory? To insulate it from the contamination of persons?

In appropriating *écriture féminine* into my course (much in the manner of Juncker et al.), I normalize it. What I refuse to do is maintain a once-powerful counterhegemonic discourse in its original radical form. I refuse, that is, to romanticize the radical. Is radicality timeless? My position is that radical critiques must be domesticated (in the sense of denominalized, made credible) to effect change.[6] I risk a metaphor here: rather than tear down old buildings to make way for new ones, I advocate rebuilding them entirely, piece by piece, in a local and ad hoc manner, starting with windows, doors, and stairways linking rooms and creating paths.[7] If remodeling persists, at some point it becomes rebuilding. With respect to universities, I advocate rebuilding through total and continuous piecemeal remodeling.[8] For example, English 111 as I taught it last year changes to the extent that I import and therefore domesticate the ideas of others. Granted, if I alter my course in a way that bears no relation to what other intellectuals are doing, the program (building) will likely remain the same because changes I make by myself are miniscule. If the program remains the same, so does the department and the university. However, if many courses change in parallel ways, programs change, departments change, and so on.

New Criticism is a historical instance of a ground swell that transformed the character of English departments across the country. The essays in this volume, which focus on the implications of postmodern thought for the teaching of composition, could inaugurate a similar ground swell. Though the authors disagree considerably, they share many concerns. On the one hand, they differ widely (as did the early proponents of New Criticism) in their motives and strategies for rethinking composition studies. On the other, they seem to agree on the general aims of teaching composition.

The Aims of Composition Programs and Courses

The general agreement among the essayists comes largely from a shared dissatisfaction with the conduct of composition studies. All the essayists— each uniquely influenced by postmodern thought—find fault with composition's continuing reliance on traditional modernist assumptions. John Schilb emphatically argues that composition needs to overcome its modernist heritage, pointing out that "modernism as a historical force . . . encouraged a certain conception of the field," a conception tied to the ideals of disciplinarity, the hallmark of modern culture. Quoting Richard Lanham, Schilb notes that composition studies "unwisely retains 'a common-sense positivism that finds a real world out there, a sincere soul inside all of us, and a prose style that opens a transparent window between the two.' " For similar reasons, the other writers in this volume complain that composition studies lacks alternatives to disciplinary discourse and argue that composition pedagogy must include such alternatives. In Schilb's words, proponents of this idea seek "to expand the stylistic repertoire of students at a time when the field is more preoccupied with training them in disciplinary prose," which Kenneth Bruffee describes as "the normal discourse of most academic, professional, and business communities."

Postmodern critiques of disciplinary discourse have shown the limitations of totalizing paradigms, metanarratives, metacommentaries, binary thinking, the logic of consistency, wholeness, integrity, centeredness, and unity, thus casting doubt, as Schilb says, on "the relevance of traditional texts and pedagogies."[9] Aware of these doubts, each writer redefines the subject matter of the traditional composition course. I focus for the moment on Vitanza's three countertheses, Herzberg's Foucauldian redefinition of rhetoric, and Harkin's notion of a postdiscipline.

Vitanza directs his three countertheses at the hold that disciplinarity has over composition studies. In opposing the "will to systematize (the) language (of composing)," he strikes at the ideal of "systemacity" that channels mere study into a discipline (Toulmin 379). He raises the question of whether composition studies can legitimate or ground its knowledge (methodologically) on some universal law or (rhetorically) on a consensus. His thesis is that the systematic logic that legitimates knowledge in the sciences cannot be a basis for a "discipline" of composition. Vitanza's second counterthesis critiques disciplinarity from a more sociohistorical point of view. In opposing the "will to be its author(ity)," he strikes at the author(ity)-power relation that maintains and regulates a modern institution through discipline (Foucault, *Discipline*). Knowledge to be accepted as knowledge has to be authorized by the institution that produces it. Hence, authorization processes control what we consider to be knowledge. Accordingly, traditional composition theories understand language to be governed by the "speaking subject." This premise establishes the "authoritarianism" of the author and, thus, "disciplines" the way these theories view communication. Although Vitanza's third counterthesis is troubling, I agree with its counterdisciplinary implications if not with the view of theory it presupposes. In opposing the "will to teach [knowledge] to students" as a means of "control," Vitanza strikes at the kind of ideological apparatuses that position students as subjects (see the essays by Clifford; Bizzell; Jarratt). Disciplines reproduce themselves through dissemination. Thus, to teach composition is to form a subject, not only in the sense of a subject matter but also in the sense of a subject materialized in students. Or, in more familiar terms, students become the subjects they study. In subjecting themselves to the subject of chemistry, students become chemists. Similarly, programs in composition make students into disciplined writers by subjecting them to its discipline. In short, the disciplinary mechanisms that humanists have borrowed from the sciences (like cognitive psychology) in the name of rationality are instruments of social control.

I believe that most of the essayists in this volume would agree with some version of these three countertheses. Correlatively, the concerns of most of the writers in this volume presuppose Herzberg's postdisciplinary redefinition of rhetoric.

Herzberg begins his essay with Foucault's discussion of the two decisive moments in the history of discourse: the defeat of the Sophists which was associated with Plato, and

> the decisive change in the nature of "true" discourse in the eighteenth century. It was then, he [Foucault] says, that the magical quality of language was dispelled and the essential similitude between signs and their referents was disrupted. . . . Discourse began to disappear or become invisible, its workings hidden by new relations of knowledge that placed truth outside language.

Herzberg points out that

> after Plato, after philosophy defeated sophistry, truth is "displaced" from the social to the ideal. The proper role of discourse in Plato's scheme is to represent truth. The truth is to be found, not created.

This view of language is the foundation of our modern world, which is structured by its disciplinarity. Knowledge production is a discipline required by the "will to truth" through which subjects objectify themselves. Subjectivity is to be curbed. Discourse aspires to the condition of truth. Rhetoric is everything that is not truthful.

Postmodern thinkers have turned this view on its head (hence the interest in sophistic thought in this volume). Herzberg quotes Edward Said's summary of this turnabout: "the will to exercise dominant control in society and history has also discovered a way to clothe, disguise, rarefy, and wrap itself systematically in the language of truth, discipline, rationality, utilitarian value, and knowledge." In short, "truth is a rhetorical construction." The implications for redefining the "subject matter" of rhetoric courses are clear.[10] A postmodern view of discourse

> embarrasses the notion that writing is the mastery of a skill, albeit a skill that may be applied to the work of knowledge. It must lead us, therefore, to question many of the available ways for representing the source and purpose of writing to students—that the source of writing is the self, one's voice, experience, or observations; that writing represents truth, describes reality, or communicates ideas.

A postmodern view of discourse redefines the subject matter of any course in rhetoric. It also invites us to abandon the notion that rhetoric is merely a servant.

The redefinition of rhetoric in this volume gives the study of writing and reading a new status within the university as a postdiscipline. Borrowing from Stephen North, Harkin describes this new but still inchoate postdiscipline. It is available to us now only as "lore," which, if understood as potentially theoretical, is the basis of a much richer understanding of the complexities of language instruction. The potential for developing nondisciplinary ways of knowing, Harkin argues, is a political issue that has been blocked by the restrictive demand that university studies be disciplinary. She calls for a new agenda that admits lore as the theoretical basis of rhetorical study.

Harkin's essay implies that claims touting rhetoric as a new discipline miss the mark and relegate rhetorical study to the basement of disciplinarity. "Lore," she writes, "is nondisciplinary: it is actually defined by its inattention to disciplinary procedures." Consequently, it is usually regarded as unreliable, even though it is "what practitioners do." Lore is the record of what happens unofficially in practice most of the time. Theoretical accounts of composition as a discipline that are published as official versions of what should go on have few referents in the classroom.[11] Lore is, so to speak, a site of resistance to the disciplining of composition. It bears the same relation to composition programs that departmental corridor talk bears to departmental reports to the dean. The corridor talk tells what is going on, and the reports make what is going on into something the dean wants to hear. In Harkin's analysis, composition scholarship exhibits this opposition, for instance in John Rouse's account of Mina Shaughnessy's practices. Rouse imposes disciplinary criteria on Shaughnessy's description of her lore. Theory—of whatever sort—is always domesticated to be of use in the classroom.[12] This fitting practice should be defended because the resulting lore is the only efficacious knowledge writing and reading teachers have. In Harkin's postdisciplinary view of theory, lore is the version of the theorem that works. Her view is consonant with post-modern critiques of disciplinarity.

Harkin's essay further implies that a reconception of rhetoric as postdisciplinary makes possible the study of new ways of knowing that have been unacknowledged and even disparaged by proponents of disciplinary criteria for knowledge production. She envisions rhetoric, freed from disciplinary constraints, opening the door to different modes of human understanding. Lore, as the version of the theorem that works, counts as understanding for teachers of writing. It is not, however, formed in the way that disciplines paradigmatically produce knowledge. It is contradictory. It disobeys the law of noncontradiction. It is eclectic. It takes feelings and emotions into account. It is subjective and nonreplicable. It is not binary. It counts as knowing only in a postdisciplinary context. Whether it counts is a political issue with many consequences.

Course Design

Once the "paradigm" of disciplinary discourse ceases to govern composition programs, a related difficulty comes to light. As Harkin notes, "disciplinary inquiries can be strategies of containment; these strategies achieve coherence by shutting out or repressing the contradictions that have their source in history." Or, in Schilb's terms, discussing the goals of composition programs often does not account for the differences among faculty members. In one sense or another, each writer in this volume supports the proposal that "contending" with disparate views is appropriate to the composition classroom. The authors agree that the desire to be a discipline has produced composition teachers who tend to teach one type, one style, one model of discourse. Instead, students should learn to compare each discourse with other types, styles, and forms of writing and to assess limitations. In Bialostosky's Bakhtinian idiom, students should hear more than one "voice" in the composition classroom.

Although most of the writers in this volume agree that alternatives to disciplinarity must be in contention, they have different strategies for contending. Patricia Bizzell, following the position she takes in her essay, presumably would design a course as a critique of hegemonic structures in discursive practices, with the critique based on the work of Paulo Freire, Fredric Jameson, and Henry Giroux. "[W]e rhetoricians," she remarks, "like to see ourselves as social reformers, if not revolutionaries." However, as a critique, her course would have some unexpected features. For instance, students would become critical members of their disciplines. Their critiques would embody not only an impulse to resist this discipline but also a utopian impulse. Like Bizzell, Herzberg advocates critique to "mend the world." "Clearly," he writes, "critics and critical teachers must make visible that which is hidden," especially the mystified and misrecognized institutional rationales. John Clifford's design would apparently be similar but starker since he focuses mainly on an Althusserian critique of ideological apparatuses like disciplinarity. His pedagogical aim to make students "agents" of their cultural formations allies him with what Bizzell calls a utopian impulse. I also associate Susan C. Jarratt with critique, one with an explicitly feminist agenda calling for "a more open acknowledgment of gender, race, and class differences among students and . . . a pedagogy designed to confront and explore [critically] the uneven power relations resulting from these differences."

Worsham and Vitanza add a different dimension to a course designed as a critique. Both encourage the development of alternatives to the dominant discourse by inviting parodies of it. "Mimicry," Worsham writes, "works indirectly to hollow out the structures of a discourse from within those structures and therefore is a form of infidelity that, like marital infidelity, operates within an institution to ruin it." For Worsham, *écriture féminine* is an "antagonistic" alternative to academic or disciplinary discourse. Unlike modern academic discourse, it is "fraught with contradictions, riddled with (theoretical) inconsistencies, and short on concrete strategies." Judged by disciplinary standards, it can only be found "lacking." It is a "spectacular discourse subculture" that arose "in response to particular historical conditions and constitutes a style and an identity for a subordinate group, the members of which seek ways to make something of what has been made of them, directly and indirectly, by phallocentrism." It disrupts the "dominant order of meanings by expressing forbidden content—specifically, consciousness of difference—in forbidden terms." Vitanza advocates "establishing the (postmodern) conditions for the possibilities of discourse in and about writing theory and pedagogy that, heretofore, the field of composition has had to disallow." He wants to place "in doubt" the traditional methods and modes of composition. He calls not so much for a critique but for "a meditative questioning . . . through an act of ironic critical in(ter)vention," which he terms "perverse comedy." It is a discourse formed as a "counteridiom" to the established disciplinary discourse that dominates the study of writing and reading. William Covino invites students to develop "true magic," a mode of discourse that they would surely see as "counter" to the "scientific" character of professional writing in their disciplines.

A program designed on a principle of contending, Schilb argues, has to encompass more than a critique of the dominant modes of discourse. As Schilb proposes in his "program," a course in composition should not only focus on writing but open up into broadly based considerations from more than one perspective of social issues in their historical contexts. Schilb writes that composition studies should become "a key force in the diagnosis of the contemporary world." For this to happen, he says, the field's "current pluralism," its "diverse topics and methods," and its "ties to numerous disciplines" need to be "productively juxtaposed" so that "broad social questions" can be analyzed. Schilb forcefully affirms that composition studies is in a better position to analyze social issues than literary studies. He writes:

> Several of us in the emerging field of composition have grown just as interested as literature colleagues in *cultural studies* and *postmodernism* and how they may relate. Indeed, I think our field can even more powerfully illuminate these two terms and examine the wisdom of linking them. Yet we should not automatically ingest a particular version of either; instead, through our scholarship and pedagogy we should ponder issues of the sort I mention here [e.g., the notion of postmodernism as a conceptual tool]. Composition would therefore examine various theories of cultural studies and postmodernism as well as how they diverge or mesh.

He adds an important caution: composition studies "need not aspire to become a supreme court for theories of culture; it can serve as an especially good arena to formulate, test, and exchange them." For Schilb, the composition program is a pluralist research endeavor into the vexed questions of our cultural formation. Like Schilb, Harkin envisions the design of a composition program (and thus of composition courses) as productive of research. For her, composition programs are "conferences" during which we accumulate lore about the formation of the culture. They are "conversations" designed to produce cultural lore.

The great virtue of Bialostosky's gloss on "contending with words," dialogics, is that it takes into account the many audients to the many voices that emerge in classrooms. Simultaneously, it attends to the "history of the discussion," marks the ideological positions inevitably involved, and invites counterdisciplinary discourses. To design a course as a dialogics brings together much of what we have been discussing.

Dialogics differs from other social theories of discourse in its vision of ideologically situated persons involved in struggles over the meanings of things and the ownership of words. It de-emphasizes rhetorical commonplaces, calling attention instead to the appropriated, if not always proper, places of persons who have identified themselves with certain words, ideas, ways of talking, and social positions. And it envisions what Bakhtin calls "an individual's ideological becoming" not just as the learning of "information, directions, rules, models" or conventions but as a struggle to make other people's language his or her own and to resist being owned completely by alien languages.

Bialostosky understands "contending with words" in terms of Bakhtin's "open forum" wherein "the word, directed toward its object, enters a dialogically agitated and tension-filled environment of alien words, value judgments and accents, weaves in and out of complex interrelationships, merges with some, recoils from others, intersects with yet a third group" and so on. This articulation seems richest in the sense that it embodies the others. Moreover, it allows for other important and interrelated redefinitions of "knowing" in this volume: eristics and lore.

Bialostosky, borrowing from Bakhtin, remarks that argumentative or disciplinary discourse produces a student whose voice is "under the influence of the authoritative word [and who therefore] repeats it thoughtlessly or imitates it confusedly or cites it passively or complies with it formally or defers to it silently." Correlatively, Jarratt challenges the traditional notion of argument as a competition in which one side wins. She views arguments as disputes characterized not by one-sided, combative wrangling or quarreling but rather by the interlocutors' ability to entertain different positions. In Bialostosky's terms, this ability is dialogic. The significant aspect of an eristics for the postmodern teacher is that it is a dispute that does not rely on a principle of noncontradiction; that is, it is not decided by the sort of logic that structures disciplinary discourse. Dialogics is also consonant with the nondisciplinary character of lore. Moreover, an open forum would be likely to engender the simultaneous development of lore. Students and teachers would develop and share strategies for coping with each other.

Teacher-Student Relationships

As my subtitle suggests, most of the writers in this volume share the conviction that a Socratic approach to teaching, especially its expressionist variant, is no longer feasible. Vitanza writes:

The basic assumption in many of the Socratic dialogues is that to know something, to call it knowledge, one has to be able to teach it, to reproduce the

means by which it is transferred to and acquired by another human being.
Socrates is always asking his interlocutors, Can *rhetoric . . . piety . . . virtue
. . . whatever . . .* be taught? This question is not innocent; it is a step in
the major language game called Socratic dialectic. If any of these concepts or
activities is unique, then it cannot be taught and is discarded as being "irrational." (This is the kind of violence that Lyotard sees perpetrated on the . . .
heterogeneity of language games.) If, however, any of the concepts or activities
is generic (or if it can fit into the scheme of a computer model, which, as
Lyotard says, determines what "knowledge is") then it can be codified, and if
codified, taught. (Plato—is it not clear by now?—with his dialectical procedure, was a protoprogrammer.)

In a Socratic situation, both the teacher's and the student's roles are troubling.
In a postmodern era, teachers who draw out students Socratically in class
seem likely to invoke expressions of the same hegemonic cultural values that
the writers in this volume question. As Clifford remarks:

> Traditional and expressive rhetorical theory . . . unproblematically assumes
> that the individual writer is free, beyond the contingencies of history and
> language, to be an authentic and unique consciousness. Since the theory boom
> of the sixties, however, the centuries-old tradition affirming the power of the
> unfettered individual writer has come under increasing pressure. . . .

Contending with Words implicitly calls for a return to a teacher-oriented classroom.

The villain in this volume seems to be the "expressive pedagogy" of Peter
Elbow, Donald Murray, and others.[13] Jarratt is most emphatic in her rejection
of the "expressionists." Her four classroom incidents reveal the limitations
of that pedagogy. As she says, "For some composition teachers, creating a
supportive climate in the classroom and validating student experience . . .
leaves [them] insufficiently prepared to negotiate the oppressive discourses of
racism, sexism, and classism surfacing in the composition classroom." Clifford
acutely summarizes the postmodern critique of the expressionist pedagogy.
The student is "a subject created or written by linguistic, sociological, and
anthropological codes. Writers do not simply express themselves or reflect
unique social realities . . . but rather mirror a general and systematic pattern
of . . . universal codes." Moreover, students are subjects formed as

> the result of multiple discourses already in place, already overdetermined by
> historical and social meanings in constant internal struggle. . . . As a result,
> the independent and private consciousness formerly endowed with plenitude
> and presence, with a timeless and transcultural essence, becomes in postmodern
> thought a decentered subject constantly being called on to inhabit overdeter-
> mined positions, the implications of which can be only dimly grasped by a
> consciousness written by multiple, shifting codes.

Jarratt shows that students are often part of the social problems teachers hope to address. They are often sexist, racist, and elitist. Worse, as Jarratt convincingly argues, they do not perceive themselves as a part of the problem. She concludes that "we must work to strengthen the goal of displacing teacher authority with a more carefully theorized understanding of the multiple forms of power reproduced in the classroom."

One of the insistent motifs in this volume is that teachers should present themselves as committed intellectuals (see, for instance, Bizzell). Students cannot claim this role (Clifford). It is one thing to treat students fairly, to attend to their painful problems, to encourage their resistance to the system, to listen between the lines of their inarticulateness, and quite another to make their interests the main concerns of the class. Not surprisingly, the essays in this volume offer different versions of the teacher as intellectual. To draw some parallels among the essayists and to mark some emphases, I group these portraits of intellectuals into three types; this grouping should not be understood as a classification system. I believe that Jarratt, Harkin, Schilb, and probably Herzberg paint the teacher as a reflexive or theoretical intellectual. Bizzell and Clifford portray the teacher as a facilitating or transformative intellectual; Bialostosky's portrait is similar. In sharp contrast to the others, Worsham and Vitanza envision the teacher as a subversive intellectual. To a surprising degree, Covino's teacher can also be drawn as a subversive.

Reflexive teachers seek to change students into intellectuals who will continue the task of challenging assumptions. Schilb is the strongest advocate of this teacher-student relationship. He sees students as "coinquirers" in the project of cultural studies: "Although theorists of cultural studies and postmodernism often write formidably, students can produce various kinds of discourse in sharing these scholars' concerns." In this role, Schilb views students as "a key force in the diagnosis of the contemporary world" when they join with their teachers in reflecting on the broad social issues he identifies as postmodern. Harkin's view of "conferencing" presupposes teachers and students as coinquirers. Because of their interest in cultural criticism and the ongoing postmodern critique of disciplinary modes of knowing, both Clifford and Jarratt presuppose a teacher-student relationship like the one Schilb describes in detail. Both speak of putting oppressive practices and interests in a "theoretical context . . . to examine the ways the infrastructures of society have created those experiences" (Jarratt). While Herzberg also believes that teachers must "make visible that which is hidden," his viewpoint resembles that of Said's "secular" critic who takes a position between the students and their culture against "negative and oppressive power." Thus Herzberg's position seems to be between those of the teacher as coinquirer and the teacher as facilitating or transformative intellectual.

The facilitating intellectual mediates between discourses so that the student can participate in them. Bizzell's teacher, for instance, mediates between students unfamiliar with academic discourse and the academic discourse community, thus facilitating the students' entry into it. For Bialostosky, the teacher initiates the dialogical situation by refusing to use the authoritative voice. This facilitates dialogue.

Subversive intellectuals encourage students' counterhegemonic tendencies. Worsham suggests that, in the initial phase of *écriture féminine,* "women assume the feminine role deliberately and thereby convert a form of subordination into an affirmation and then into a process of subversion." Vitanza's teacher turns almost everything on its head. Though I do not wish to pigeonhole everyone, in many respects Covino's tactic of getting students to recognize the magical elements in the disciplinary discourse is also subversive.

I agree with Jarratt that the "teacher's role in the writing classroom . . . varies greatly depending on the makeup of the class in relation to the teacher's subjectivity." Teachers and students need to be themselves in their classrooms. For this reason, we must have many models of student-teacher relationships. The problem with a single profile for teachers—a problem characteristic of modern pedagogical imperatives—is that everyone must fit that Procrustean ideal. One of the implications of this volume is that teachers are multiple subjects just as their students are. Hence, it makes sense for postmodern teachers to be reflexive, transformative, and subversive at different moments in recognition of different contexts in order to elicit different voices.

I do not wish to romanticize the teacher-student relationship, however, by making believe that it is not a power relation. For instance, I believe that students need to *become* intellectuals and that this process is a worthwhile pedagogical goal even though it clearly entails a directive to students not to be who they are. At the same time, I do not mean by this directive that students should have a lot of information about current theories. Students should learn to theorize their own pain and help others in similar situations to do so. As emergent intellectuals, they should be able to turn an inarticulate feeling into an articulate emotion as well as to take an inchoate problem and articulate it as a theorem. Intellectuals deal with both emotions and ideas. This conception of intellectuals is one of the implications of feminist theory (see Worsham). In this scheme, students do not disappear. Teachers address "the forces that shape . . . students' lives," namely their pains (Weiler, qtd. in Jarratt).

Classrooms

Each view of the teacher-student relationship commits us to a correlative view of a classroom. These classrooms do not have to follow a single blueprint and should change according to the situation.

At times, classrooms can be self-selecting communities. This conception, however, is full of perils. Bizzell advocates "designing freshman composition as an initiation into the academic discourse community."

She argues for classrooms as experiences of community but looks for a "more diverse, less smoothly integrative notion of community to allow us to discuss . . . social disjunctions" and encourage resistance. Jarratt agrees but criticizes expressionists for their simplistic view of community building:

> This vision of communication fails to acknowledge fundamental clashes in values that underlie issues of style, effect, and meaning. How would those differences be negotiated in Elbow's writing group? They wouldn't, because the group is essentially value-free.

She envisions the classroom as a forum (part of the polis) in which sophistics is the governing protocol. The Sophists, she remarks, "place at the center of their practice *dissoi logoi*—conflicting views about an issue." This view, of course, immediately reminds us of Bialostosky's description of Bakhtin's "open forum" that

> excludes no prior or contemporary voices [and that] is the ultimate forum in which the voices we learn in our disciplinary and pedagogical communities get their hearings and find their meanings. Its manners are rough-and-tumble, its genres are mixed, its commonplaces are always getting appropriated, and its only convention is the taking of turns by all the voices it has convened, though there is no guarantee they will not interrupt one another.

Bialostosky finds the conventional classroom insular and isolating, a means of indoctrinating students in the departmentalization of understanding that characterizes the modern university in its disciplinarity. As he notes, traditional classrooms "protect the young from [the open forum's] full cacophony so that they can cultivate students' capacities to speak up and be heard in it, but they offer no permanent refuge from it." The mention of "cacophony" brings me to Vitanza.

It is difficult to imagine what sort of classroom either Vitanza or Worsham would favor. Probably, the best answer is none. I will let that answer stand for Worsham, but I suggest a special category of classroom for Vitanza: the playground. Vitanza wants to "deterritorialize" students, to turn them into "drifters." The playground is a chaotic and anarchistic drifting of responses to what has happened indoors in the classroom. The playground is a kind of anticlassroom. There are no walls. It is outdoors. The constraints are lifted. Games get played for fun, and rules are always in question. What is disallowed indoors is allowed outdoors.

As Harkin suggests, classrooms should sometimes be conferences; this approach has two enormous advantages. First, it links classrooms to one another and to other kinds of forums (even internationally). As Schilb points out, "students can also benefit from relating their research into cultural studies and postmodernism to the whole composition program." His view of the process through which this might be accomplished parallels Harkin's view of conferencing. "The process," he writes, "involves forging connections among the program's individual classes, through such activities as team teaching, joint section meetings, program colloquia, letters between classes, and even program publications." He adds that "if the literature camp is willing to join in, so much the better." The second advantage of this expanded view of a classroom is that it anticipates the kind of electronic educational environments we are likely to see in the twenty-first century.

Courses in a postmodern program take place in a range of environments, from the formalities of the conference to the free-for-all of the playground. Moreover, the movement from one to the other will be speedy in the inevitable electronic environments that will be the classrooms of the future. The inevitable question that follows is, Are there texts in these classrooms?

Syllabi and Textbooks

The essays in this volume contain almost no discussion of appropriate textbooks for postmodern courses in writing and reading. When texts are mentioned, the reference is usually to instances of the inadequacy of modern composition courses. Harkin criticizes the Linda Flower and John Hayes model; Jarratt, the expressionist model; Vitanza, the idea of a textbook. This aversion to textbooks leaves us in something of a vacuum. Covino is the most suggestive of the writers in the volume on the question of syllabus content. Though he spends much time on the *National Enquirer* in his essay, I don't think he intends us to use it as the content of our course—as a text in the course. However, with this example, he makes an important point about writing and reading—that it is a habit to which persons subscribe. Talking, writing, listening, and reading become habitual. At one extreme (as Bizzell points out), students have trouble because they are not in the habit of writing in a disciplinary idiom, preferring a highly personal and regional idiom instead. At the other extreme, teachers are in the habit of writing, speaking, listening to, and reading highly professional prose of a national, if not international, character. Covino's essay suggests ways of bridging this gap. He speaks in analogous, specific, and concrete terms that help students translate to their own experiences the theoretical considerations about language that preoccupy teachers. Further, he gives accessible examples—for instance, his discussion of the ways in which "false" magic restricts action and reduces complexity. The implications are obvious.

The content of our course should include habits of talking, writing, listening, and reading that belong to our students. It should also include writing that is habitually professional. But, most important, courses should include "bridging" discourse. In Covino's essay, the material he cites from the *National Enquirer* functions as a bridge to the understanding of the rhetorical effects of disciplinary discourse. This is an exemplary instance. We can develop similar strategies for bridging the gap between students' habitual discourse and professional discourse, strategies that show the value and limitations of both discourses.

However, we do not need a textbook as such. As this volume's critique of dominant discourse clearly shows, it probably makes most sense for students to construct their own textbooks.

Assignments

Although, for the most part, the writers in this volume give us few details, they imply several kinds of assignments. I can even imagine an arrangement that uses all the different assignments to involve students in alternative modes of discourse.

Assignment 1. A likely first assignment would be based on Freire and would involve students in a personal understanding of their "oppression."[14] It could take a narrative form. Students, as Bialostosky notes, usually begin writing in a state of frustration. He quotes Elaine Maimon's moving description:

> The lonely beginner condemned to the linearity of ink on the blank page hears all the wrong voices. As he tries to imagine those absent strangers to whom he must write, he hears the voices of doubt and despair: "You don't belong here. This paper will show your smart English teacher how stupid you are. You never could write anyway."

As Bialostosky points out, "the voices in this drama are all voices from the pedagogical situation itself." These pains are occasioned by discourse, the discourse of parents, former teachers, and other authorities who place students in particular subject positions (see Bizzell; Clifford; Herzberg). Freire's pedagogy addresses the ways in which persons are oppressed by their positions in society. We can relate his insights to the idea of being oppressed by a subject position forced on one by another's discourse.

Exploring the painfulness of student writers' situations could make the classroom a community. Whereas students are accustomed to "discouraging voices," the class could provide an environment in which "encouraging voices" are heard (Bialostosky). Thus, the first assignment could establish an environment in which students feel comfortable dealing with their problems as writers. This initial community would later be problematized as contentious voices became increasingly audible.

Assignment 2. Early on, teachers should give assignments that acquaint students with disciplinary discourse because, as Bizzell contends, learning professional discourse is desirable.

Assignment 3. Teachers could follow this work with an assignment of the sort Richard Ohmann proposes in his *Politics of Letters*, which would expose the limitations of professional discourse from a political point of view. Or, the second assignment might have as a sequel one that contrasts "true" magic with "false" magic, so that students understand the personal as well as the impersonal dimensions of discourse in terms of effects, including political effects.[15] In this respect, Covino's essay is quite suggestive. He provides us with a way of making the coercive aspect of disciplinary discourse come alive to students over whom its magic has already cast a spell. We might juxtapose proper disciplinary discourses with uses of them, such as the *Dictionary of Cultural Literacy* and the *Enquirer*. Considering the marginal uses of disciplinary discourse in "self-help" contexts like Hirsch's ties those uses to the sort of "spells" the invocation of disciplinary work casts in the discourse of the *National Enquirer*. We can contrast this false magic with true magic, which is "the result not of formulaic incantation that attempts to suspend or control . . . but of action that creates action, words that create words." It is "practiced as *constitutive inquiry*, . . . while false-incorrect magic . . . is practiced as *enforced doctrine*." True magic is interpersonal or dialogical. This contrast provides a bridge to a "dialogic assignment."

Assignment 4. Bialostosky's essay is rich in specific suggestions for assignments that would acquaint students with the interplay of voices in various uses of langauge and that would help students understand many of the conventions we use. Teaching the conventions per se seems sterile compared with the powerful sense of interaction in the dialogic matrix Bialostosky proposes as a classroom environment. This assignment could be designed to place the first three assignments, which contrast personal and disciplinary discourse, into the broader frame of a dialogic universe that is polyvocal.

Assignment 5. At some point, teachers should give an assignment that allows students to vent their distrust of the dominant disciplinary discourse in ways that Vitanza calls "perverse," Worsham calls "subversive," and Schilb calls "satiric."[16] Such an assignment could actually help students master the codes of disciplinarity instead of being unconsciously mastered by them. As Worsham notes, mimicry "repeats and parodies phallocentric modes of argument to exaggerate their effects and expose their arbitrary privilege." In Schilb's words, "students might satirize the languages of various cultural phenomena and then consider what leverage they have gained." This assignment would also allow students to give free play to their feelings—their resentment of the constraints of disciplinary discourse, their fear of exposure in personal discourse, their contempt for schooling, their prejudices—as matters to be negotiated. In this assignment the "body" would be privileged (see Worsham), and the articulation of feeling and emotion would be paramount. Contradictions would not be errors. The assignment would, as Worsham puts it, "[break] up the orderly arrangement of discourse," perhaps by following Cixous's manner of beginning many different times from several points of view in a diffuse and circular manner, all the while miming academic or business discourse. In "jumbling the order of space, in disorienting it, in changing around the furniture, dislocating things and values, breaking them all up, emptying structures, and turning propriety upside down," the effect would be laughter, but earned laughter in the sense that the object of the mimicry was discernible because the mime had control of its conventions (Cixous).

Assignment 6. The final assignment might be an instance of *dissoi logoi*. Postmodern environments require us to be multivalent; hence, students need to be flexible. They need to learn to go both ways while being committed to contradictory alternatives. It is difficult to conceive of an assignment that could accomplish this. Schilb suggests a possibility, pointing out that postmodern thinkers

> have probed what it means to lead a concrete existence in the contemporary world—what it means to experience the influence of the media, the lure of commodities, the pressures of schooling, the limits of a certain social status, the virtues and illusions of theories themselves. Of course, teachers may have to encourage students to see how their personal narratives tie into larger geopolitical conditions. In particular, students may need help recognizing that autobiographies can differ with shifts in gender, race, class, sexual preference, and nation.

In the final assignment, students might be asked, as Schilb proposes, to link what they wrote in the first assignment to "larger geopolitical conditions." This activity might allow middle-class students, for example, to see how their oppression as subjects of the discourse they have introjected links them to the oppression of minorities whose problems usually seem threateningly other.

Although developing a sequence of assignments of this sort might seem intimidating, it may comfort teachers to realize that most of these assignments already exist in composition lore. Though we may be tempted to think of the body of lore as conservative, its marginality makes it a site of resistance. There is, no doubt, even lore about assignments that induce "perverse comedy."

Grading

It is instructive, though not surprising, that this volume contains no theses about grading. Clifford is the only author to speak about it at any length, but he focuses on it as an aspect of ideology and hierarchization. He does argue that grammar is not a good basis for grading writing, remarking that "grammar instruction is probably harmful to writing." That no one proposes a system of evaluation is an informative lacuna.

For the postmodern teacher, grading is a particularly difficult problem. Since disciplines use hierarchization to individuate subject positions, any evaluation scheme entails subjugation. However, this problem cannot be left unanswered. Though the pedagogies described in this volume suggest that teachers should not give grades, most readers will not consider this alternative viable. Hence, I briefly suggest what a postmodern, postdisciplinary grading procedure might involve.

As these essays imply, the criteria for evaluation should not be exclusively disciplinary. We need to recognize abilities in other forms of discourse and to develop criteria for different groups of students that take into account the value of their differences. While these ideas may seem impractical at the moment, such systems can be developed. Students might, for instance, agree to "work contracts" in which grading is related to problems students identified as their own (as in the first Freirean assignment). Further, if a modern composition course subjugates students, then, in some way, we must reward their efforts to become agents of their own "style." Grades should also include evaluations of student's abilities not only to write in a certain mode but to be critical of that mode as well. As the criticisms of expressionist composition theories in this volume suggest, for instance, grading should constrain students' self-expression. Writing and reading would *not* be regarded as private matters, and thus socially irresponsible self-expression could not be condoned. Our lore about teaching writing and reading needs to include ways to conduct evaluations without undermining the aims of a postmodern teacher.

In conclusion, I understand theories as sets of theorems that can be infinitely rearranged to address different problems. Theorems are lore, not in their pristine state as cogs in a theory, but in their appropriated ad hoc hypothetical state. In humanistic research, teaching, and practice, lore is a body of understandings. It has the same conceptual status for us as theory has for scientists. Lore is disparaged only by those whose criteria for well-formed theories are scientifically derived. In the humanities, theory is radically ad hoc because it has to account for specific and concrete instances of behavior too complex to be uniformly specifiable.

Lore has the same diagnostic value as symptomology does in medicine.

Though we are not accustomed to thinking of ourselves as healers, we do help reduce pain. Of course, we cannot reduce every pain conceivable, but we can help with those pains having to do with discourse, that is, with rhetoric—namely, the frustration of not making sense, humiliation, insult, shame, and so on. The problem rhetoric teachers face is not illiteracy but inarticulateness—a very painful condition.[17] This pain must be theorized even if we have to "domesticate" theory, a phrase that needs to be understood in its most metaphoric sense. Domesticating theory helps us to feel "at home" with theorizing, "sheltered," through theorizing, from oppression.

I have always been attracted to Frank Smith's definition of "meaning" as the reduction of the tension accompanying the frustration of not being able to make sense of a text (see his *Understanding Reading*). I believe that we should understand the problems associated with writing in a similarly strategic way. Writing poorly is due not to ignorance but to a particular kind of pain—inarticulateness. That pain parallels the pain of not being able to make sense of a text, which Smith associates with reading problems. It has several registers. At the lowest, persons have feelings and cannot name the emotions that would convey to others their sense of what has happened to them. At another register, persons make no sense to others because what makes sense for them is tremendously convoluted and abstract. Inarticulateness is the painful condition of not being able to find words for the sense persons have made of their experiences.

Writing is painful. Students hurt. Teachers hurt. Postmodern theorizing helps.

NOTES

[1] One question I asked myself was, What will a postmodern classroom look like? It probably will not even resemble our present classrooms since it is likely to be an electronic environment. The postmodern period is, after all, inaugurated by an electronic revolution. This consideration is extremely important. Patricia Harkin's essay is suggestive in this regard. Although my reflections here assume present classrooms, some implications of the essays in this volume fit an electronic environment quite well.

[2] The issue of whether an institution can be changed from within is beyond the scope of this paper and the essays it addresses; thus I simply refer to Michel Foucault's advocacy of the local intellectual as a defense of my interest in changing a "local" subinstitution (see "Revolutionary Action").

[3] I use the word *theorizing* to speak about a discourse that generalizes discursive practices across various "fields" by juxtaposing the practices so that their differences reveal what the discourses presuppose.

[4] Though students find themselves inescapably placed in highly restrictive subject

positions, they are not to be equated to any of them. See Paul Smith's *Discerning the Subject* for a detailed discussion of this point.

⁵Although the discourse I use in speaking about a classroom can be called pedagogical, I have no concern for its authorship. See Foucault's "What Is an Author?" for a defense of this stratagem.

⁶I have altered my position on this point. Though I still object to the notion that the discursive practices of literary criticism can be justified because they enable (as well as disable) practitioners, I accept the notion that incorporating radical critiques into the university system alters it (see Culler; Sosnoski). If I ask the question, Do I become a revolutionary or leave the academy? I create a false opposition.

I believe that university structures change in ad hoc and rather random ways. Moreover, since university structures operate largely by committee, any change put in place is first denominalized, that is, reduced to its lowest common denominator of agreement. At first, this realization made me despair, but more recently I have found hope in the circumstance that changes do occur. Intellectuals who insist on the "integrity" of their theoretical concerns and refuse to have these concerns denominalized seem to be making a tactical error.

⁷Windows, doors, and stairways are the linking structures that make buildings suitable for particular uses. They stand for the "structuring structures" of institutions. In this analogy, disciplinarity is a structuring structure. If we "remodeled" what we mean by *theory*, then many other structures would be structured by that change because theory has a crucial function in the production of knowledge.

⁸This pattern is the pattern of historical change in the university system. Over the years university structures have been entirely revamped. Within the next decade or two, the modern university as we now know it will be replaced by an electronic educational environment. This change will occur, as did the changes that brought the preprofessional university into the age of disciplinarity, in small and uneven increments over a period of years. The pattern is evolutionary not revolutionary. Even though some changes may seem catastrophic or disruptive, they remain ad hoc because they are not planned and because they take years to filter down to underfunded universities.

⁹The essays in *Contending with Words* suggest alternatives to disciplinary discourse that would partially or completely change the current aims of most composition courses as they are described in departmental programs, though not necessarily as they are taught by practitioners whose eclectic use of lore subverts those departmental programs. The disparity between the official aim of composition programs and the unofficial aims of composition instruction (not always identified in course descriptions) underscores that composition teachers live in a postmodern era and do not invariably think like modernists. They often appeal for a discourse that contrasts with scientific discourse. But their postmodernism is usually not self-reflexive. For instance, their objections to scientism are more widespread than their objections to "discipline," which they often translate into a rejection of standards. The essays in this volume call for aims that practitioners often advocate, but the essayists caution us to articulate those aims with care. A return to "humanistic" modes of thought would create as many problems as submission to disciplinary modes of thought would from a postmodern standpoint. The idiomatic rhetoric of liberal humanism that has often been

used to justify nonscientistic aims of writing courses in terms of self-expression and self-understanding now seems a dangerous invitation to maintain the status quo.

[10]I intend the expression *subject matter* as a kind of pun. Subjects are formed in and through discourse; hence the subject matter of a course in rhetoric is inevitably subjectivities materialized.

[11]Harkin's account of lore parallels Pierre Bourdieu's delineation of the "unofficial" discourse natives use among themselves versus the "official" accounts of what they do that they provide for outside investigators (*Outline*).

[12]It is more accurate to say not that theory is domesticated by classroom use but that theoretical concepts can never remain in their purely conceptual state when they become ad hoc hypotheses used in the resolution of pedagogical problems. This is as it should be.

[13]Clifford criticizes the "process approach" to writing instruction as well.

[14]I use the word *oppression* here to underscore a possible link with Freire's work. The word can be understood here only in the sense of an oppressive subject position. We have not sufficiently explored the ways in which discourse occasions pain.

[15]In some ways, the designations "true" and "false" magic are thoroughly post-modern when applied to, say, disciplinary discourse. The idea of discipline as embodying true magic, for example, seems quite appropriate to postmodern critiques of disciplinarity. However, the binary opposition that Covino introduces by enumerating the characteristics of the two seems inappropriate. We can easily avoid this slippage into modernism if we supply less binary designations. For instance, we can speak of a spectrum of magic that goes from yellow to blue. But even these terms are risky because of the potential reverberations of the phrase "black magic." Nonetheless, to speak of discourse in concrete analogies rather than in abstract concepts seems very desirable both as a way of relating discourse to experience and as a way of making its character polyvalent.

[16]According to Worsham, teachers cannot give an assignment in "doing" *écriture féminine*, but I believe that such a normalization would nonetheless be beneficial. In the spirit of lore, we could just call it something else—and perhaps not even credit Cixous or Irigaray with the inspiration. Though the assignment would no longer be radical, it could nevertheless allow a valuable voice to emerge in the dialogue among students.

[17]By "inarticulateness," I mean a state during which one cannot formulate an experience in words. Though the experience may be comprehensible, the understanding involved is tacit and unspecifiable. Within one's own discursive community, inarticulateness may be broached by tags, but in public situations the tags are not idiomatic.

❖ *Notes on Contributors* ❖

Don H. Bialostosky contends with words as professor of English and coordinator of the program in rhetorical theory at the University of Toledo. He is currently working on book-length projects entitled "Wordsworth, Literary Study, and Liberal Education" and "Dialogics and the Arts of Discourse."

Patricia Bizzell is professor of English at the College of the Holy Cross. She has published several articles on composition, rhetoric, and literacy in journals such as *College English, College Composition and Communication, Pre/Text, Rhetoric Review*, and *Curriculum Inquiry*. With Bruce Herzberg, she has edited *The Bedford Bibliography for Teachers of Writing* (3rd ed., 1991) and *The Rhetorical Tradition: Readings from Classical to Contemporary Times*.

John Clifford is professor of English at the University of North Carolina, Wilmington. He has published essays on Louise Rosenblatt, Kenneth Burke, Terry Eagleton, Ann Berthoff, Alice Walker, and various critical theorists in *College English, Rhetoric Review, Reader*, and *Teaching English in the Two-Year College* as well as in the anthologies *Audits of Meaning, The Territory of Language*, and *Perspectives on Research and Scholarship in Composition*. He has co-edited two textbooks and the collection *Modern American Prose* and has edited *The Experience of Reading: Louise Rosenblatt and Reader-Response Theory*.

William A. Covino is associate professor of English at the University of Illinois, Chicago, where he teaches in the graduate program in language, literacy, and rhetoric. His articles on rhetorical theory and history have appeared in several journals, and his recent books include *The Art of Wondering: A Revisionist Return to the History of Rhetoric* and *Forms of Wondering: A Dialogue on Writing for Writers*.

Sharon Crowley is professor of English at Northern Arizona University, where she teaches the history of rhetoric. Her articles have appeared in *Pre/Text, College Composition and Communication*, and *College English*. Her recent books are *A Teacher's Guide to Deconstruction* and *The Methodical Memory*.

Patricia Harkin is associate professor of English and associate chair for writing programs at the University of Toledo. Her articles on composition, rhetoric, and literary theory have appeared in *Pre/Text*, *Folklore Forum*, *Critical Exchange*, *Dispositio*, and *Works and Days*.

Bruce Herzberg is associate professor of English, director of the freshman English program, and coordinator of writing across the curriculum at Bentley College. His publications include *The Bedford Bibliography for Teachers of Writing* and *The Rhetorical Tradition: Readings from Classical to Contemporary Times* (both with Patricia Bizzell) and several articles on composition and rhetoric in journals and books. He has made frequent presentations at CCCC and MLA conventions.

Susan C. Jarratt is associate professor of English at Miami University of Ohio, where she teaches the history of rhetoric and women's studies. She is the author of *Rereading the Sophists: Classical Rhetoric Refigured*, as well as of articles in *Pre/Text* and *College English*.

John Schilb directs the freshman writing program at the University of Maryland, College Park. He has published on the relation between composition theory and critical theory in journals such as *College Composition and Communication*, *Pre/Text*, *Rhetoric Review*, the *Journal of Advanced Composition*, and *Writing Instructor*.

James J. Sosnoski is professor of English at Miami University of Ohio. His writing has appeared in *College English*, *Boundary 2*, the *North Dakota Review*, the *Journal of the Midwest Modern Language Association*, and the *Dalhousie Review*. He has recently completed *The Magister Implicatus: The Call to Orthodoxy in Literary Studies*.

Victor J. Vitanza is associate professor of English and director of the Center for Rhetorical and Critical Theory at the University of Texas, Arlington. He is editor of *Pre/Text*, and he has published articles in that journal as well as in *Rhetoric Review*, *College Composition and Communication*, *Style*, *CEA Forum*, *Argumentation* and *Texas Studies in Literature and Language*. He is currently writing a book on historiographies of rhetoric.

Lynn Worsham is assistant professor of English at the University of Wisconsin, Milwaukee, and was a fellow at the Center for Twentieth-Century Studies there in 1989. She has published an article on Heidegger's theory of invention in *Pre/Text* and review essays in the *Journal of the American Forensic Association* and *Rocky Mountain Review*. She is currently at work on a book that employs postmodern theories of discourse and culture to examine aspects of composition theory and teaching.

❖ *Works Cited* ❖

Allen, Michael. "Writing away from Fear: Mina Shaughnessy and the Uses of Authority." *College English* 41 (1980): 857–67.

Althusser, Louis. "Ideology and Ideological State Apparatuses." Althusser, *Lenin* 127–86.

———. *Lenin and Philosophy and Other Essays*. Trans. Ben Brewster. New York: Monthly Review, 1971.

Althusser, Louis, and Etienne Balibar. *Reading Capital*. Trans. Ben Brewster. London: NLB, 1970.

Arac, Jonathan, ed. *After Foucault: Humanistic Knowledge, Postmodern Challenges*. New Brunswick: Rutgers UP, 1988.

———, ed. *Postmodernism and Politics*. Minneapolis: U of Minnesota P, 1986.

Aristotle. *The* Rhetoric *and* Poetics *of Aristotle*. Trans. Rhys Roberts (*Rhetoric*) and Ingram Bywater (*Poetics*). New York: Modern Library, 1984.

———. *Topics*. Trans. W. A. Pickard-Cambridge. *The Complete Works of Aristotle: The Revised Oxford Translation*. Vol. 1. Ed. Jonathan Barnes. Princeton: Princeton UP, 1984. 167–277. 2 vols.

Arnett, Ronald C. *Communication and Community: Implications of Martin Buber's Dialogue*. Carbondale: Southern Illinois UP, 1986.

Aronowitz, Stanley. "Postmodernism and Politics." Ross 46–62.

Atkins, G. Douglas, and Michael Johnson, eds. *Writing and Reading Differently: Deconstruction and the Teaching of Composition and Literature*. Lawrence: UP of Kansas, 1985.

Axelrod, Rise B., and Charles Cooper. *The St. Martin's Guide to Writing*. 2nd ed. New York: St. Martin's, 1988.

Bakhtin, Mikhail. *The Dialogic Imagination*. Trans. Caryl Emerson and Michael Holquist. Ed. Holquist. Austin: U of Texas P, 1981.

Barthes, Roland. *Mythologies*. Trans. Annette Lavers. New York: Hill, 1972.

Bartholomae, David. "Inventing the University." *When a Writer Can't Write: Studies in Writer's Block and Other Composing Problems*. Ed. Mike Rose. New York: Guilford, 1985. 134–65.

Baudrillard, Jean. *Selected Writings*. Stanford: Stanford UP, 1988.

Bauer, Dale Marie, et al. "Feminist Pedagogy." Unpublished ms., 1988.

Baumlin, James S., and Tita French Baumlin. "Psyche/Logos: Mapping the Terrains of Mind and Rhetoric." *College English* 51 (1989): 245–61.

Berlin, James A. "Rhetoric and Ideology in the Writing Class." *College English* 50 (1988): 477–94.

———. *Rhetoric and Reality: Writing Instruction in American Colleges, 1900–1985*. Carbondale: Southern Illinois UP, 1987.

Bernstein, Basil B. *Class, Codes, and Control*. 3 vols. London: Routledge, 1975.

Bersani, Leo. "Pedagogy and Pederasty." *Raritan* 5.1 (1985): 14–21.

Berthoff, Ann E. "Is Teaching Still Possible? Writing, Meaning, and Higher Order Reasoning." *College English* 46 (1984): 743–55.

———. "Recognition, Representation, and Revision." *Journal of Basic Writing* 3.3 (1981): 19–32. Rpt. in *A Sourcebook for Basic Writing Teachers*. Ed. Theresa Enos. New York: Random, 1987. 545–56.

Bizzell, Patricia. "Beyond Anti-Foundationalism to Rhetorical Authority: Problems Defining 'Cultural Literacy.' " *College English* 52 (1990): 661–75.

———. "Cognition, Convention, and Certainty: What We Need to Know about Writing." *Pre/Text* 3 (1982): 213–44.

———. "College Composition: Initiation into the Academic Discourse Community." *Curriculum Inquiry* 12 (1982): 191–207.

———. "Composing Processes: An Overview." *The Teaching of Writing: 85th Yearbook of the NSSE. Part II*. Ed. Anthony R. Petrosky and David Bartholomae. Chicago: U of Chicago P, 1986. 49–70.

———. "Foundationalism and Anti-Foundationalism in Composition Studies." *Pre/Text* 7 (1986): 37–56.

———. "On the Possibility of a Unified Theory of Composition and Literature." *Rhetoric Review* 4 (1986): 174–79.

Bloom, Allan. *The Closing of the American Mind: How Higher Education Has Failed Democracy and Impoverished the Souls of Today's Students*. New York: Simon, 1987.

Booth, Wayne. *Critical Understanding: The Powers and Limits of Pluralism*. Chicago: U of Chicago P, 1979.

Bourdieu, Pierre. *Homo Academicus*. Trans. Peter Collier. Stanford: Stanford UP, 1988.

———. *Outline of a Theory of Practice*. Trans. Richard Nice. Ed. Jack Goody. Cambridge: Cambridge UP, 1977.

Bourdieu, Pierre, and Jean-Claude Passeron. *Reproduction: In Education, Society, and Culture*. Trans. Richard Nice. Los Angeles: Sage, 1977.

Bové, Paul A. *Intellectuals in Power: A Genealogy of Critical Humanism*. New York: Columbia UP, 1986.

Bruffee, Kenneth A. "Collaborative Learning and the 'Conversation of Mankind.' " *College English* 46 (1984): 635–52.

———. "Kenneth Bruffee Responds." *College English* 49 (1987): 711–16.

————. "Social Construction, Language, and the Authority of Knowledge: A Bibliographical Essay." *College English* 48 (1986): 773–90.

Buchloh, Benjamin H. D. "From Faktura to Factography." *October* 30 (1984): 82–119.

Burger, Peter. *Theory of the Avant-Garde*. Trans. Michael Shaw. Minneapolis: U of Minnesota P, 1984.

Burke, Kenneth. *Counter-statement*. New York: Harcourt, 1931.

————. *A Grammar of Motives*. Berkeley: U of California P, 1969.

————. *The Philosophy of Literary Form: Studies in Symbolic Action*. Los Angeles: U of California P, 1974.

————. *A Rhetoric of Motives*. Berkeley: U of California P, 1969.

————. "Rhetoric, Poetics, and Philosophy." *Rhetoric, Philosophy, and Literature*. Ed. Don M. Burkes. W. Lafayette: Purdue UP, 1978. 15–34.

Butler, Judith P. *Subjects of Desire*. New York: Columbia UP, 1987.

Carroll, David. *Paraesthetics*. New York: Methuen, 1987.

Caywood, Cynthia L., and Gillian R. Overing, eds. *Teaching Writing: Pedagogy, Gender, and Equity*. New York: State U of New York P, 1986.

Chase, Geoffrey. "Accommodation, Resistance, and the Politics of Student Writing." *College Composition and Communication* 39 (1988): 13–22.

Cixous, Hélène. "Castration or Decapitation?" Trans. Annette Kuhn. *Signs* 7 (1981): 41–55.

————. "The Laugh of the Medusa." Trans. Keith Cohen and Paula Cohen. *The Signs Reader: Women, Gender, and Scholarship*. Ed. Elizabeth Abel and Emily K. Abel. Chicago: U of Chicago P, 1983. 279–99.

————. "Rethinking Differences." Trans. Isabella de Courtivron. *Homosexualities and French Literature*. Ed. George Stambolian and Elaine Marks. Ithaca: Cornell UP, 1979. 70–86.

Cixous, Hélène, and Catherine Clément. *The Newly Born Woman*. Trans. Betsy Wing. Minneapolis: U of Minnesota P, 1986.

Clifford, John. "Burke and the Tradition of Democratic Schooling." L. Z. Smith 29–40.

Cocks, Joan. *The Oppositional Imagination: Feminism, Critique, and Political Theory*. New York: Routledge, 1989.

Coles, William E., Jr. *The Plural I—and After*. Portsmouth: Boynton, 1988.

Collins, Jim. *Uncommon Culture: Popular Culture and Postmodernism*. New York: Routledge, 1989.

Conley, Verena Andermatt. *Hélène Cixous: Writing the Feminine*. Lincoln: U of Nebraska P, 1984.

Cooper, Marilyn M. "Why Are We Talking about Discourse Communities? Or, Foundationalism Rears Its Ugly Head Once More." Cooper and Holzman 202–20.

Cooper, Marilyn M., and Michael Holzman. *Writing as Social Action*. Portsmouth: Boynton, 1989.

Covino, William A. *The Art of Wondering*. Portsmouth: Boynton, 1988.

Crowley, Sharon. "The Perilous Life and Times of Freshman English." *Freshman English News* 14.3 (1986): 11–16.

Culler, Jonathan. "Problems in the 'History' of Contemporary Criticism." *JMMLA* 17 (Spring 1984): 3–15.

Culley, Margo, and Catherine Portuges, eds. *Gendered Subjects: The Dynamics of Feminist Teaching*. Boston: Routledge, 1985.

Culley, Margo, et al. "The Politics of Nurturance." Culley and Portuges 11–20.

D'Angelo, Frank. *A Conceptual Theory of Rhetoric*. Cambridge: Winthrop, 1975.

Daniell, Beth. "Re-reading Ong: Literacy and Social Change." CCCC Meeting. St. Louis, 18 Mar. 1988.

Darnton, Robert. "What Was Revolutionary about the French Revolution?" *New York Review of Books* 35.21–22 (1989): 3–4, 6, 10.

Däumer, Elisabeth, and Sandra Runzo. "Transforming the Composition Classroom." Caywood and Overing 45–62.

Davis, Mike. "Urban Renaissance and the Spirit of Postmodernism." Kaplan 79–87.

de Beaugrande, Robert. "In Search of Feminist Discourse: The 'Difficult' Case of Luce Irigaray." *College English* 50 (1988): 253–72.

de Lauretis, Teresa. *Alice Doesn't: Feminism, Semiotics, Cinema*. Bloomington: Indiana UP, 1984.

———. *Technologies of Gender*. Bloomington: Indiana UP, 1987.

Deleuze, Gilles. *Foucault*. Trans. and ed. Seán Hand. Minneapolis: U of Minnesota P, 1988.

———. "Nomad Thought." *The New Nietzsche*. Ed. David B. Allison. Trans. Brian Massumi. New York: Dell, 1977. 142–49.

Deleuze, Gilles, and Félix Guattari. *Anti-Oedipus: Capitalism and Schizophrenia*. Trans. Robert Hurley, Mark Seem, and Helen R. Lane. Minneapolis: U of Minnesota P, 1983.

———. *A Thousand Plateaus: Capitalism and Schizophrenia*. Trans. Brian Massumi. Minneapols: U of Minnesota P, 1987.

de Man, Paul. "Aesthetic Formalization: Kleist's *Uber das Marionettentheater*." *The Rhetoric of Romanticism*. By de Man. New York: Columbia UP, 1984. 263–90.

———. *Allegories of Reading*. New Haven: Yale UP, 1979.

———. "The Resistance to Theory." *Yale French Studies* 63 (1982): 3–20.

de Romilly, Jacqueline. *Magic and Rhetoric in Ancient Greece*. Cambridge: Harvard UP, 1975.

Derrida, Jacques. "Differance." *Margins of Philosophy*. Trans. Alan Bass. Chicago: U of Chicago P, 1982. 1–28.

———. *Of Grammatology*. Trans. Gayatri Chakravorty Spivak. Baltimore: Johns Hopkins UP, 1976.

———. *Positions*. Trans. Alan Bass. Chicago: U of Chicago P, 1981.

Dews, Peter. *Logics of Disintegration: Post-Structuralist Thought and the Claims of Critical Theory*. New York: Verso, 1987.

Doane, Mary Ann. *The Desire to Desire: The Woman's Film of the 1940s*. Bloomington: Indiana UP, 1987.

Douglas, Wallace. "Rhetoric for the Meritocracy." Ohmann, *English* 97–132.

Dowling, William C. *Jameson, Althusser, Marx: An Introduction to the Political Unconscious*. Ithaca: Cornell UP, 1984.

Duren, Brian. "Cixous' Exorbitant Texts." *SubStance* 32 (1981): 39–51.

Eagleton, Terry. *Literary Theory: An Introduction*. Minneapolis: U of Minnesota P, 1983.

Eco, Umberto. *Semiotics and the Philosophy of Language*. Bloomington: Indiana UP, 1984.

Elbow, Peter. "Appendix Essay: The Doubting Game and the Believing Game—An Analysis of the Intellectual Enterprise." Elbow, *Writing* 147–91.

———. *Embracing Contraries*. New York: Oxford UP, 1986.

———. "Methodological Doubting and Believing: Contraries in Inquiry." Elbow, *Embracing Contraries* 254–300.

———. *Writing without Teachers*. New York: Oxford UP, 1973.

Ellsworth, Elizabeth. "Why Doesn't This Feel Empowering? Working through the Repressive Myths of Critical Pedagogy." Tenth Annual Conference on Curriculum Theory and Classroom Practice. Dayton, 26–29 Oct. 1988.

Farenga, Vincent. "Periphrasis on the Origin of Rhetoric." *MLN* 94 (1979): 1033–55.

Fekete, John, ed. *Life after Postmodernism: Essays on Value and Culture*. New York: St. Martin's, 1987.

Felman, Shoshana. "Psychoanalysis and Education: Teaching Terminable and Interminable." *Yale French Studies* 63 (1982): 21–44.

Feyerabend, Paul. *Against Method: Outline of an Anarchistic Theory of Knowledge*. London: Verso, 1978.

Fiore, Kyle, and Nan Elsasser. "Strangers No More: A Liberatory Literacy Curriculum." *College English* 44 (1982): 115–28.

Fish, Stanley. "Anti-Foundationalism, Theory Hope, and the Teaching of Composition" and "Interview with Stanley Fish." *The Current in Criticism*. Ed. Clayton Koelb and Vergil Lokke. W. Lafayette: Purdue UP, 1987. 65–98.

————. "Consequences." *Against Theory*. Ed. W. J. T. Mitchell. Chicago: U of Chicago P, 1985. 106–31.

————. *Doing What Comes Naturally: Change, Rhetoric, and the Practice of Theory in Literary and Legal Studies*. Durham: Duke UP, 1989.

————. *Is There a Text in This Class?* Cambridge: Harvard UP, 1980.

Fisher, Walter R. *Human Communication as Narration: Toward a Philosophy of Reason*. Columbia: U of South Carolina P, 1987.

Flax, Jane. "Postmodernism and Gender Relations in Feminist Theory." *Feminism/Postmodernism*. Ed. Linda J. Nicholson. New York: Routledge, 1990. 39–62.

Flower, Linda, and John R. Hayes. "The Cognition of Discovery: Defining a Rhetorical Problem." *College Composition and Communication* 31 (1980): 21–32.

————. "A Cognitive Process Theory of Writing." *College Composition and Communication* 32 (1981): 365–87.

Flynn, Elizabeth. "Composing as a Woman." *College Composition and Communication* 39 (1988): 423–35.

Fogarty, Daniel. *Roots for a New Rhetoric*. New York: Columbia UP, 1959.

Foss, Sonja K., Karen A. Foss, and Robert Trapp. *Contemporary Perspectives on Rhetoric*. Prospect Heights: Waveland, 1985.

Foucault, Michel. *The Archaeology of Knowledge*. 1969. Trans. A. M. Sheridan Smith. New York: Pantheon, 1972.

————. *Discipline and Punish: The Birth of the Prison*. Trans. Alan Sheridan. New York: Vintage, 1979.

————. "The History of Sexuality." Foucault, *Power/Knowledge* 183–93.

————. *The History of Sexuality: An Introduction*. Trans. Robert Hurley. New York: Pantheon, 1978. Vol. 1 of *The History of Sexuality*.

————. *Language, Counter-Memory, Practice*. Trans. Donald F. Bouchard and Sherry Simon. Ed. Donald F. Bouchard. Ithaca: Cornell UP, 1977.

————. *Madness and Civilization: A History of Insanity in the Age of Reason*. Trans. Richard Howard. New York: Vintage, 1973.

————. "The Order of Discourse." 1970. *Untying the Text*. Ed. Robert Young. Trans. Ian McLeod. Boston: Routledge, 1981. 48–78.

————. *The Order of Things*. 1966. New York: Vintage, 1973.

————. *Power/Knowledge: Selected Interviews and Other Writings, 1972–1977*. Trans. and ed. Colin Gordon. New York: Pantheon, 1980.

————. "Revolutionary Action: 'Until Now.'" Foucault, *Language* 218–33.

————. "The Subject and Power." *Michel Foucault: Beyond Structuralism and Hermeneutics*. Ed. Hubert L. Dreyfus and Paul Rabinow. Chicago: U of Chicago P, 1982. 208–26.

————. *The Use of Pleasure*. Trans. Robert Hurley. New York: Pantheon, 1985. Vol. 2 of *The History of Sexuality*.

————. "What Is an Author?" *Textual Strategies: Perspectives in Post-Structuralist Criticism.* Trans. and ed. Josué V. Harari. Ithaca: Cornell UP, 1979. 141–60.

Francesconi, Robert. "The Implications of Habermas's Theory of Legitimation for Rhetorical Criticism." *Communication Monographs* 53 (1986): 16–35.

Freedman, Carl. "Marxist Theory, Radical Pedagogy, and the Reification of Thought." *College English* 49 (1987): 70–82.

Freire, Paulo. *Education for Critical Consciousness.* Trans. Myra Bergman Ramos. New York: Continuum, 1973.

Freire, Paulo, and Donaldo Macedo. *Literacy: Reading the Word and the World.* S. Hadley: Bergin, 1987.

Fussell, Paul. *Class.* New York: Summit, 1983.

Gadamer, Hans-Georg. *Philosophical Hermeneutics.* Trans. David E. Linge. Berkeley: U of California P, 1976.

————. *Truth and Method.* New York: Crossroad, 1975.

Gallagher, Catherine. Address. Forum on What Is Cultural Studies? Div. on Sociological Approaches to Literature, MLA Convention. New Orleans, 28 Dec. 1988.

Gallop, Jane. *The Daughter's Seduction: Feminism and Psychoanalysis.* Ithaca: Cornell UP, 1982.

————. "The Immoral Teachers." *Yale French Studies* 63 (1982): 117–28.

————. *Reading Lacan.* Ithaca: Cornell UP, 1985.

Gearhart, Sally Miller. "The Womanization of Rhetoric." *Women's Studies International Quarterly* 2 (1979): 195–201.

Gilligan, Carol. *In a Different Voice: Psychological Theory and Women's Development.* Cambridge: Harvard UP, 1982.

Giroux, Henry. *Theory and Resistance in Education: A Pedagogy for the Opposition.* S. Hadley: Edward Arnold, 1978.

Goleman, Judith. "Reading, Writing, and the Dialectic since Marx." L. Z. Smith 107–121.

Grady, Hugh H., and Susan Wells. "Toward a Rhetoric of Intersubjectivity: Introducing Jurgen Habermas." *Journal of Advanced Composition* 6 (1985–86): 33–47.

Graff, Gerald. "The Politics of Composition: A Reply to John Rouse." *College English* 41 (1980): 851–56.

————. *Professing Literature: An Institutional History.* Chicago: U of Chicago P, 1987.

Gramsci, Antonio. *An Antonio Gramsci Reader: Selected Writings, 1916–1935.* Trans. Quintin Hoare, Geoffrey Nowell-Smith, John Matthews, and William Boelhower. Ed. David Forgacs. New York: Schocken, 1988.

Graves, Richard L., ed. *Rhetoric and Composition: A Sourcebook for Teachers and Writers.* Upper Montclair: Boynton, 1984.

Grossberg, Lawrence. "Putting the Pop Back into Postmodernism." Ross 167–90.

Guattari, Félix. "Towards a Micro-Politics of Desire." *Molecular Revolution: Psychiatry and Politics.* Trans. Rosemary Sheed. New York: Penguin, 1984. 82–107.

Habermas, Jürgen. *Communication and the Evolution of Society.* Trans. Thomas McCarthy. Boston: Beacon, 1979.

———. "Entwinement of Myth." Habermas, *Philosophical* 106–30.

———. *Knowledge and Human Interests.* Trans. Jeremy L. Shapiro. Boston: Beacon, 1971.

———. *Legitimation Crisis.* Trans. Thomas McCarthy. Cambridge: MIT P, 1975.

———. *The Philosophical Discourse of Modernity: Twelve Lectures.* Trans. Frederick Lawrence. Cambridge: MIT P, 1987.

Harris, Joseph. "The Idea of Community in the Study of Writing." *College Composition and Communication* 40 (1989): 11–22.

Hassan, Ihab. *The Dismemberment of Orpheus: Toward a Postmodern Literature.* New York: Oxford UP, 1971.

Havelock, Eric A. "The Linguistic Task of the Pre-Socratics." *Language and Thought in Early Greek Philosophy.* Ed. Kevin Robb. La Salle: Monist Library of Philosophy, 1983. 7–82.

Hebdige, Dick. *Subculture: The Meaning of Style.* London: Methuen, 1979.

Hellman, Lillian. *Pentimento: A Book of Portraits.* New York: NAL, 1973.

Hirsch, E. D., Jr. *Cultural Literacy: What Every American Needs to Know.* Boston: Houghton, 1987.

Hirsch, E. D., Jr., Joseph F. Kett, and James Trefil. *The Dictionary of Cultural Literacy: What Every American Needs to Know.* Boston: Houghton, 1988.

Hohendahl, Peter U. "Critical Theory, Public Sphere, and Culture: Jürgen Habermas and His Critics." *New German Critique* 16 (1979): 89–118.

———. "*The Dialectic of Enlightenment* Revisited: Habermas' Critique of the Frankfort School." *New German Critique* 35 (1985): 3–26.

Holzman, Michael. "A Post-Freirean Model for Adult Literacy Education." *College English* 50 (1988): 177–89. Rpt. in Cooper and Holzman 14–27.

———. "Teaching Is Remembering." Cooper and Holzman 221–32.

Hooks, Bell. *Talking Back: Thinking Feminist, Thinking Black.* Boston: South End, 1989.

Horkheimer, Max, and Theodor W. Adorno. *Dialectic of Enlightenment.* Trans. John Cumming. New York: Continuum, 1989.

Hunter, Carman St. John, and David Harman. "Who Are the Adult Illiterates?" *Perspectives on Literacy.* Ed. Eugene R. Kintgen, Barry M. Kroll, and Mike Rose. Carbondale: Southern Illinois UP, 1988. 378–90.

Huyssen, Andreas. *After the Great Divide: Modernism, Mass Culture, Postmodernism*. Bloomington: Indiana UP, 1986.

Irigaray, Luce. *Speculum of the Other Woman*. Trans. Gillian G. Gill. Ithaca: Cornell UP, 1985.

———. *This Sex Which Is Not One*. Trans. Catherine Porter with Carolyn Burke. Ithaca: Cornell UP, 1985.

———. "Women's Exile." *Ideology and Consciousness* 1 (1977): 57–76.

Jackman, Mary R., and Robert W. Jackman. *Class Awareness in the United States*. Berkeley: U of California P, 1983.

Jameson, Fredric. "On *Habits of the Heart*." *South Atlantic Quarterly* 86 (1987): 545–65.

———. *The Political Unconscious: Narrative as a Socially Symbolic Act*. Ithaca: Cornell UP, 1981.

———. "Postmodernism: Or, The Cultural Logic of Late Capitalism." *New Left Review* 146 (1984): 53–92.

Jardine, Alice. *Gynesis: Configurations of Woman and Modernity*. Ithaca: Cornell UP, 1985.

———. "Opaque Texts and Transparent Contexts: The Political Difference of Julia Kristeva." Miller 96–116.

Jarratt, Susan C. "The First Sophists and Feminism: Discourses of the 'Other.'" *Hypatia* 5 (1990): 27–41.

———. *Rereading the Sophists: Classical Rhetoric Refigured*. Carbondale: Southern Illinois UP, 1991.

Johnson, Barbara. *A World of Difference*. Baltimore: Johns Hopkins UP, 1987.

Jones, Ann Rosalind. "Writing the Body: Toward an Understanding of *L'Ecriture Féminine*." *The New Feminist Criticism: Essays on Women, Literature, and Theory*. Ed. Elaine Showalter. New York: Pantheon, 1985. 361–77.

Juncker, Clara. "Writing (with) Cixous." *College English* 50 (1988): 424–35.

Kail, Harvey. "Narratives of Knowledge: Story and Pedagogy in Four Composition Texts." *Rhetoric Review* 6 (1988): 179–89.

Kameen, Paul. "Rewording the Rhetoric of Composition." *Pre/Text* 1 (1980): 73–93.

Kaplan, E. Ann, ed. *Postmodernism and Its Discontents: Theories, Practices*. New York: Verso, 1988.

Kearney, Richard. *The Wake of Imagination: Toward a Postmodern Culture*. Minneapolis: U of Minnesota P, 1988.

Kennedy, George A. "Some Reflections on Neomodernism." *Rhetoric Review* 6 (1988): 230–33.

Kinneavy, James L. "Restoring the Humanities: The Return of Rhetoric from Exile." Murphy, *Rhetorical Tradition* 19–28.

———. *A Theory of Discourse*. 1971. New York: Norton, 1980.

Knoblauch, C. H., and Lil Brannon. *Rhetorical Traditions and the Teaching of Writing*. Upper Montclair: Boynton, 1984.

Kozol, Jonathan. *Illiterate America*. Garden City: Anchor, 1985.

Kristeva, Julia. "Freud and Love: Treatment and Its Discontents." Trans. Leon S. Roudiez. Moi, *Kristeva* 238–71.

———. "Postmodernism?" *Romanticism, Modernism, Postmodernism*. Ed. Harry R. Garvin. Lewisburg: Bucknell UP, 1980. 136–41.

———. *Powers of Horror: An Essay on Abjection*. Trans. Leon S. Roudiez. New York: Columbia UP, 1982.

———. "Psychoanalysis and the Polis." Trans. Margaret Waller. Moi, 301–20.

———. "The System and the Speaking Subject." Moi, *Kristeva* 25–33.

———. "Women's Time." Trans. Alice Jardine and Harry Blake. Moi, *Kristeva* 188–213.

Kuhn, Thomas S. *The Structure of Scientific Revolutions*. Chicago: U of Chicago P, 1970

Lacan, Jacques. *Ecrits: A Selection*. Trans. Alan Sheridan. New York: Norton, 1977.

———. *Four Fundamental Concepts of Psycho-analysis*. Trans. Alan Sheridan. New York: Norton, 1978.

———. "The Function and Field of Speech and Language in Psychoanalysis." Lacan, *Ecrits* 30–113.

———. "Television." Trans. Jeffrey Mehlman. *October* 40 (1987): 7–50.

Lakoff, George, and Mark Johnson. *Metaphors We Live By*. Chicago: U of Chicago P, 1980.

Langer, Susanne. *Philosophy in a New Key*. Cambridge: Harvard UP, 1957.

Lanham, Richard A. "The Rhetorical Paideia: The Curriculum as Work of Art." *College English* 48 (1986): 132–41.

LeFevre, Karen Burke. *Invention as a Social Act*. Carbondale: Southern Illinois UP, 1987.

Leff, Michael. "Serious Comedy: The Strange Case History of Dr. Vitanza." *Rhetoric Review* 6 (1988): 237–45.

Lentricchia, Frank. *After the New Criticism*. Chicago: U of Chicago P, 1980.

———. *Criticism and Social Change*. Chicago: U of Chicago P, 1983.

Lewis, Magda, and Roger I. Simon. "A Discourse Not Intended for Her: Learning and Teaching within Patriarchy." *Harvard Educational Review* 56 (1986): 457–72.

Liddell, H. G., and Robert Scott. *A Lexicon, Abridged from Liddell and Scott's Greek-English Lexicon*. Oxford: Clarendon P, 1983.

Lunsford, Andrea. "Composing Ourselves: Politics, Commitment, and the Teaching of Writing." Opening General Sess. CCCC Meeting. St. Louis, 16 Mar. 1989.

Lyman, Rollo. *Summary of Investigations Relating to Grammar, Language, and Composition*. Chicago: U of Chicago P, 1929.

Lyotard, Jean-François. "Adrift." Trans. Roger McKeon. *Driftworks*. By Lyotard. New York: Semiotext(e), 1984. 9–18.

———. *The Differend: Phrases in Dispute*. Trans. Georges Van Den Abbeele. Minneapolis: U of Minnesota P, 1988.

———. "For a Pseudo-Theory." *Yale French Studies* 52 (1975): 115–27.

———. *The Postmodern Condition: A Report on Knowledge*. Trans. Geoff Bennington and Brian Massumi. Minneapolis: U of Minnesota P, 1984.

———. "Theory as Art: A Pragmatic Point of View." *Image and Code*. Ann Arbor: U of Michigan P, 1981. 71–77.

Lyotard, Jean-François, and Jean Loup Thebaud. *Just Gaming*. Trans. Wlad Godzich. Minneapolis: U of Minnesota P, 1985.

Macdonell, Diane. *Theories of Discourse*. New York: Blackwell, 1986.

MacLaine, Shirley. *Out on a Limb*. New York: Bantam, 1983.

Maimon, Elaine P. "Maps and Genres: Exploring Connections in the Arts and Sciences." *Composition and Literature: Bridging the Gap*. Ed. Winifred Bryan Horner. Chicago: U of Chicago P, 1983. 110–25.

Maranhao, Tullio. *Therapeutic Discourse and Socratic Dialogue*. Madison: U of Wisconsin P, 1986.

Marcuse, Herbert. *One-Dimensional Man*. Boston: Beacon, 1964.

Marrou, H. I. *A History of Education in Antiquity*. New York: Sheen, 1956.

Massumi, Brian. "Translator's Foreword." Deleuze and Guattari, *Thousand* ix–xv.

McCarthy, Thomas. *The Critical Theory of Jürgen Habermas*. Cambridge: MIT P, 1978.

Mendelson, Jack. "The Habermas-Gadamer Debate." *New German Critique* 18 (1979): 44–73.

Merod, Jim. *The Political Responsibility of the Critic*. Ithaca: Cornell UP, 1987.

Miller, Nancy K., ed. *The Poetics of Gender*. New York: Columbia UP, 1986.

Moi, Toril. "Feminism, Postmodernism, and Style: Recent Feminist Criticism in the United States." *Cultural Critique* 9 (1988): 3–22.

———, ed. *The Kristeva Reader*. New York: Columbia UP, 1986.

———. *Sexual/Textual Politics: Feminist Literary Theory*. London: Methuen, 1985.

Montag, Warren. "What Is at Stake in the Debate on Postmodernism?" Kaplan 88–103.

Morris, Meaghan. *The Pirate's Fiancée: Feminism, Reading, Postmodernism*. New York: Verso, 1988.

Mulvey, Laura. "Visual Pleasure and Narrative Cinema." *Screen* 16.3 (1975): 6–18.

Murphy, James J. "Rhetorical History as a Guide to the Salvation of American Reading and Writing: A Plea for Curricular Courage." Murphy, *Rhetorical Tradition* 3–12.

———, ed. *The Rhetorical Tradition and Modern Writing*. New York: MLA, 1982.

Murray, Donald M. "Teach Writing as a Process not Product." Graves 89–94.

———. *Write to Learn*. 2nd ed. New York: Holt, 1987.

Myers, Greg. "Reality, Consensus, and Reform in the Rhetoric of Composition Teaching." *College English* 48 (1986): 154–74.

Nägele, Rainer. *Reading after Freud*. New York: Columbia UP, 1987.

Neel, Jasper. *Plato, Derrida, and Writing*. Carbondale: Southern Illinois UP, 1988.

Nelson, Cary, ed. *Theory in the Classroom*. Urbana: U of Illinois P, 1986.

Nietzsche, Friedrich. "Ancient Rhetoric." *Friedrich Nietzsche on Rhetoric and Language*. Trans. and ed. Sander L. Gilman, Carole Blair, and David J. Parent. New York: Oxford UP, 1989. 2–206.

———. "On Truth and Lies in a Nonmoral Sense." 1873. *Philosophy and Truth: Selections From Nietsche's Notebooks of the Early 1870s*. Trans. and ed. Daniel Beazeale. Atlantic Highlands: Humanities, 1979. 79–97.

———. Twilight of the Idols *and* The Anti-Christ. Trans. R. J. Hollingdale. New York: Penguin, 1968.

Noack, Paul. "Crisis instead of Revolution: On the Instrumental Change of Social Innovation." *Innovation/Renovation: New Perspectives on the Humanities*. Ed. Ihab Hassan and Sally Hassan. Madison: U of Wisconsin P, 1983. 65–84.

Norris, Christopher. *Paul de Man: Deconstruction and the Critique of Aesthetic Ideology*. New York: Routledge, 1989.

North, Stephen M. *The Making of Knowledge in Composition: Portrait of an Emerging Field*. Upper Montclair: Boynton, 1987.

Ohmann, Richard. *English in America: A Radical View of the Profession*. New York: Oxford UP, 1976.

———. *Politics of Letters*. Middletown: Wesleyan UP, 1987.

O'Keefe, Daniel Lawrence. *Stolen Lightning: The Social Theory of Magic*. New York: Continuum, 1982.

Ong, Walter J. *Fighting for Life: Contest, Sexuality, and Consciousness*. Amherst: U of Massachusetts P, 1989.

———. *Orality and Literacy: The Technologizing of the Word*. London: Methuen, 1982.

Owens, Craig, "The Discourse of Others: Feminists and Postmodernism." *The Anti-Aesthetic: Essays on Postmodern Culture*. Ed. Hal Foster. Post Townsend: Bay, 1983. 57–82.

Pattison, Robert. *On Literacy: The Politics of the Word from Homer to the Age of Rock.* New Haven: Yale UP, 1982.

Phelps, Louise Wetherbee. *Composition as a Human Science: Contributions to the Self-Understanding of a Discipline.* New York: Oxford UP, 1988.

Plato. *Phaedrus. The Collected Dialogues of Plato.* Trans. R. Hackforth. Ed. Edith Hamilton and Huntington Cairns. Princeton: Princeton UP, 1961. 475–525.

———. *Protagoras.* Ed. Gregory Vlastos. Trans. B. Jowett. Rev. Martin Ostwald. Indianapolis: Bobbs, 1956. 475–525.

———. *Theaetetus and Sophist.* Trans. Harold North Fowler. Cambridge: Harvard UP, 1961.

Plaza, Monique. " 'Phallomorphic Power' and the Psychology of 'Woman.' " *Ideology and Consciousness* 4 (1978): 4–36.

Polan, Dana. "Postmodernism and Cultural Analysis Today." Kaplan 45–58.

Polanyi, Michael. *Personal Knowledge: Towards a Post-Critical Philosophy.* Chicago: U of Chicago P, 1958.

Poulakos, John. "Rhetoric, the Sophists, and the Possible." *Communication Monographs* 51 (1984): 215–26.

Prigogine, Ilya, and Isabelle Stengers. "Postface: Dynamics from Leibniz to Lucretius." Serres 137–55.

Rabine, Leslie W. *"Ecriture Féminine* as Metaphor." *Cultural Critique* 8 (1988): 19–44.

Rabinow, Paul. Introduction. *The Foucault Reader.* Ed. Rabinow. New York: Pantheon, 1984. 3–29.

Reif, Rita. "A Record for Beuys." *New York Times* 4 Aug. 1989: 19.

Resnick, Stephen A., and Richard D. Wolff. *Knowledge and Class: A Marxian Critique of Political Economy.* Chicago: U of Chicago P, 1987.

Richman, Michele. "Sex and Signs: The Language of French Feminist Criticism." *Language and Style* 13 (1980): 62–81.

Riley, Denise. *"Am I That Name?" Feminism and the Category of "Woman" in History.* Minneapolis: U of Minnesota P, 1989.

Rooney, Ellen Frances. *Seductive Reasoning: Pluralism as the Problematic of Contemporary Literary Theory.* Ithaca: Cornell UP, 1989.

Rorty, Richard. "Habermas and Lyotard on Postmodernity." *Habermas and Modernity.* Ed. Richard J. Bernstein. Cambridge: MIT P, 1985. 161–76.

———. *Philosophy and the Mirror of Nature.* Princeton: Princeton UP, 1979.

Rose, Mike. *Lives on the Boundary: The Struggles and Achievements of America's Underprepared.* New York: Free, 1989.

Ross, Andrew, ed. *Universal Abandon? The Politics of Postmodernism.* Minneapolis: U of Minnesota P, 1988.

Rouse, John. "The Politics of Composition." *College English* 41 (1979): 1–12.

Ryan, Michael. *Marxism and Deconstruction: A Critical Articulation*. Baltimore: Johns Hopkins UP, 1982.

Said, Edward. "Criticism between Culture and System." Said, *The World* 178–225.

———. *The World, the Text, and the Critic*. Cambridge: Harvard UP, 1983.

Schilb, John. "Pedagogy of the Oppressors?" Culley and Portuges 253–64.

———. Rev. of *Composition as a Human Science: Contributions to the Self-Understanding of a Discipline*, by Louise Wetherbee Phelps. *Rhetoric Review* 8 (1989): 162–66.

Scholes, Robert. *Textual Power: Literary Theory and the Teaching of English*. New Haven: Yale UP, 1985.

Scott, Robert L. "Non-Discipline as a Remedy for Rhetoric? A Reply to Victor Vitanza." *Rhetoric Review* 6 (1988): 233–37.

Sedgwick, Peter. *Psycho Politics*. New York: Harper, 1982.

Serres, Michel. *Hermes: Literature, Science, Philosophy*. Ed. Josué V. Harari and David F. Bell. Baltimore: Johns Hopkins UP, 1982.

Shaughnessy, Mina. *Errors and Expectations: A Guide for the Teacher of Basic Writing*. New York: Oxford UP, 1977.

Shor, Ira. *Critical Teaching and Everyday Life*. Boston: South End, 1980.

———, ed. *Freire for the Classroom*. Portsmouth: Boynton, 1988.

Silverman, Kaja. *The Subject of Semiotics*. New York: Oxford UP, 1983.

Sloterdijk, Peter. *Critique of Cynical Reason*. Trans. Michael Eldred. Minneapolis: U of Minnesota P, 1987.

Smit, David W. "Some Difficulties with Collaborative Learning." *Journal of Advanced Composition* 9 (1989): 45–58.

Smith, Frank. *Understanding Reading*. New York: Holt, 1982.

Smith, Louise Z., ed. *Audits of Meaning*. Portsmouth: Boynton, 1988.

Smith, Paul. *Discerning the Subject*. Minneapolis: U of Minnesota P, 1988.

———. "Visiting the Banana Republic." Ross 128–48.

Synder, Carol. "Analyzing Classifications: Foucault for Advanced Writers." *College Composition and Communication* 35 (1984): 209–16.

Sosnoski, James. "The Token Professional." *JMMLA* 18 (Fall 1984): 1–12.

Spender, Dale. *Man Made Language*. London: Routledge, 1980.

Spivak, Gayatri Chakravorty. *In Other Words: Essays in Cultural Politics*. New York: Methuen, 1987.

Sprague, Rosamund Kent, ed. *The Older Sophists*. Columbia: U of South Carolina P, 1972.

Stanger, Carol A. "The Sexual Politics of the One-to-One Tutorial Approach and Collaborative Learning." Caywood and Overing 31–44.

Stanton, Domna C. "Difference on Trial: A Critique of Material Metaphor in Cixous, Irigaray, and Kristeva." Miller 157–82.

Street, Brian V. *Literacy in Theory and Practice.* Cambridge: Cambridge UP, 1984.

Suleiman, Susan Rubin. "(Re)Writing the Body: The Politics and Poetics of Female Eroticism." *The Female Body in Western Culture: Contemporary Perspectives.* Ed. Suleiman. Cambridge: Harvard UP, 1986. 7–29.

Tate, Gary, and Edward P. J. Corbett, eds. *The Writing Teachers' Sourcebook.* 2nd ed. New York: Oxford UP, 1988.

Tinburg, Howard B. "On Reading Freire and Macedo's *Literacy.*" *Correspondences* 10 (Winter 1988): n. pag.

Tompkins, Jane. "Me and My Shadow." *New Literary History* 19 (1987): 169–78.

Toulmin, Stephen. *Human Understanding: The Collective Use and Evolution of Concepts.* Princeton: Princeton UP, 1972.

Trebilcot, Joyce. "Dyke Methods or Principles for the Discovery/Creation of the Withstanding." *Hypatia* 3 (1988): 1–13.

Trimbur, John. "Beyond Cognition: The Voice in Inner Speech." *Rhetoric Review* 5 (1987): 211–21.

———. "Consensus and Difference in Collaborative Learning." *College English* 51 (1989): 602–16.

———. "Cultural Studies and Teaching Writing." *Focuses* 1.2 (1988): 5–18.

Ulmer, Gregory L. *Applied Grammatology: Post(e)-Pedagogy from Jacques Derrida to Joseph Beuys.* Baltimore: John Hopkins UP, 1985.

———. "Textshop for Post(e)pedagogy." Atkins and Johnson 38–64.

———. "Textshop for Psychoanalysis: On De-Programming Freshman Platonists." *College English* 49 (1987): 756–69.

Untersteiner, Mario. *The Sophists.* Oxford: Basil Blackwell, 1954.

Vesey, Laurence R. *The Emergence of the American University.* Chicago: U of Chicago P, 1965.

Vitanza, Victor J. "Concerning a Post-Classical *Ethos,* as a Para/Rhetorical Ethics, the 'Selphs,' and the Excluded Third." *Ethos: New Essays in Rhetorical and Cultural Theory.* Ed. James Baumlin and Tita Baumlin. Dallas: Southern Methodist UP (forthcoming).

———. "Critical Sub/Versions of the History of Philosophical Rhetoric." *Rhetoric Review* 6 (1987): 41–66.

———. " 'Some More' Notes, towards a 'Third' Sophistic." *Argumentation* (forthcoming).

Ward, John O. "Magic and Rhetoric from Antiquity to the Renaissance: Some Ruminations." *Rhetorica* 6 (1988): 57–118.

Watson, Sam, Jr. "Breakfast in the Tacit Tradition." *Pre/Text* 2 (1981): 9–31.

Watson, Stephen. "Jürgen Habermas and Jean-François Lyotard: Postmodernism and the Crisis of Rationality." *Philosophy and Social Criticism* 10.2 (1984): 1–24.

Weidner, Hal Rivers. "Three Models of Rhetoric: Traditional, Mechanical, and Vital." Diss. U of Michigan, 1975.

Weiler, Kathleen. *Women Teaching for Change: Gender, Class, and Power.* S. Hadley: Bergin, 1988.

West, Cornel. *The American Evasion of Philosophy: A Genealogy of Pragmatism.* Madison: U of Wisconsin P, 1989.

White, Eric Charles. *Kaironomia: On the Will-to-Invent.* Ithaca: Cornell UP, 1987.

Williams, Raymond. *Keywords.* New York: Oxford UP, 1976.

———. *Marxism and Literature.* New York: Oxford UP, 1977.

Wittgenstein, Ludwig. *Philosophical Investigations.* Trans. G. E. M. Anscombe. Oxford: Basil Blackwell, 1953.

Wojick, David E. "Issues Analysis: An Introduction to the Use of Issue Trees and the Nature of Complex Reasoning." Unpublished ms., n.d.

Worsham, Lynn. "The Question concerning Invention: Hermeneutics and the Genesis of Writing." *Pre/Text* 8 (1987): 197–244.

———. "The Question of Writing Otherwise: A Critique of Composition Theory." Diss. Univ. of Texas, Arlington, 1988.

Young, Richard E. "Paradigms and Problems: Needed Research in Rhetorical Invention." *Research on Composing: Points of Departure.* Ed. Charles R. Cooper and Lee Odell. Urbana: NCTE, 1978. 29–47.

Young, Richard, Alton Becker, and Kenneth Pike. *Rhetoric: Discovery and Change.* New York: Harcourt, 1970.

Zavarzadeh, Mas'ud. "Theory as Resistance." *Rethinking Marxism* 2.1 (1989): 50–70.

Zavarzadeh, Mas'ud, and Donald Morton. "Theory, Pedagogy, Politics: The Crisis of 'The Subject' in the Humanities." *Boundary 2* 15.1–2 (1986–87): 1–22.

❖ *Index* ❖